ANIMAL AND SHAMAN

Animal and Shaman

Ancient Religions of Central Asia

JULIAN BALDICK

I.B. Tauris Publishers
LONDON • NEW YORK

Published in 2000 by I.B.Tauris & Co Ltd
Victoria House, Bloomsbury Square, London WC1B 4DZ
175 Fifth Avenue, New York NY 10010
Website: http://www. ibtauris.com

ISBN 1 86064 431 7

A full CIP record for this book is available from the British Library

Typeset in New Baskerville by Hepton Books, Oxford
Printed and bound in Great Britain by WBC Ltd, Bridgend

Contents

Acknowledgements   viii

Introduction   1
1   Early Inner Eurasia   15
2   The Turks   38
3   The Mongols   92
4   The Tunguz and the Manchus   126

Conclusions   150

Notes   171
Bibliography   189
Index One: Names of Persons, Deities etc.   193
Index Two: Names of Peoples   198
Index Three: Subjects   201

*To Amir and Dilu
and all our family in Bangladesh*

Acknowledgements

I must acknowledge an enormous indebtedness to the pioneering work on Turkic and Mongol religion done by Jean-Paul Roux, who has laid the foundations for all future research in this field. Thanks are also due to King's College London for granting me sabbatical leave, and to Sergei Andreyev and Brian Horne for carrying out my duties during my absence. I must also express my thanks to a number of scholars who have contributed useful information: Oleg Akimushkin, Nick Allen, Didier Bouillon, Gérard Colas, Simon Digby, John Penney, Alexis Sanderson, Sergei Turkin and Stephanie West. Finally, I must thank the staff of I.B.Tauris, and in particular Anna Enayat; my sons for their help in the field of information technology and, above all, my wife for her great patience and help.

Introduction

This book presents a comparative study of the indigenous religions of Central Asia. It argues that there is a common inheritance to be found in the religions of various peoples who have lived in Central Asia or have migrated from there: Scythians, Huns, Turks, Mongols, Tunguz, Manchus, Finns and Hungarians. This common heritage is to be found in myths, rituals and epics: what is observed by anthropologists today goes back to a past studied by ancient historians. I call this common inheritance 'Inner Eurasian', and argue that it is extremely important for the study of European as well as oriental literature.

Thus we have to begin with a number of questions. What is meant by the terms 'Inner Eurasia' and 'Inner Eurasian'? Who are the various peoples whose geography and religious heritage are designated by these terms? What methods and concepts are to be used in examining their religions?

Inner Eurasia

Inner Eurasia may be defined as the part of the Eurasian land mass which, in history, has been surrounded by the civilizations of Europe, the Middle East, India and China. So the term 'Inner Eurasia' is historical and cultural as well as geographical. Inner Eurasia has never had fixed political boundaries to give it definition. 'Central Asia', by contrast, is a term of modern political

1

geography: sometimes it has been restricted in its use to the five
ex-Soviet republics to the east of the Caspian Sea, while sometimes north-west China and Afghanistan have been thrown in for
good measure. But the term 'Central Asia' cannot convey the unity
and range of the Inner Eurasian domain, with its vast sweep of
nomadic and barbarian culture, stretching from the former Yu-
goslavia and Hungary in the west to the Pacific Ocean in the east,
and from Lapland and the Bering Strait in the north to Azerbaijan
and the Khyber Pass in the south.[1]

Although the term 'Inner Eurasia' is more cultural than geographical, it is also, to a large extent, a reflection of the harsh
realities of physical geography. Most of Inner Eurasia has been
unsuitable for agriculture, and thus for sedentary civilization. The
population has been poor, in an excessively dry climate, which is
also exceptionally cold in winter, while being often warm or hot
in summer, so that the differences in temperature are the highest
in the world. Seas and rivers are of little use for transport. Mountains are particularly prominent, their water flowing down into
oases. In the far north, on the shores of the Arctic, there is the
zone called the tundra, a wasteland with stunted vegetation, suitable only for reindeer breeding and hunting foxes and lemmings.
South of this is the forest zone, with Norway spruce, pine and fir
trees in the west, larches in the east and birches to the south.
Here the hunter finds larger animals: elk, bears and tigers. Further south lie the steppes, with their rich grasslands and black
earth, well suited for grazing five types of animal: cattle, sheep,
goats, horses and camels. Finally, in the far south-east of the region, are the deserts stretching from the Caspian to Mongolia.
The difficulties presented by these deserts are partly relieved by
oases, with excellent soil watered by the thawing of mountain snow
and glaciers.[2]

These geographical factors are all-important in religion, myth,
ritual and epic. Elsewhere in the world fertility rites for the pro-
motion of agriculture are dominant, but not here, where primacy
is accorded to rituals which ensure success in hunting and breeding livestock. Whereas elsewhere the male-female opposition is
prominent, as symbolizing the union of the forces of nature in
producing crops, in Inner Eurasia there is instead an emphasis
on the opposition between summer and winter. Trees are

particularly significant in Inner Eurasian religion, largely because they serve to link the earth to Heaven, to which their tops belong. Animals, however, constitute the most important element in the indigenous religions of Inner Eurasia: hunted or bred, they are humans' guides, rescuers, ancestors, totems and sacrificial victims. The horse is the main form of transport and corresponds to the ship in Greek epic, just as the steppe replaces the sea. Mountain, water and earth form a triad: the summit, like a tree top, is in the sky, and the river flows in the middle to the grasslands below.

The poverty produced by the Inner Eurasian climate has determined the history of the region: the population has consisted of hungry nomads jealous of the rich sedentary civilizations on the periphery. Thus the Inner Eurasian barbarians have constantly posed a military threat to their prosperous neighbours, and this threat has been increased by the extraordinary strength of the Inner Eurasian horse, inured to cold, frugal in its eating and able to reproduce itself in enormous numbers. In battle the Inner Eurasian horse has always proved victorious, and the colossal size of its herds has allowed their owners to operate a relay system with each fighter using between three and eighteen mounts. The result has been exceptional rapidity in the movement of troops, and a distinctively Inner Eurasian 'war machine'.[3]

This military background has also been all-important in Inner Eurasian religion. Warriors have believed that the massacres committed by them were due to Heaven's 'making pressure', and that the enemies whom they killed would be transformed into slaves to serve them in the next world. Horses and arms have been buried or burnt with their deceased owners, in the belief that the latter will need them to journey to the land of the dead and live there. Swords, arrows and banners have all been leading elements in the religions of Inner Eurasia, along with the veneration of the tombs of conquering leaders.

The prehistory of Inner Eurasia

The Inner Eurasian preoccupation with hunting and animals is already manifest in the prehistory of the region, especially in the art of the Palaeolithic era's final stages (dated to c.13,000 to c.8000 BCE). Extremely impressive cave paintings of this period have been

found in western Mongolia, on the banks of the Khoit-Tsenker
river. These paintings resemble those found in western Europe in
the same period, with the interweaving of animal figures: mountain goats and large birds resembling ostriches. There are also
enormous animals with trunks, evidently elephants or mammoths,
and symbols in the forms of arrows and trees. It is noteworthy that
no humans are represented, but there is one drawing of a camel
and another of a horse, with two tails but no head. Scholars have
taken the view that the paintings not only reflect the observations
of hunters but were produced as magical means of ensuring success in hunting.[4]

Magic hunting rites are probably also reflected in the ensuing
Neolithic period. In the sixth millennium BCE, in the south of
what is now ex-Soviet Turkmenistan, clay figurines of animals were
made in which small stab wounds are often to be found. Later, in
the third millennium, in western Siberia, fishermen and hunters
produced pottery decorated with flying ducks and wavy lines indicating water, along with sculptural representations of the bear
(echoing the art and myths of the later ancestors of the Finns and
Hungarians).[5]

With the advent of the Bronze Age in the third millennium
BCE more evidence of religious practices is found in the region of
Lake Baikal in southern Siberia. Bone images of fish have been
discovered in burials, along with figures of elk heads: these resemble the horse heads on the staffs of modern Mongol shamans,
the main religious and magical practitioners of the region, whom
we shall discuss at length below. In the first millennium BCE, as
the Bronze Age gives way to the Iron Age, the area from Lake
Baikal to Mongolia is filled with standing stones covered by figures of stags, which have markedly human traits and are
accompanied by depictions of daggers, bows and axes. At the same
time drawings appear on cliffs, showing soaring eagles – a bird
most important in Mongol myth and religion. Also in this period,
in the mountains of Tuva in the south of Siberia, we encounter an
enormous tomb constructed for a tribal leader, who is surrounded
by the bodies of several humans and dozens of horses, grouped in
70 sections made of huge logs, with a stone circle enclosing the
whole.[6]

The peoples of early Inner Eurasia

In my first chapter consideration is given to various early Inner Eurasian peoples whose identities are not clear. This uncertainty is due to various factors, such as the sparseness of the historical sources in which these peoples are mentioned, and the difficulties involved in equating the European and Chinese names with which they are labelled. It must be borne in mind that a label like 'Scythian' or 'Hun' may designate very different groups of people. Sometimes such a label is the name of a dominant ethnic unit in some loosely-knit confederacy of nomadic tribes, and sometimes it refers to all the members of such a confederacy and is as misleading as the term 'English' as applied to all the inhabitants of Britain. Inner Eurasian confederacies have constantly absorbed one another and changed their names, identities and languages, while their religious beliefs and practices have often remained very much the same.

The first great Inner Eurasian people to enter history are called the 'Scythians' and appear in the work of the Greek historian, Herodotus, who wrote in the fifth century BCE. He gives an account of an Iranian invasion of 'Scythia', the region to the north of the Black Sea. It must be said at once that the Scythians are considered by some modern scholars to have dominated a far wider area, stretching eastwards into Siberia, while other researchers see the 'Siberian Scythians' as constituting a number of different, albeit related peoples.[7] The Scythians described by Herodotus have as their present-day descendants the Ossetians of the Caucasus whose legends have been collected in the nineteenth and twentieth centuries and closely reflect ancient Scythian customs. Linguistically the Ossetians are Iranian, but Ossetian and Scythian religious materials are often closest to what is found among Turks and Mongols and belong to a clearly Inner Eurasian heritage.

After the Scythians come a people called by the Chinese name of Hsiung-nu, who lived in Mongolia from the fourth century BCE to the second century CE. It has been observed that although the Chinese sources present the Hsiung-nu as fierce warriors they had plenty of entertainments: horse jumping, camel races and singing in a very slow tempo (as evidenced among the Mongols). In their portable dwellings the left side of the entrance was used by

men and the right by women (this was to be the case among the
Turks and Mongols, for whom the left side of the human body is
the side of honour, as containing the heart).[8] The Hsiung-nu are
often identified with the Huns, who attacked the later Roman
Empire in the fourth and fifth centuries CE and whose religion
seems to have been typically Inner Eurasian. When their great
king Attila died in 453 CE he was buried with precautions observed
in Scythian and Mongol royal funerals: the tomb's location had to
be kept secret. The Huns possessed the widespread Inner Eurasian legend of an animal acting as a guide in their migrations: a
doe or cow is supposed to have led them into the Crimea.

Succeeding waves of barbarian military activity show us similar
peoples of uncertain identity but common religious practices. The
Avars, who invaded Europe in the mid-sixth century, may have
been descended from the Juan-juan, who had previously been
fighting on the northern frontiers of China. Both these peoples
followed the Inner Eurasian practice of horse riding at funerals,
and both exposed the corpse before burial while the mourners
rode round it. The Khazars, who flourished from the seventh to
the eleventh century in the Volga delta and the North Caucasian
steppes, also concealed their royal tombs. Some subjects of the
Khazar state would, like many Inner Eurasian peoples, worship
trees, sacrificing horses to them and hanging their heads and skins
over the branches. The Bulghars, who migrated to the Balkans in
680 and founded Bulgaria, seem to have been a mixture of Turks,
Huns and other nomads before they adopted a purely Slavic culture. They used to swear solemn oaths with the accompanying
sacrifice of a dog, who was cut in half – a custom observed by
Turks and Hungarians.

Finally, we must mention the Khitans, who conquered China
in 907 and ruled it until 1125. It is not clear whether they were
Mongols or belonged to the linguistically-related Tunguz-speakers. They would also sacrifice dogs, along with horses, cattle, sheep
and geese, in special double and triple combinations, the victims
often being white. The Khitans, as hunters, would often use arrows in their rituals, symbolizing men, as is frequently the case in
Inner Eurasia. Trees and sacrosanct royal tombs also figure prominently in the Khitans' religion, as do mountains and the veneration
of ancestors, who are sometimes animals in a thin human disguise.

The Turks

Our second chapter is devoted to the national religious inheritance of the Turks. Here it is mainly the Turks' original Inner Eurasian homeland (along with the Turks who have stayed there) which will concern us, although some attention is given to present-day Turkey, in which some branches of the Turks settled from the eleventh century CE onwards. Turks are divided into a variety of peoples, who, like their languages, are called 'Turkic', while 'Turkish' is used to denote the language of the modern Republic of Turkey. The Turkic group of languages itself belongs to a wider language family, termed 'Altaic' after the Altai mountains on the frontiers of China, Mongolia, Russia and ex-Soviet Kazakhstan. Linguists have posited the existence of a hypothetical 'Proto-Altaic' language, which would have been spoken before 5,000 BCE. It is thought that the western speakers of Proto-Altaic would have broken off shortly afterwards before becoming the linguistic ancestors of the Turks.[9]

The first Turkic-speaking empire known to history is that of the Türks (552–744), whose name has to be carefully spelt with two dots above the 'u': they ruled from Mongolia to the Aral Sea and, like their successors, are known to us from their inscriptions and from Chinese historians. We know that originally they were engaged in the mining or processing of iron, while their legends present them as being descended from a wolf.[10] As was the case with other Turkic-speaking peoples, their holy number was seven. They were succeeded by the Uighurs, who ruled in Mongolia from 744 to 840 and now live mainly in north-west China. The Uighurs are recorded as possessing the Turks' famous magic stone, which could produce rain and snow. After them come the Kirghiz (840–924), who have given their name to the ex-Soviet republic of Kyrgyzstan. Their funerary inscriptions reflect the belief that a man will be served in the hereafter by the animals, not just the warriors, whom he has killed. In the following centuries, as some groupings of Turks converted to Islam and took over the central Islamic lands, a lot of evidence about indigenous Turkic religion was preserved in Islamic and Christian sources, as well as in the Turks' own literature. Legends of the Turks' origins and early, warlike past are particularly informative, and stories of Muslim holy men sometimes yield glimpses of ancient Turkic myths.

From the eighteenth century onwards there are plenty of valuable descriptions of Inner Eurasian Turkic religion, provided first
by travellers and later by anthropologists. These descriptions give
us first-hand accounts of the performances of the Turkic shamans,
the religious specialists who, with the help of a drum, go into a
trance, foretell the future and heal the sick by means of a supernatural journey, in which they retrieve the sick person's soul, stolen
by an evil spirit. We hear how the shaman climbs a tree in order to
travel through the heavens, and how he uses imaginary animals
or birds to carry him on his way, or actually turns himself into
them to go faster.

In the nineteenth and twentieth centuries Turkic oral epics
have been collected, to constitute the world's richest and most
instructive treasury of such materials. The nineteenth-century
Russian pioneers in this field were quick to point out the importance of studying a Turkic singer's oral performance in order to
understand the Homeric epics and recent scholarship has confirmed the validity of their insights. A Turkic singer is very like a
shaman, going into a state of inspiration when performing and
seeing himself as riding his stringed instrument as a horse. A horse
is indeed often as important in the epic as the hero himself and
the archaic relationship between the two reflects the ancient roots
of Turkic epic in Inner Eurasian folk tales, which, it has been con-
tended, are the sources of the Greek legends of Odysseus.

The Mongols

In our third chapter we examine the traditional religion of the
Mongols. Linguistically the Mongols also belong to the Altaic family. It is thought that they represent descendants of the eastern
speakers of 'Proto-Altaic'. These 'Proto-Eastern-Altaic' speakers
would have separated into different groups around 5000 BCE and
the group which migrated to the Mongolian steppes would have
been the linguistic ancestors of the Mongols of today.[11]

The Mongols enter history with the invasions led by Genghis
Khan (d.1227). In the thirteenth and fourteenth centuries there
are plenty of sources for the study of their religion, beginning
with the famous *Secret History of the Mongols*, which may have been

composed by an adopted son of Genghis. This gives us legends of Genghis' ancestors and mentions plenty of Mongol beliefs and rituals: we read of the Mongols' being descended from a blue wolf who came to a holy mountain, and we also learn that they have nine as a holy number and possess a great white banner with nine corners symbolizing the people's protective spirits. Christian and Muslim sources are particularly informative about the Mongols, as a result of their far-ranging conquests and empire, which extended from China to Turkey and included present-day Afghanistan, ex-Soviet Central Asia, Russia, Iran and Iraq. The Mongol court received visits from western Christian monks and they and the Mongols' Muslim collaborators wrote a lot about the barbarian conquerors. The famous traveller Marco Polo (c.1255–c.1325) is also a valuable source, whose truthfulness has now been confirmed after recent doubts about his reliability.[12] We hear that the Mongols sacrifice to images, severely punish violations of taboos and respect the advice of powerful shamans. These shamans consecrate all white mares, foretell the destinies of all new-born boys and are called in to diagnose the causes of all illnesses.

In the sixteenth and seventeenth centuries more evidence is forthcoming from Mongol law codes, which penalize breaches of taboos with fines consisting of sets of five or nine animals. A Chinese administrator tells us of the precautions that are still taken to hide the graves of kings and nobles. It is in this period that Buddhism triumphs over indigenous religion in Mongolia. However, the Mongolian chronicles which recount this triumph often give us glimpses of the old faith, and in particular the offerings made by shamans to spirits in order to protect humans and livestock from disaster. Eighteenth-century travellers provide useful descriptions of Mongol spirit-images, and nineteenth-century scholarship has obtained extremely detailed accounts of how a shaman is initiated. Twentieth-century anthropologists have given us extensive lists of the numerous Mongol gods or spirits, along with elaborate analyses of the various rituals performed to guarantee the fertility of the herds. They have also discussed the relationship between shamans on the one hand, with their primary function of curing illnesses, and 'elders' on the other, who often seem to be more important in specifically religious matters such as annual public sacrifices.

The Tunguz and the Manchus

Our fourth chapter surveys the religion of the Tunguz-speaking peoples, along with that of the Manchus, who have a closely-related language. Their linguistic ancestors, like those of the Mongols, are thought to have been 'Proto-Eastern-Altaic' speakers who formed a different group around 5000 BCE and migrated to the north-east, into the Siberian forests.[13]

Tunguz-speaking peoples are first known to historians in the twelfth century CE, when one of them, the Jurchens, conquered northern China, which they ruled from 1125 to 1234. Chinese sources present them as having plenty of shamans and shamanesses, who would sacrifice pigs or dogs when treating illnesses. In one ritual a white dog was impaled on a pole and its head raised on another pole towards Heaven (the recipient of the sacrifice). The seventeenth century witnessed another conquest of China, by the Manchus, who ruled it from 1644 to 1912. In the seventeenth century we hear already of the Manchus' holy mountains and how they honoured their ancestors there. Eighteenth-century travellers tell us of the Tunguz-speakers of Siberia and their shamans' costumes and performances, in which antlers are worn and bears, dogs and cats are imitated.

It is, however, the twentieth-century anthropological descriptions of Tunguz and Manchu religion that give us the most useful evocations of the roles of animals and shamans. We are told of the vast knowledge of animals which the Tunguz possess, and of the elaborate paraphernalia which the shamans use: rattles, trinkets, bells and mirrors. We also hear of how the Tunguz shamans use ecstasy, hallucinations and hypnosis, and of the great strains imposed on them by their profession. There is also plenty of information about how some Tunguz-speakers go to great lengths to allay their fear of the spirit of someone who has recently died. Tunguz bear-hunting rituals have been analysed in minute detail, in which we see the terror inspired by the spirit of the animal which has been killed.

The Uralic family

In a concluding section I have briefly considered the religions and epics of the Uralic language family, which includes Finnish, Hungarian and Samoyed and is so called after the Ural mountains to the west of Siberia. Linguists have often seen this language family as somehow connected with the Altaic one, and perhaps forming a super family with it. It is thought that the original Proto-Uralic speakers may have lived near the Ural mountains in the seventh millennium BCE. At some point in the period stretching from the sixth millennium to the fourth some of the Proto-Uralic speakers broke away to form the Samoyedic group, now represented by the Samoyeds of the shores of the Arctic. The remainder, the Finno-Ugrians, split up in the third and second millennia and some groups migrated westwards: these are the Finns. Among the rest, the Ugrians, some were to conquer Hungary in the ninth century CE: these are the Hungarians. The remaining Ugrians are found today on the River Ob in western Siberia.[14]

It is clear that the religions of Uralic-speakers have been heavily influenced by their neighbours. I have not attempted to survey these religions in any detail, but have simply tried to indicate how an understanding of them can be enhanced by comparing them with the Inner Eurasian materials set out earlier in this book. In particular, I have offered a reinterpretation of the famous Finnish national epic, the *Kalevala*, in the light of Inner Eurasian parallels. It must be emphasized that the *Kalevala* is a nineteenth-century compilation which must be viewed as a work of literature and never as a primary source for the study of Finnish myths.

Methods

The methods which I have used are generally those of French scholars, and reflect the French domination of the history of religions (in the European sense of 'history as applied to religions' as opposed to the North American sense of 'studies relating to religion'). In this academic tradition the investigator seeks first of all to gather the evidence available and then to establish the internal logic of the religion of a given people. Only then does one proceed to make comparisons with the patterns found in the religions of other peoples and to draw inferences of a general character.

Thus I have begun by reviewing the sources listed by Jean-Paul Roux in his surveys of Turkic and Mongol religion. I am enormously indebted to the pioneering work which he has done. Without his thorough and painstaking exhumation of the European and Asian materials it would have been impossible for me to find my way to the evidence needed for the present study. I have added further sources where it has seemed appropriate, notably from Turkic epics, modern anthropological literature and my own work on Islamicized legends from north-west China. I have excluded Mongolian epics, as they seem to reflect foreign influences and a late stage of development.

I have also taken inspiration from the work done in comparative mythology by Georges Dumézil (1898–1986) and his followers. Comparative mythology compares the myths of a given language family, so that the patterns in the religion of one people cast light on that of another. Work in this discipline has been done almost entirely in the Indo-European language family, which includes English, Latin, Greek, Russian, Persian and Sanskrit. It is thought that these languages are descended from a hypothetical proto-language or group of dialects, called 'Proto-Indo-European', spoken sometime between 8000 and 2500 BCE in a homeland which might have been in Eastern Europe, Turkey, the Caucasus or the area to the north of the Black Sea. Thus comparative Indo-European mythology is highly relevant to our study of Inner Eurasian religions: specialists consider that there were large groups of Indo-European speakers in Inner Eurasia in the last few millennia BCE and the first millennium CE, before they migrated or were absorbed into groups of Altaic-speakers. This is particularly the case with the Indo-Iranian sub-family of Indo-European, whose speakers lived in what is now ex-Soviet Central Asia before splitting up and conquering Iran and India in the second millennium BCE.[15]

Dumézil argued that early Indo-European ideology was centred round an articulation of three concepts, as follows:

[1]   religious sovereignty (notably in its magical and legal aspects);
[2]   physical force (notably that of the warrior);
[3]   fertility (notably in its erotic and agricultural aspects).

I have argued elsewhere that this schema needs to be adapted, in particular to allow for the reflection of all three concepts as sub-concepts within each member of the triad, and also to include the figure of the wise old man who serves as a 'frame' for myths, along with the craftsmanship of the smith, placed at the bottom of the social scale. My adaptation runs:

[o]   the 'frame-figure', who lives or comes before and after everyone else and gives wise advice

[1]   religious sovereignty (including reason, intelligence and education)

[1.1]   sovereignty within sovereignty

[1.1a] the magical, arbitrary, terrifying and remote aspect of sovereignty

[1.1b] the legal, contractual and familiar aspect of sovereignty within sovereignty

[1.2]   force within sovereignty: the protection of the community's solidarity and continuity, notably by its young armed force

[1.3]   fertility within sovereignty: the distribution of goods

[2]   physical force (including anger)

[2.1]   sovereignty within force: either the warrior's intelligence, allied with speed, or his respect for religious sovereignty

[2.2]   force within force: either the warrior's brute force or his respect for its proper use

[2.3]   fertility within force: the warrior's respect for fertility

[3]   fertility (including desire, wealth, beauty and medicine)

[3.1]   sovereignty within fertility: prophecy

[3.2]   force within fertility: archery, horse breeding

[3.3]   fertility within fertility: luxury, pacificness, music and cattle breeding

[4]   the craftsmanship of the smith.[16]

Now Dumézil also saw his tripartite schema as reflecting Indian and Roman views of the universe. Thus the ancient Indians saw the universe as being divided into [1] the heavens; [2] the atmosphere, between the heavens and the earth; and [3] the earth itself. The Romans had three groups of gods: [1] gods of the heavens; [2] gods of the earth; and [3] gods of the underworld.[17] It seems to me that Inner Eurasian religions have had a view of the universe which resembles the Indian and may be represented as follows:

[1]   the space taken up by the sky, including tree tops and mountains, in particular their summits;
[2]   the space between the sky and the earth's surface, a space including seas and rivers, the trunks of trees and the scope of usual human activity, such as hunting and fishing, and sometimes also the slopes of mountains;
[3]   the space stretching from the earth's surface downwards, a space including the earth itself and graves, mines and other holes in the ground made by humans or animals.

I call this last schema 'typically Inner Eurasian' when using the numbers 1, 2 and 3 in this book; sometimes it has to be made clear that a tripartite pattern in the evidence discussed is partly 'typically Inner Eurasian', partly Indo-European.

1

Early Inner Eurasia

In this chapter we will consider the religions of a number of early Inner Eurasian peoples who have in common a lack of clear ethnic identity. We will begin with the famous 'Scythians', looking at them through the eyes of Herodotus, then move on to the Hsiung-nu, whose attacks on China resulted in the building of the Great Wall and who figure prominently in Chinese sources. After them we must briefly examine the T'o-pa, who first appeared on China's frontiers in the third century CE and who, by succeeding in establishing an empire in northern China, also obtained a place in Chinese records. Then we will survey the Huns, as described in the work of Roman historians; the Avars, as mentioned by Christian and Muslim authors, and the Juan-juan, their eastern counterparts, as evoked by the Chinese; and the Khazars and Bulghars, who also appear in Christian and Islamic sources. Finally, we will consider the Khitans, who, as rulers of China, gave their name to 'Cathay' and have left plenty of evidence in the Chinese official histories.

The Scythians

Herodotus' picture of Inner Eurasian religion is given to us as part of his account of an invasion of 'Scythia', the region to the north of the Black Sea, led by the famous Persian emperor Darius I (reigned 522–486 BCE), probably between 515 and 510. It must

be said that the Greek historian's narrative of the invasion displays considerable geographical confusion and his depiction of
the 'Scythians' is also ethnographically imprecise. Herodotus is
always trying to present them as the exact opposite of the Egyptians: whereas the latter are for him the oldest of peoples, the
'Scythians' are the youngest. Here he is not without good grounds,
since recent research has demonstrated that nomads, far from
being older than agriculturalists, as was previously imagined, have
to depend on them and thus post-date them. Herodotus often
says that he knows the 'Scythians' from first-hand experience, and
he probably did visit Greek colonies on the Black Sea's north coast.
His testimony regarding 'Scythian' religion is largely confirmed
by modern anthropological and archaeological studies and by comparisons with the folklore of the Ossetians of the Caucasus, the
linguistic descendants of the Iranian-speaking Scythians of classi-
cal antiquity.[1]

We are told by Herodotus that the Scythians claim to be descended from Zeus, the king of the Greek gods, and a daughter
of the River Dnieper who had a son and three grandsons. These
grandsons were confronted by three golden objects which fell from
the sky: a cup, a sword and a plough joined to a yoke. The eldest
and second of the three brothers tried to seize these objects, but
were thwarted when the gold started to burn as they approached.
When the youngest brother drew near the burning stopped, and
so he was recognized as king. To this day the sacred gold is honoured with sacrifices in an annual festival. If any man falls asleep
at this festival he is said not to live out the year, and thus, as a
consolation prize, is given as much land as he can ride around in
a day.[2]

Now the three golden objects are interpreted by Dumézil as
symbolizing the three leading concepts which he found in Indo-
European ideology: the cup, as often, represents religious
sovereignty [1], being used to pour libations to the gods, whereas
the sword naturally stands for the force of the warrior [2] and the
plough with its yoke symbolizes fertility [3]. As for the succession
to the throne of the youngest son, this seems to be common among
Inner Eurasian nomads: nomadism requires that the elder brothers should migrate elsewhere, while the youngest stays as heir to
the home. The annual festival in honour of the gold appears to

require staying awake in a kind of ordeal. An Ossetian folk tale tells of a magic golden apple which has to be guarded at night: if the guards fall asleep death and disaster will befall their family.[3]

Further information about other Inner Eurasian peoples is given by Herodotus, notably concerning a people called the Issedones. It is said of them that when a man's father dies the relatives eat his flesh, mixed with that of livestock which they bring. The dead man's skull is gilded and kept as an object of worship: his son will make an important sacrifice to it every year. A recent Italian commentator on Herodotus, Aldo Corcella, notes that cannibalism is attributed to various Inner Eurasian societies, along with the use, for magical purposes, of skulls as drinking vessels. We shall find further examples of the use of skulls, along with sacrifices to ancestors, in due course.[4]

As for the religion of the Scythians themselves, Herodotus informs us that they worship Hestia (the Greek personification of the hearth) in particular, and after her Zeus and the Earth (seen as married to him) followed by Apollo, 'the heavenly Aphrodite', Heracles and Ares. Only the last of these is worshipped with images, altars and sanctuaries.[5]

This list of Scythian gods, presented in the forms of their Greek equivalents, has been the subject of much comment by modern scholars. The cult of the hearth is widespread among nomadic Turks and Mongols, and also among Indo-European speakers. Here Hestia seems to enter into a particularly Indo-European configuration, as has been observed by Dumézil, who points out that the list corresponds closely to the enumeration of spirits and saints in the famous 'Prayer of the Ossetian Women' transcribed around 1870. Further Caucasian parallels have been adduced by Dumézil's Georgian follower Georges Charachidze, both from among Georgians living in the mountains in the east of the Caucasus and from among the Svans, a people who live in the high valleys in the south of the same region and whose unwritten language (like Georgian, belonging to the Caucasian family) is noted for its many archaic features. Hestia and Zeus appear to represent the usual Indo-European pair of supreme sovereign gods, the former close to humans, the latter remote [symbolizing subconcepts 1.1b and 1.1a respectively in my notation – see above, p. 13]. They are reflected, in the Prayer of the Ossetian Women, by the Spirit of God on the one hand and God himself on the other both of whom are invoked together at the start of the prayer. The Earth, in the list of Scythian deities, seems to be echoed, in the Ossetian prayer, by Mary the mother of Jesus, to whom the Ossetian women pray next, as the protectress of the solidarity and continuity of the community formed by the women [sub-concept 1.2]: they ask her to kill their enemies and protect their children. Apollo, the next god in the Scythian list, is paralleled by the next figure invoked by the Ossetian women, the spirit of Smallpox: in Greek religion Apollo is a deity of medicine, who also grants a peaceful death and can bring an epidemic, so that he has an appropriate counterpart in this Ossetian spirit, who is much venerated, surrounded by strict taboos and propitiated with sacrifices when an epidemic occurs.

Charachidze points out that whereas in the rest of the Indo-European domain medicine belongs to the third of Dumézil's concepts, fertility, in the Caucasus illness is seen above all as a matter of divine possession, and thus belongs to the first concept, that of religious sovereignty. I have argued elsewhere that there are other examples of a figure's being promoted from the third concept to what I call 'sub-concept 1.3', fertility within sovereignty. Here, naturally, the Ossetian women beg the spirit of Smallpox to grant good health to their children. The next Scythian deity, the 'heavenly Aphrodite', presumably symbolizes fertility as such [3], and is echoed on the Ossetian side by 'Saint Elias', invoked in the third section of the women's prayer in a call for an abundant harvest. As for the two final gods in the Scythian list, Heracles and Ares, they doubtless represent the common Indo-European pair of a clever war-deity [sub-concept 2.1: sovereignty, in its aspect of intelligence, reflected within the concept of warlike force] and a brutish, stupid war-god [sub-concept 2.2: force within force]. In the Ossetian prayer they are paralleled by two figures invoked in the prayer's second section, 'Saint George', venerated in the Caucasus as the patron of manly, warlike activity, and 'The Bad One', a spirit called Tyhost – a savage and extremely violent being who gouges out eyes and tears limbs off.[6]

When Herodotus says that there is a particular enthusiasm for producing religious sculpture and architecture in honour of Ares the comparatist is reminded of a similar enthusiasm for a brutal

war-god, Gish, among the warlike Nuristani of north-east Afghanistan, who, linguistically, also belong to the Indo-Iranian sub-family
of Indo-European and had an archaic set of gods of the same
kind at the end of the nineteenth century CE: Nuristani villages
always had one shrine dedicated to Gish, by far their most popular deity and would often pride themselves on having two.
Otherwise, the absence of sanctuaries among the Scythians is paralleled by the absence of temples among the Turks and Mongols
who declare that God is to be worshipped everywhere.[7]

Herodotus goes on to explain that the Scythians sacrifice animals by strangling them. This is clearly to avoid spilling blood:
many Altaic-speaking peoples have a similar taboo and prefer to
kill animals (and humans) in such a way that no blood is spilt. So
far as the cult of Ares is concerned, however, Herodotus says that
the Scythians do spill blood. Every year they make an enormous
pile of sticks and put an ancient sword, symbolizing Ares, on it.
Along with the usual bloodless animal sacrifices, performed on a
greater scale than to other gods, the Scythians cut the throats of
prisoners of war and pour their blood on the sword; they also cut
off the prisoners' right arms and throw them away. Corcella comments that the cult of the sword is attested among other early
Euroasiatic nomads, while maiming the corpses as the ultimate
humiliation is found elsewhere in the Iranian linguistic domain.
We may add that the exceptionally large-scale sacrificing of animals to the war-god is paralleled in Nuristan, where prisoners of
war have also been taken to religious services in honour of the
war-god before being executed.[8]

Proceeding to purely military matters, Herodotus reports that
the Scythians scalp their enemies and make cups of their heads.
Every year those warriors who have killed enemies drink wine from
a special bowl, while those who have killed none sit apart in dis-
grace. Ossetian folklore also has stories of scalping and a magic
cup, filled with beer, which rises of its own accord to a warrior's
lips, but only if his boasts of killings are true.[9]

According to Herodotus the Scythians have many diviners who
foretell the future by means of willow rods which they put on the
ground. There are also some diviners who are feminized men and
claim to have acquired their art from Aphrodite: they practise it
with the help of lime tree bark, cut into three parts, which they

plait and unplait as they prophesy. Corcella explains that such
methods are still used by the Ossetians, while the feminized male
diviners are reminiscent of Siberian shamans who often practise
ritual transvestism.[10]

Herodotus also tells us that the Scythians give each other sworn
pledges by pouring their blood, mixed with wine, into a bowl in
which they dip a sword, arrows, an axe and a javelin before drinking from it. We may note that the use of arrows in making a
'blood-brother' agreement is evidenced in the case of Genghis
Khan and also in East (or Chinese) Turkistan (now Sinkiang or
Xinjiang in north-west China): there, as generally among the Turks
and Mongols, the weapons represent the souls of men themselves.[11]

Scythian royal funerary customs are described in great detail
by Herodotus. When a king dies the mourners cut their faces and
take the body to a distant spot. Some of his servants are strangled
and buried with him. A year later 50 more of them are strangled,
along with 50 horses, and the bodies of the men and animals are
impaled around the tomb. Here Herodotus' testimony is echoed
by descriptions of various Inner Eurasian royal funerals: self-lac-
eration and transporting the corpse to a secret, remote location
are standard usages, evidenced for Attila and the Mongol conquerors, while human sacrifice for the purpose of serving the king
in the hereafter is also well-evidenced: one of Genghis Khan's sons
killed 40 concubines as presents for his father.[12]

Ordinary Scythians, according to Herodotus, have their bodies carried around in waggons for 40 days after death, as their
families visit their friends and food is placed before the corpse.
After the burial the Scythians purify themselves by taking a vapour bath of hemp smoke in a tent. Corcella comments that in
the beliefs of many Indo-European speakers 40 days are needed
for the soul to leave the body, and that Altaic-speaking shamans
purify the tent of the deceased 40 days after death. Archaeological discoveries in Siberia have shown the great antiquity of the
practice of inhaling the smoke of ordinary hemp (Cannabis
Sativa), a practice which was widespread before the medieval Islamic adoption of Cannabis Indica.[13]

Later on Herodotus, in his account of Darius' invasion of
Scythia, tells us about a people called the Getae, a subdivision of
the Thracians living to the north of Greece. These Getae, he says,

:laim that after death they go to a god called Zalmoxis. Every five
years they choose a messenger and send him to tell Zalmoxis what
they need. They do so by throwing the messenger on to their spear
points: if he is killed this is taken as a good omen, and if not another messenger is chosen. The Getae also respond to thunder
and lightning by shooting arrows at the sky to threaten their god.
This Zalmoxis, according to a Greek story re-told by Herodotus,
was a man who tricked the Thracians into believing in life after
death by vanishing into an underground chamber, where he lived
for three years, making the Thracians believe that he was dead
before reappearing to them. Corcella comments that shooting
arrows at the sky is a practice paralleled among various peoples in
their attempts to drive inclement weather away; we shall find it
again in Inner Eurasia. As for the sending of the messenger and
Zalmoxis' underground retreat, the American classicist Rhys Carpenter, writing in 1946, pointed out that the Ainu, a people of
northern Japan, kill a bear after telling him that he is going to
their god as a messenger who must ask for plenty of game.
Zalmoxis, according to other ancient sources, fasted in a 'cave-
like place' and was dressed in a bearskin. Other Greek writers
speak of a Thracian cult in which people would descend into a
hole in a mountain cave, after a ritual in which references were
made to the Underworld.[14]

As for Darius' invasion itself, Herodotus relates that the
Scythians responded to it with a strategic retreat and a mocking
message to Darius to try and find the graves of their fathers, the
only things for which they would be prepared to fight. Here we
see again the importance of the secret and sacred royal tombs.
Subsequently the Scythians sent Darius a bird, a mouse, a frog
and five arrows. An Iranian noble interpreted these gifts as a message meaning 'Unless you become birds and fly up into the sky,
Persians, or become mice and go down into the earth, or become
frogs and leap into the lakes, you will be hit by these arrows and
not return home.' The tripartition looks typically Inner Eurasian:
it presents [1] the sky, [3] the space stretching from the surface
of the earth downwards and [2] water above the surface of the
earth. Scholars have noted a close parallel to this story. In 1303
CE a Mongol prince, Toktai, sent a hoe, an arrow and a handful of
earth to a rival who took this to mean: 'If you hide beneath the

earth, I shall dig you out. If you fly up to the sky, I shall shoot you.
Choose a battlefield.'¹⁵ Another close parallel, however, has been
overlooked by recent scholarship. In 1730 a Swedish former prisoner of war, Philipp Johann von Strahlenberg (1676–1747),
published a description of north-eastern Eurasia. In it he mentioned a people of north-west Siberia who were to die out in the
eighteenth century, the Arins: they, on seeing Russian colonial
expansion threatening their region, sent the Russians an arrow, a
black fox and a piece of red earth as an offer of the choice of
peace or war.¹⁶

Finally, says Herodotus, some Scythians did confront Darius,
and it looked as if a battle was about to start, but a hare ran out
between the two armies and the Scythians all chased after it. Now
the hare has long had great religious significance for Inner Eurasian nomads, as we shall see in East Turkistan where it assumes
the role of a spiritual guide to humans: thus, as Corcella observes,
it may well have had a symbolic value in an earlier version of
Herodotus' story.¹⁷

The Hsiung-nu

The Inner Eurasian people known by the Chinese name of Hsiung-
nu were active militarily from the fourth century BCE to the second
century CE. We have evidence concerning them from Chinese historical sources and twentieth-century archaeological discoveries.
The materials for the study of the Hsiung-nu's religion have been
studied by Roux, but his references to them are scattered throughout his writings under various subject headings, and so here we
must try to use these references and his sources to produce an
overview.

Chinese historians refer to Hsiung-nu specialists in divination
and healing, and tell us that the Hsiung-nu's 'sorcerers of the
nine heavens sacrificed to the nine heavens'. The historians seem
to be referring to shamans. We are told that in order to cure illnesses recourse was had to human sacrifice: Roux points out that
the medieval Mongols believed that a man could, by volunteering
to die, save an invalid from death. With regard to the 'nine heavens', the Chinese historians say that the Hsiung-nu believed that
each heaven possessed its own spirits. 'Heaven' as a single entity

was God himself, 'Tengri': the name is preserved by both the Turks and the Mongols. The Hsiung-nu also venerated a holy mountain. It was from God-Heaven, however, that there came the vital force (*qut*, again a word preserved by the Turks) which gave a sovereign his kingship. Another sort of force seems to have been discerned in bones: in 202 BCE the Hsiung-nu king made a cup out of the skull of a rival chieftain. Plaits of hair were similarly important, as is shown by their presence in Hsiung-nu tombs. Light is also charged with vital force in a Hsiung-nu myth: a man sees a huge fish with two horns, and then his wife sees this fish transformed into a man who gives her an object with an extraordinary light emanating from it and says that she will have a son – this son becomes the founder of a dynasty.[18]

This motif of the animal as a portent is evidenced elsewhere in the Chinese sources: for the Hsiung-nu a bird is always a presage of good fortune. (The same is the case if one sees the ginseng plant.) Eagle feathers are used to feather Hsiung-nu arrows. Hsiung-nu children kill birds, weasels and rats as a preparation for killing foxes and hares when they grow up. The Hsiung-nu, like the Scythians, sacrifice horses. Non-animal offerings, however, are also made by them when a king dies: the whole army gathers to give the corpse wine and rice. When a treaty is concluded a white horse is sacrificed, and afterwards the two leaders mix its blood in a cup made from the skull of an enemy chieftain. The Hsiung-nu also make funerary sacrifices and have special 'houses' for sacrificing. They have special sacrifices in the first, fifth and ninth months of the Chinese year (corresponding to February, June and October). Those performed on the fifth day of the month are particularly important. It is on this day that they sacrifice to 'the spirit of Heaven'.[19]

The Hsiung-nu figure together with animals in various myths reproduced in Chinese sources. One myth has a Hsiung-nu boy thrown into a marsh: he is rescued and brought up by a she-wolf and later has intercourse with her, thereby becoming the ancestor of a whole people: the Turks. (We shall refer to this myth below.) Another myth involves another Inner Eurasian nation, the Wu-sun, who lived on the north-east side of the Ti'en Shan mountains (in what is now north-west China) in the second and first centuries BCE. The father of their first king had reigned over a tiny amount of land and had been killed by his neighbours. His son survived as a baby in a desert, being given milk by a wolf. The Hsiung-nu's king, impressed by this miracle, brought the boy up. In a similar myth a Hsiung-nu king has two daughters who are too beautiful to be given to men, and whom he therefore offers to Heaven, imprisoning them in a tower. One daughter finds a husband in a wolf which makes its lair at the base of the tower, and she becomes the ancestress of a new tribe. It would appear that such legends are reflected in animal sacrifices: the Hsiung-nu sacrifice to the tutelary god of the ground in honour of their ancestors, and the Türks sacrifice in a cave where their ancestral she-wolf is believed to have given birth.[20]

Chinese historians have preserved a brief prayer uttered by a Hsiung-nu king on finding a city abandoned to him. On horseback, he lifted his arms, bowed his head and cried out, 'O Heaven! Thank you for having delivered it up to me!' Roux points out that elsewhere the Hsiung-nu are described as dismounting before praying.[21]

We are also told by the Chinese sources that the Hsiung-nu, like other Inner Eurasian peoples, despise the old. As Roux observes, this seems to be linked to the widespread practice of killing old people. However, both archaeological and literary evidence shows that the practice of killing a widow immediately after the death of her husband, attested in Siberian burials before the Hsiung-nu period, was not continued by the Hsiung-nu. By contrast, it is clear from Chinese writings that they, like their successors in the same region, would give the wives of a dead father or brother to his sons (though avoiding a mother–son marriage) or surviving brothers. However, again like their successors, the Hsiung-nu would kill large numbers of slaves, concubines and prisoners of war at an important man's funeral. They would also bury gold, silver, and clothing with the corpse. No mound would be erected over the grave, and the ancient practice, often found among the steppe peoples, of planting a tree upon it was not observed by the Hsiung-nu.[22]

Some elements of Hsiung-nu religion, which we have not adduced from Roux's works, are listed in a brief summary of the Chinese evidence published by the German orientalist Wolfram Eberhard in 1942. For the Hsiung-nu the left is the side of honour this is normal among the Turks and Mongols, the reason given being that the heart is on the left side). They venerate the sun and the moon and have particular respect, not just for the fifth day of the month (as we have seen), but for the sixth as well. We also hear of 'sorcerers' who bury the bones of sheep and cattle beneath roads in order to work black magic against invaders.[23]

Finally, we may note an important article on Hsiung-nu worship of the sword, published by the Chinese scholar Kao Ch'ü-hsün in 1960. The Hsiung-nu, we hear, possessed special shrines in which a sword was venerated as a god and had prisoners of war immolated to it. They also had metal images in human form: these are echoed in the circumstantial evidence for the existence of 'idols' among the Huns.[24]

The T'o-pa

Very little is known about the religion of the T'o-pa people, who apparently were Altaic-speakers and appeared on the northern frontiers of China in the third century CE. The T'o-pa were to establish an empire in northern China under the dynastic name of Wei, ruling from 386 to 534. Roux notes that the T'o-pa would worship the moon on the evening of the autumnal equinox and the sun on the morning of the spring equinox. Further information is provided by Eberhard in his study of the T'o-pa's empire, published in 1949 and based on the Chinese historical sources. The T'o-pa performed a great sacrifice to the sky on the fourth day of the fourth month of the year, with 49 wooden figures on the altar. These figures wore a white headdress, a silk robe and a horse's tail. Eberhard points out that 49 is 7 x 7 and that these figures sound like ones found in Hsiung-nu sites, representing 'sky-gods'. The Chinese sources give further details of this T'o-pa sacrifice: the offerings consisted of a white calf, a yellow horse and a white sheep. Shamanesses stood by with drums, and the figures were sprinkled with wine. Another festival took place in the tenth month, presumably corresponding to that in the fourth month as being half a year later and thus in a symmetrical relationship with it. Similarly, there was a sacrifice on a mountain at the end of the sixth month, to summon the warm weather. Eberhard points out that the Central Asian Turks had a corresponding festival at the end of the twelfth month, to summon the cold weather. He also observes that when a new T'o-pa emperor was enthroned he was presented to the sky on a carpet held by seven men. (This custom was observed by other Altaic speaking rulers.) The T'o-pa buried their dead simply, without a mound, and burned all the deceased's possessions. Roux remarks that their empress was killed when one of her sons succeeded to the throne. He further notes that the T'o-pa would sacrifice to their ancestors at a cave transformed into a temple at the solstices and equinoxes.[25]

Roux has also collected further evidence relating to the role of animals in T'o-pa religion. The T'o-pa, according to one of their myths, migrated across mountains and were guided by a supernatural animal which looked like a horse but had the voice of a bull. In one of their sacrifices their ruler would mount a horse before daybreak and, heavily armed and followed by 20 horsemen, would ride round a special mound before going to its summit. There he would perform the sacrifice before remounting and circling the mound again: this was called 'going round the sky'.[26]

The Huns

As with the T'o-pa, little is known about the Huns' religion. We have very hostile reports about them from the historians of the later Roman Empire, which they attacked in the fourth and fifth centuries CE, and there is some archaeological evidence. Here we shall use the fine survey of the Huns left by the erudite Viennese scholar Otto Maenchen-Helfen at his death in 1969.

Maenchen-Helfen notes that the Huns, like medieval Turks and Mongols, did not wash their clothes, probably for the same reason: to avoid offending the water spirits. They did not persecute their Christian subjects, and had no reason to do so. A couple of Christian writers claimed that huge successes had been made in converting the Huns, but Maenchen-Helfen shows that this is just a stock apologetic commonplace, used by Christian writers when speaking of all barbarians. When the Huns invaded they killed Christian monks, raped the nuns and burnt the churches after stealing the sacred vessels: if, afterwards, they permitted the Christians under their rule to pray and fast this was presumably due to difference rather than any pre-existing sympathy for Christianity. We know that the Huns had diviners and shamans, who may have been the same people. The Huns practised divination by examining the bones of livestock: this is an ancient Inner Eurasian practice, in which, as a rule, the shoulder blades of sheep are exposed to fire and the resulting scorch marks are interpreted.[27]

When the Huns' great king Attila died they cut off part of their hair and made deep cuts in their faces, as was their normal custom when mourning. Maenchen-Helfen comments that cutting the face as a sign of mourning has been well attested from Eastern Europe to Central Asia, and combining this with cutting off one's hair is evidenced among the Turks, Hungarians and Slavs. According to the Roman historians Attila's body was laid in state in a silken tent and the Huns' finest horsemen provided a cavalcade. A dirge was sung, and then revels ensued. Afterwards, at night, the body was secretly buried. In order to keep the tomb's location hidden the men who did this were killed. Maenchen-Helfen observes that horse races at funerals are evidenced among the Huns of the Caucasus and the Turks, as well as a great variety of peoples, and that mixing grief with joy is also widespread. We have already noted that the Scythian custom of keeping the locations of royal tombs secret is paralleled among the Mongols.[28]

The Roman historians also tell us that the Huns (like the Scythians and the Hsiung-nu) worshipped the god of war in the form of a sword. However, Maenchen-Helfen points out that this custom (which is reflected in that of swearing by one's sword) is attested among a number of diverse peoples, such as the Franks and the Indians. The Huns, like other northern Eurasian nomads, have left masks, depicting human heads, in their burials: these masks are imitations of Greek and Iranian models and tell us nothing about the Huns' own gods. One Byzantine historian says that the Huns who lived in the Crimea in the sixth century had sacred figures made of gold and electrum (an alloy of gold and silver). As Maenchen-Helfen comments, there is no reason to doubt this and Attila's followers probably also had sacred images in human form.[29]

Archaeologists have found plenty of Hunnic bronze cauldrons, from central Europe to Siberia. These cauldrons have often been discovered buried in or near running water, as is also the case

with non-Hunnic cauldrons in Inner Eurasia. Maenchen-Helfe
agrees with the theory that the nomads used such cauldrons i
rituals at watercourses in spring and stored them by the wate
when they moved to their summer pastures.[30]

Roux, in his notes on the Huns' religion, naturally emphasize
the classic Altaic motif of the animal as guide. This appears ir
their legend, mentioned by the Byzantine historians, that the
were led in their invasion of the Crimea by a doe or cow. Extremely
similar legends of animals going before conquering armies are
found among the Turks and Mongols.[31]

The Juan-juan and the Avars

After the Huns, the next barbarian invaders of Europe were the
Avars who appeared in the mid-sixth century and lived on in Eastern Europe until the first half of the tenth. As we have noted, it is
not clear whether they were descended from (or in some way originally belonged as subjects to) the Juan-juan, a people who fought
the Chinese from the fourth to the sixth centuries and ruled from
what is now north-west China to northern Korea. Here we shall
look first at the Juan-juan, as they appear in the work of Chinese
historians and then at the literary and archaeological evidence
concerning the Avars.

The Juan-juan evidently had female shamans. According to the
Chinese sources one of their rulers became devoted to a shamaness
who pretended that his youngest brother had been taken up to
heaven and claimed that she had the power to bring him down. A
tent was erected beside a lake and the shamaness offered a sacrifice to the spirit of Heaven. The prince reappeared in the tent
and declared that he had indeed been staying in the sky. Along
with venerating the sky, the Juan-juan fired arrows at it during
thunderstorms. Otherwise we know only of their funerary rites.
They buried their dead in a sitting position: Roux thinks that this
means a foetal one, as often in the world, symbolizing a new ges-
tation. The grave was left open while mourners rode round it 100
times.[32]

As for the Avars, we again learn little of their religion from
literary sources. The Christian writers used by Maenchen-Helfen
say that the Avars swear by their swords and defeat their enemies

•y producing illusions through magic. An Iranian geographer, •bn Rusta, who lived at the start of the tenth century, reports: The Avars, near their capital, possess an enormous barren tree. Everyone gathers round it on Wednesdays in order to hang all •orts of fruit on it, and they prostrate themselves before the tree and make offerings to it.'[33] Ibn Rusta also reports, laconically, that the Avars all worship a skull. He is more forthcoming about Avar funerals. A man had his corpse exposed in public for three days, and the inhabitants, wearing armour, charged at it and wheeled around it, pointing their lances in its direction. The aim, it was explained to Ibn Rusta, was to bring the soul back to the body.[34]

The archaeological evidence concerning the Avars was briefly reviewed by the Hungarian historian Samuel Szádecky-Kardoss in 1990. An Avar warrior would be buried with an indication of his military rank, consisting of one or more arrows laid beside the corpse. Eggs were put in women's tombs, doubtless as symbols of fertility. An Avar bone jar depicts the famous Inner Eurasian world-mountain, along with the column seen as standing at the world's centre: above there is engraved the tree of life, with its nine branches, reaching to the sky.[35]

The Khazars

The Khazars, who first emerged as a political grouping in the seventh century and then existed as a people until the eleventh, had their heartland in the Volga delta and the North Caucasian steppes. Information about their indigenous religion is furnished by Christian and Muslim writers. Of particular interest is their bizarre ritual performed at the accession of a new king. He is strangled, almost to death (so that he loses consciousness), and the words which he utters during this are interpreted to predict the length of his reign. At the end of this period he is put to death. This practice, Roux notes, is also found among the early Turks. When a married man dies, we are told, his widow is burnt. If a man dies a bachelor he is given a wife after his death. (A similar custom is described by Marco Polo as being observed in the Inner Eurasia of his day, and, as we shall see, the practice has survived in Hungary up to our own time.) A Khazar king would be buried near a river, which was diverted to flow over the mausoleum. This mausoleum was in the form of a

house with 20 rooms, each containing a tomb. The men who had
buried the king were beheaded afterwards so that no-one would
know which room contained the body. When one Khazar governor died, 300 Byzantine prisoners were executed.[36]

Further information about religion beneath the Khazar state is
provided in an Armenian *History* attributed to one Movsês
Kağankatouaçi and apparently compiled in the tenth century. According to this source, in 681 the Khazars had as vassals some
North Caucasian 'Huns'. These 'Huns' worshipped trees and considered men or objects struck by lightning to be sacrificed to a
god. At funerals they beat drums and whistled over corpses, lacer-
ated their cheeks and limbs and engaged naked in sword fights at
the graves, as well as taking part in wrestling matches and galloping their horses. They sacrificed horses to a supreme god called
'Tengri'. The 'Huns' also sacrificed to fire, water, 'gods of the
roads', the moon and 'all creatures considered in their eyes to be
in some way remarkable'. In addition they sacrificed horses to
specially dedicated oak trees, pouring the blood over them and
throwing the heads and skins over the branches. The 'Huns', we
are told, had priests and sorcerers who used dice for 'witchcraft',
and royal graves which were important sanctuaries.[37]

The Bulghars

The Bulghars appear to have been a mixture of various peoples,
notably Turks, and also Huns surviving to the north of the Black
Sea. From there, in 680, they migrated to the Balkans. As found-
ers of Bulgaria they mingled with the local Slavs and became
Slavicized. Here it is of course the pre-Slavic Bulghars who interest us. Their religion also appears in brief glimpses given by
Christian and Muslim sources, analysed by Roux. The Bulghars,
we learn, paid the greatest attention to divination and treated
illnesses with specific prayers and ligatures, along with a special
'healing stone', attested in ancient north-east Asia and (today) in
Central Asia and southern Turkey. Like other Altaic-speaking peoples, they worshipped the sun. The Bulghars held the howling of
dogs to be a good omen, presaging a whole year of prosperity.
They swore solemn oaths with the accompaniment of the sacrifice of a dog, cut in half, as did some medieval Turks and

Hungarians (the Mongols used a horse instead). The Bulghar men wore a phallus, which they would kiss and worship, saying, 'It is our sole creator.' Like other Inner Eurasian peoples, the Bulghars made a cup out of the skull of a leading enemy and would keep the skulls of lesser ones. We are told that whenever they found a man who was particularly clever and knowledgeable they would sacrifice him in order to make him serve a spirit: they would hang him from a tree until his body turned to dust. It is also recorded that the Bulghars of the Danube, when burying an important man, would burn some people and send others (his wives and servants) into the tomb to die of hunger.[38]

The Khitans

By contrast, we have a lot of materials concerning the religion of the Khitans, a Mongol or Tunguz people who ruled China from 907 to 1125. The main source, the *Liao History* (so called after the name of the Khitans' reigning dynasty), was not finished until 1343, but is based on records which go back to the tenth century, and can be supplemented from passages in other dynastic histories. It has been translated, with commentaries, by the Parisian researcher Rolf Stein (in 1940) and the famous German Sinologist Karl Wittfogel and his Chinese colleague Feng Chia-Sheng (in 1949).

The Khitans had shamans who performed a special ceremony on the first day of the year. Twelve master shamans would jingle small bells, while holding arrows, singing and shouting in order to frighten the demons. There was also a head shaman, who took part in the twelve-yearly 're-birth' ceremony performed by the Khitan emperor. Thus the head shaman and his colleagues formed an official priesthood, which was commanded to worship 'Heaven and Earth and the god of War'. There were also female shamans. Divination was practised by heating the shoulder blade of a white sheep: if this cracked the Khitans would go to war. Various rites were performed to produce rain, notably firing arrows at willow trees. Perhaps here the male symbol of the arrow reflected Khitan cosmology in which the sky, male, had the female earth as his complement, represented by a goddess in the form of an old woman on a cart drawn by a grey bovine. She, the ancestress of

the Khitans, had met her husband at a place where two river
joined, at the foot of the holy mountain called Mu-yeh (in th
east of the Inner Mongolian Region of the Chinese Republic)
He had come riding a white horse.[39]

These animals, along with others, are all-important in Khita
religion. Special festivals accompanied the catching of the firs
fish and the first wild goose of the year: success or failure was seer
as determining the luck of the next twelve months. Game would
be hunted by specialists (often furnished by the Jurchen people
considered below), who were experts in the art of imitating the
cries of different species: thus we hear of 'animal-men', 'deer-men',
'boar-men', etc. The hunters would sacrifice to the spirit of the
animal and put on its skin and head before going hunting: Stein
comments that this was not just to deceive the animal, but rather
to enter into the community of the species. In another ceremony
the Khitans would fire arrows at a wooden hare. Annual sacrifices
of animals were made to the sky and the earth, the ancestors,
mountains and rivers, 'the earl of the wind', 'the Divine Lady',
'the spirit of the deer' and 'the spirit of the white horse'. At the
winter solstice every Khitan man would sacrifice a white horse, a
white sheep and a white goose, mixing the blood with his wine.
The emperor would sacrifice to the Black Mountain (near Tsaghan
Khoton, Jehol), which was believed to take care of the souls of all
the Khitan dead. Ten thousand sets of paper men and horses would
be burnt as offerings to the mountain. On the eighth day of the
eighth month the Khitans sacrificed white dogs seven paces in
front of their tents and buried them with their muzzles pointing
out above the ground: seven days later the tents were placed on
top of them. (It is known that a Khitan taboo prohibited the use
of the word for 'dog'.)[40]

Double sacrifices of animals were particularly significant. The
Khitans (like Homer's Trojans) would sacrifice a white sheep to
Heaven and a black one to Earth. They would also, more frequently, immolate a grey bovine and a white horse (in memory of
the original pair of ancestors). As Stein observes, there is alterna-
tion between human and animal on the level of the symbol:
according to Khitan legend there had once been a chief in the
form of a skull, who lived in a tent and occasionally donned human form to come out and see the double sacrifice. (Evidently

his skull corresponds to the dogs' muzzles just mentioned.) Similarly, there was a second legendary chief who wore a wild boar's
head and a pigskin, and also left his tent only on important occasions. Both these rulers disappeared for good when someone
peeked curiously into the tent. Afterwards there was a third chief
who used to keep 20 sheep and eat 19 of them every day: the next
day they were miraculously replaced. We may observe that the
trio of chiefs looks like an Indo-European one: the first seems to
represent religion as well as sovereignty [1], while the second, in
the form of a wild boar, seems to symbolize the force of the war-
rior-hunter [2] and the third evidently stands for fertility [3]. What
is more important for our purposes, however, is the role of the
animal as ancestor: this appears in the legend of a Khitan empress who dreamt that a black hare jumped into her bosom – as a
result she conceived a future emperor.[41]

Sacrifices were also made after the death of a Khitan nobleman: food would be burnt at the new and the full moon. The
body itself was exposed on a tree in the mountains. After three
years the bones were gathered and cremated. Afterwards the
mourners, while pouring a libation of wine, addressed the deceased:

> During the winter months eat facing the sun
> During the summer months eat facing the cold
> If I go to the hunt make me catch
> Plenty of boars and plenty of deer.

The idea, explains Stein, is that the dead are seen as exposed
to the sun in winter, to have their flesh eaten by birds or animals,
whereas the bones live on in the cold tomb in summer. Giving
their flesh and skin is a preliminary to obtaining the flesh and
skin of the animals hunted.[42]

Human sacrifices were made at the funerals of emperors early
on in Khitan rule over China. The emperor himself, at his investiture ceremony, had to go through a ritual which seems to
correspond to the simulated human sacrifice of the Khazar ruler:
he was obliged to gallop off, fall from his horse and be covered
with a felt rug. He also had to lean against a black bearskin, which
hid some children: this apparently reflects the ancient T'o-pa

investiture ritual in which the ruler stood on a black felt blanket covering seven men. The investiture itself was preceded by the 'rebirth' ceremony, performed by the emperor in a specially erected building outside which there stood an old man carrying a quiver and arrows. After the emperor had passed under three timbers in the form of an inverted 'V', the old man hit the quiver and called out, 'A boy is born!' At this point the emperor's head was covered by the chief shaman. Stein remarks that the use of an arrow to represent the birth of a boy is a well-known symbol in ancient China. We may add that so-called 'devil arrows' were fired by the Khitans at criminals, prisoners-of-war and captured spies in a magic technique used against rebels and enemies. Arrows (along with bows, saddles, horses and gowns) also figure in ritual exchanges made between two men who agree to be blood-brothers.[43]

Various other elements of Khitan religion are of special interest. The Khitans' tents always faced east, and they gave honour to the left side. They paid particular reverence to the sun, but neglected the moon. According to one Chinese observer the Khitans had 'a predilection for spirits'. They often practised marriage by abduction – evidently with the collusion of the bride. Another Chinese writer, an eye-witness, mentions a burial-place between two mountains with tall pine trees, beautiful plants, rare birds and wild herbs, and relates how the Khitan emperor entered a building there in order to sacrifice. 'Of the various tribal chieftains only those who carried the sacrificial utensils could go in; when they had entered the door was locked. The next day the door was opened, with the statement "The ceremony of the 'throwing back of the cups' is over." When we asked about this ceremony everyone became mysterious and refused to reply.'[44]

It must be added that the Khitans named the first seven days of the year after animals: cock, dog, pig, sheep, bovine, horse and man. Here we may note the important position of the bovine–horse pair (explicitly named as the most significant couple in Khitan astrology), occupying days five and six.[45]

The logic of early Inner Eurasian religions

The materials surveyed in this chapter echo various aspects of the

geography and prehistory of Inner Eurasia noted in our Introduction. There is a strong emphasis on the opposition between
summer and winter, which corresponds to the huge differences
in temperature common in the region. As appears to have been
the case in prehistoric times, there are prominent hunting rituals. Just as prehistoric figures of stags have human traits, historical
accounts of human hunters show them turning themselves into
animals. The soaring eagles of ancient cliff drawings are reflected
in the Hsiung-nu practice of using eagle feathers to feather arrows. As in the prehistoric tribal leader's tomb in the mountains
of Tuva, we find kings buried with other humans and horses.

In spite of these obvious correspondences, the rules of method
demand that we should concentrate first on the internal logic of
a given people's religion. During this chapter we have encountered only three peoples described in sufficient detail for this to
be done: the Scythians, the Hsiung-nu and the Khitans. Thus we
must briefly re-examine these three peoples before proceeding
to make comparisons.

We have seen that the religion of the Scythians is partly Indo-
European, partly typically Inner Eurasian. The legend of their
origin gives us the classic Indo-European tripartition of religious
sovereignty, warlike force and fertility, and this triad is echoed in
the list of their gods. However, other aspects of Scythian religion
are Altaic: avoiding the spilling of blood in sacrifices, scalping,
the employment of feminized male diviners, the use of arrows in
'blood brother' agreements and the concealment of royal tombs.
Also Altaic, or typically Inner Eurasian, is the tripartition of [1]
the sky, [2] the water upon the earth and [3] the space from the
earth's surface downwards.

Much has been written about the Scythian practice in which,
after a burial, people purify themselves with hemp smoke. It has
often been claimed that these people are shamans (though
Herodotus just calls them 'the Scythians') and that they are producing a trance. However, Herodotus makes it clear that a vapour
bath of this kind is a substitute for a water bath, never used by the
Scythians. This tallies with other Inner Eurasian evidence: water
must not be used for self-purification, since this defiles the water
spirit, and so one has to purify oneself with fire and smoke.[46]

As regards the Hsiung-nu, their religion appears to be more

Altaic. It is dominated by the worship of Heaven, seen as the source
of vital force. The theme of intercourse between human and ani
mal is important in the myths of the Hsiung-nu's origins, and is
echoed in the sacrifices of animals made in honour of the ancestors. Also noteworthy is the sacrificing of humans at the funerals
of leading men in order to give them servants in the next world.
Accordingly, the internal logic seems to be one of ensuring the
continuity of life, from the original ancestors through the present
day and into the hereafter.

Khitan religion is also heavily Altaic in its internal logic. Heaven
is again dominant, represented by a white horse and comple-
mented by the Earth, represented by a grey bovine. Again, the
myth of origins is reflected in animal sacrifices. In Khitan religion, however, there is a greater emphasis on the logic of hunting:
when alive, humans imitate animals in order to catch them; when
dead, humans have their flesh and skin eaten by animals in order
that surviving humans may obtain the flesh and skin of the latter.

Apart from the internal logic to be discerned in Scythian,
Hsiung-nu and Khitan religions there is also a logic that can be
found only by comparing the different religions surveyed so far.
This is most evident when one looks at the motif of the cup. As we
have seen, in the Indo-European domain this symbolizes concept
1, that of religious sovereignty: the Scythians use it for pouring
libations to the gods. It also symbolizes wisdom and reason, elements of concept 1. Scalping is typically Altaic, and so is the custom
of turning the skull of a defeated leader into a cup and using it
for ritual purposes. However, this latter custom may reflect the
Indo-European view of the tripartition of the human body: the
head, as representing intelligence, also symbolizes concept 1, while
the upper torso and the arms naturally symbolize concept 2, warlike strength, and the lower torso, as possessing the organs of
digestion and procreation, symbolizes concept 3, fertility. Thus it
is not surprising that the Issedones sacrifice to a skull, the Scythians
make cups out of heads, while the Ossetians speak of a magic cup
which rises automatically to one's lips. It is apt that Hsiung-nu
leaders should use a cup made from a skull to solemnize a treaty,
and not surprising that the Avars all have a skull as an object of
worship, while the Bulghars keep the skulls of dead enemies.
Among the Khitans the muzzles of sacrificed dogs, covered by

ents, clearly correspond to their legendary first chief who had
he form of a skull concealed in a tent and, as we have seen, seems
o represent concept 1 in an Indo-European triad.

As regards the nine heavens venerated by the Hsiung-nu, these
evidently reflect the widespread belief in the number of heavens
corresponding to the visible planets (including the sun and moon)
– a number which has sometimes been seven (as with the Turks),
sometimes nine (as with the Mongols).[47] The importance given
to the fifth day of the month (and to some extent also the sixth)
by the Hsiung-nu is paralleled, as we have seen in the case of the
Khitans by whom the fifth and sixth days of the year are named
after the highly significant bovine–horse pair (while the seventh
is named after man). For the Hsiung-nu the fifth is the day for
sacrificing to the 'spirit of heaven'. By contrast, the T'o-pa sacrifice to the sky on the fourth day of the month, and prefer the
number seven or its square in their ceremonies (they have been
seen as 'proto-Turkic').

What is most striking, however, is the logic of transformations
between humans and animals. Among the Hsiung-nu a huge fish
with two horns turns into a man, and wolves, through intercourse
with humans, produce more of the latter. The Huns are guided
by a doe or cow, and the T'o-pa by a supernatural animal which
looks like a horse but sounds like a bull. Among the Khitans men
become 'deer-men' or 'boar-men', imitating animals' cries and
donning their skins and heads, while animals and humans also
turn into each other through mutual consumption. This motif of
'becoming-animal' has been analysed by the French post-struc-
turalist philosopher Gilles Deleuze, in collaboration with the
psychiatrist Félix Guattari: they point out that 'becoming-animal'
involves anomalous animals like the horned fish or bovine horse
which we have just encountered, and which have to distinguish
themselves from ordinary animals in order to lead humans into
new adventures. They also point out that 'becoming-animal' is
necessary not only for hunting, but also for warfare: warriors turn
into animals on battlefields, owing to the demand for speed and
fury.[48]

2

The Turks

This chapter surveys a very wide range of materials. It examines
the evidence for the study of Turkic religions from the sixth century CE to the present. Thus we shall begin with the Türks, who, it
will be recalled, must have their name spelt with two dots over the
'u', as opposed to the Turks in general. Then we shall consider
their successors in Inner Eurasia, the Uighurs and the Kirghiz,
who, like the Türks, have left inscriptions and traces in the Chinese records. After this we shall look at medieval Turkic literature
and Islamic and Christian sources before proceeding to the evidence of eighteenth-century European travellers in Inner Eurasia.
Nineteenth-century collections of Turkic poetry will be of special
interest to us. Finally, we shall examine the labours of twentieth-
century anthropologists and students of oral epics.

The empire of the Türks (552–744)

The empire of the Türks, which replaced that of the Juan-juan in
Mongolia in 552, stretched as far west as the Aral Sea. We have
plenty of information about it, partly from a few inscriptions left
by the Türk rulers, but mainly from Chinese and Byzantine historians. It is again Roux who is the main modern writer on Türk
religion, and we shall follow his survey of the materials, while noting contributions by the American-based orientalist Denis Sinor
and the Chinese scholar Tang Chi.

There seem to have been shamans among the Türks. Byzantine sources say that the Türks had priests who foretold the future, and these priests intervened when a Byzantine envoy came to visit a Türk ruler. They made the envoy and his attendants pass between two fires, in order to purify them. Then the priests 'pronounced certain words, burnt some kinds of incense to the sound of several instruments, and then, having entered into a sort of frenzy, they made the envoy go round a fire, claiming that by so doing they were driving away all the misfortunes which could befall him.'[1]

The Byzantine sources also tell us that the Türks had a holy mountain, noted for its abundance of fruits and pastures and immunity to epidemics and earthquakes. This mountain was, by law, given to the most powerful of the Türk rulers. Now a Türk inscription exhorts the people to stay on one particular mountain (called Ötükän) and says that if it remains there it will survive for ever, dominating other peoples, but if it goes elsewhere it will die. We are further informed by the Byzantine historians that the Türks hold fire in the most extraordinary respect, and also venerate air, water and earth, but do not worship and call 'god' anyone except the creator of heaven and earth: to him they sacrifice horses, oxen and sheep.[2]

Chinese sources and Türk inscriptions show that the Türk rulers constantly orientated themselves towards the east. These rulers would be called 'divine' (or 'celestial', *tengri*) and designated as 'heaven-like' or 'heaven-created'. Heaven was also credited with giving them their empire. This 'heaven-god' was called 'the Tengri of the Türks'. He was 'high' and 'blue', and gave men strength. Tengri punished with death refusal to obey the legitimate ruler. However, the inscriptions show that there was also a 'god of time' (*öd tengri*), both independent and part of Heaven. They also show the ultimate creator as making the sky: 'When the blue sky above and the reddish-brown earth below were created, between the two human beings were created.'[3]

Along with Tengri, the Türk inscriptions also mention a benevolent goddess called Umay, who seems to have been borrowed from the Mongols, as *umai* is the usual Mongol term for 'placenta' or 'womb'. Umay is still venerated among some Turkic peoples in the Altai region, and by the Tunguz: she is seen as protecting the souls of unborn and small children.[4]

We know from the inscriptions that the Türks had holy rivers, and the Chinese sources say that they gathered on the banks of one of these to sacrifice to Tengri on the 18th day of the fifth month of the Chinese year (Roux explains that this meant between late May and mid-June, and was certainly a sacrifice marking the start of summer). The inscriptions show 'the Tengri of the Türks' acting in concert with 'the holy earth and water of the Türks'. They also indicate that the holiness of the mountain called Ötükän is due largely to its having a forest. As we have seen, dwelling on this mountain brings success: the inscriptions speak repeatedly of 'good luck' (qut, 'fortune'), something given by Tengri and constituting an essential part of a human being, but which also has to be 'confirmed' in one's life. On the other hand, the Chinese historians relate that the Türks have another holy mountain which is bare of all vegetation: this is called 'the god of the earth'. The inscriptions show that the Türks are impressed by stone, which they often call 'eternal'. Their cosmic ideas, expressed in number-symbols, are reflected in Chinese accounts of ceremonies: a new ruler is spun round nine times on a felt blanket, and mourners ride seven times round the tent of the deceased.[5]

Holy places naturally figure in Chinese references to the Türks' sacrifices. A bridge, aptly, is used for concluding a treaty of alliance, before which a white horse is immolated. An ancestral cave is visited every year by the Türk ruler, who brings the nobles to sacrifice there. This ruler, we are told, is descended from a wolf. One myth, preserved in a Chinese version, features a beggar with a wolf's head. A shepherd and his wife give him a meal, and she (but not the husband) notices his peculiar form. Out of curiosity they follow him and reach the holy mountain of Ötükän, where the beggar catches sight of them and prophesies that their tribe will be destroyed. Roux points out that the reason why the wife alone notices the wolf's head is that women are used to the appearances of animals who come to make them conceive. This myth reflects another, according to which the Türks are descended from a she-wolf who took refuge in a cave. According to the Chinese sources a Hsiung-nu boy was thrown into a marsh, rescued by a she-wolf and brought up by her. Afterwards they had intercourse, and became the ancestors of the Türks. When the she-wolf became

pregnant there was an attempt to kill her, and she fled to a cave
on a mountain, where she gave birth to ten sons. One of these
became a king who put a wolf's head on his flag.[6]

At this point the myth (which has been presented and analysed in detail by Sinor) takes on, in my view, a typically Inner
Eurasian tripartite pattern, the details of which are echoed, as we
shall see, in an Arabic source describing the Bashkir Turks. The
king with the wolf's head emblem clearly belongs to the sky [1]:
we are told that he had supernatural gifts, being able to make the
wind and rain come, and married two wives, the daughters of the
god of the summer and the god of the winter. He had four sons,
who belong to the space between the sky and the earth [2]: one
changed into a white swan, and the others established their king-
doms beside rivers and on the slopes of a mountain. His many
grandsons belong to the earth's surface [3]: to decide which of
them would succeed as king they held a competition to see who
could jump the highest from the foot of a great tree.[7]

With reference to the wolf symbolism, it is to be noted that the
Türks' royal guards were called 'wolves' in memory of their part
animal origin. Roux comments that Chinese references to a golden
wolf's head, used by the Türks as a heraldic emblem, probably
indicate the gilding of a skull, placed on a flagpole to precede
and guide an army.[8]

It is in the army, say the Chinese historians, that a Türk man is
supposed to die, killed in action, whereas to die of an illness is
shameful. The Türks despise men who live into old age. As for the
enemies whom they kill, the inscriptions tell us of a specifically
Altaic practice, that of dedicating an enemy (or one of his various
souls) to a Türk in the hereafter, in order to serve him. In this
connection a special word, *balbal*, is used to designate both the
slain enemy (or a soul of his) and a stone monument which is set
up to represent him. Thus the enemy is turned into a *balbal*: he
becomes the stone monument. Accordingly, the Türk nobleman
(or one of his souls) would live on in his tomb, organized as a
home, and the various enemies dedicated as his *balbal*s would serve
him there. His wives, say the Chinese, would be married by his
surviving sons (excluding their own mothers) and younger
brothers.[9]

As we have seen in the case of the ancestral cave, the Türks

sacrificed in memory of their ancestors. The start of the ancestor
cult for a Türk nobleman (and its sacrifices) naturally began with
the burial, which took place (as we know from both Chinese
sources and the inscriptions) several months after his death, in
autumn if he died in spring or summer, in spring if he died in
summer or winter, and on the 27th day of the month. As Roux
remarks, both the observation of the seasonal cycle and the day
of the month reflect both death and the expectation of resurrection. The Chinese documents tell us that in the sixth century the
Türks would burn the corpse before burial, along with the deceased's horse, clothes and personal belongings. By the seventh
century the custom of burning the corpse had been largely abandoned. Like the Hsiung-nu, the Türks would sacrifice large
numbers of slaves at their funerals. These slaves could on occasion be charged with conveying a message to the dead man. Gold
and silver would be buried with him. Princes had splendid tombs
built for them, and hundreds of *balbals* in the form of roughly
hewn stones placed standing around. (The tombs of the Türk
rulers have not been well preserved, but archaeologists have found
tens of thousands of *balbals*, in large groups, confirming the Chinese evidence.)[10]

The Türk rulers, as we have already noted, were supposed to
undergo a peculiar ritual on their accession, a ritual which, Sinor
observes, was probably ignored in real life and closely resembles
that attributed to the Khazars. After being spun round on a felt
blanket nine times the new ruler had to ride a horse, and then
was strangled almost to death. Then he was asked, 'How long will
you be our ruler?' The incoherent mutterings which he produced
in reply were interpreted to forecast the length of his reign.[11]

We have already mentioned the use of the numbers seven and
nine in the numerical symbolism of the Türks. An extended survey of this symbolism was published in 1989 by the Chinese
historian Tang Chi. He points out that the Türks, in addition to
the numbers seven and nine, also used numbers including seven
for symbolic purposes, such as 17, 70 and 700. In the Chinese
sources we read that one of the Turks' ancestors had 17 brothers,
and in the inscriptions we are told that a Türk ruler set out with
17 men and was then repeatedly joined by others, so that his forces
numbered 70 and then 700. The inscriptions also allege that one

prince died on the 17th day of the year, aged 47. In Chinese documents we also encounter the symbolism of the arrow, used to represent chieftains and tribes. The drum (along with the wolf head) appears as a symbol of royal authority, bestowed by the Chinese on Türk rulers.[12]

The Uighur empire (744–840)

After the Türks a new empire, that of the Uighurs, existed in Mongolia from 744 to 840. Here the inscriptional and Chinese evidence is less rich than for the Türks, but we also have a report from an Arab traveller. The conversion of the Uighurs to Manichaeanism in 762 naturally reduces the value of the materials for the study of indigenous Turkic religion (officially proscribed in 763), but this conversion was very far from universal, and some authentically Inner Eurasian elements are apparent. In addition to Roux' work we shall consider contributions by the Australian orientalist Colin Mackerras.

The Chinese sources presented by Mackerras show us that the Uighurs had shamans, who, in 765 (two years after the official proscription of the old national faith), were brought to their leaders to predict the fate of a military expedition. These shamans were also taken along on the expedition, and allegedly summoned up wind and snow when it was thought advantageous. Doubtless they did this with the help of the famous Turkic rainmaking stone, since the Arab traveller Tamim ibn Bahr, who visited the Uighurs around 821, long after their conversion to Manichaeanism, relates that the ruler alone possessed stones of this kind, used to produce rain, snow, cold and so on. Evidently the stones had passed from the proscribed shamans to the ruler himself.[13]

As Roux observes, the ruler (before the conversion) calls himself 'divine' (*tengri*) in his inscriptions. He identifies God with Heaven (Tengri), but says that the earth has a certain power: 'Because on high Blue Heaven has ordained, because below the Dark Earth has guided ... .' The Uighur ruler, like his predecessors, spends his summers high up on the holy mountain of Ötükän and visits holy rivers. Apparently the forest of Ötükän was important for sacrificial purposes: a Chinese historian says that the Uighurs used to gallop round the trees of a forest when sacrificing, and, if they were in a treeless area, would plant willow branches in the ground instead. It seems that the most important sacrifice was that of the winter solstice. The inscriptions indicate that the shamans were involved in the sacrifice, notably in a preliminary ritual which involved inscribing magical texts and tying up offerings to the spirits in a dangerous spot. Here the ultimate recipient is designated as Tengri himself, while the spirits below him are asked to grant 'that there be no war', 'a good welcome', 'a good road' and 'good fortune' (*qut*). These spirits are called 'the 22 wise lords of life and luck', and 'my fathers'.[14]

Little is known of the ancient Uighurs' funerary customs. The Chinese sources state that the Uighur warriors were buried standing up and armed. They add that the Uighurs in the middle of the eighth century were still burying widows alive with the corpses of their husbands, but only if the latter had left no sons to look after them. A Chinese princess whose royal Uighur husband died was urged by his court to go into the tomb with him, but she insisted on following Chinese mourning customs instead. She slashed her face and wept loudly, in the Uighur manner, and, as she had no sons, was allowed to go back to China. A similar problem occurred when a Chinese prince visited a Uighur ruler and refused, on the grounds that he was in mourning, to perform a ceremonial dance in front of his tent, although his father and the Uighur sovereign had sworn an oath of brotherhood. On a happier occasion a Chinese princess was married to another Uighur ruler according to the native ritual. He sat on a tower facing east, and she was installed in a felt tent facing him. Then she was carried round the court nine times on a sedan chair by representatives of the Uighurs' nine clans, following the movement of the sun.[15]

The Kirghiz (c.750–924)

The last Turkic empire in Mongolia was founded by the Kirghiz people in 840. However, the Kirghiz had existed as a political entity in Inner Eurasia for a very long time: just before the Christian era they appear in Chinese sources, which describe them as being tall with blond hair and blue eyes. Thus scholars have seen them as having been originally Indo-European speakers who later adopted a Turkic language. They supplied iron ore to the Türk empire to their south in the late sixth century CE when, one Chinese emperor noted, they were eager to establish their own rule in Mongolia. Their surviving inscriptions date from around 750 to 924, but are nearly all funerary ones and tell us little about their religion except for their attitude to death. The Chinese evidence is also relatively uninformative. Again, Roux is our only secondary source.[16]

According to the Chinese, the Kirghiz had shamans in the ninth century. These shamans seem to have their activities reflected in the inscriptions: a dead man is presented as rejoining his family through a shamanic summoning of his spirit, so that he comes down to his country. An epitaph of around 750 may be translated 'He wandered in the three storeys of the universe,' suggesting that the deceased was a shaman and had travelled in the heavens, on the surface of the earth and in the underworld, but the translation is not certain. What is clear from the inscriptions is that Heaven (Tengri) looks after the Kirghiz and protects them from misfortune, and that their ruler has a divine mission, his country itself being called 'divine'. The funerary inscriptions are for important, but not royal people, who are shown as regretting, after their death, their previous close connections with the sun and the moon.[17]

One Kirghiz inscription has the dead man say, 'I have killed seven wolves.' Roux comments that the idea, as in the representation of animals in Turkic funerary sculpture, is that the animals killed will serve the hunter in the next world. The Chinese sources depict the Kirghiz as venerating bovines and say that they have a myth according to which their ancestor lived in a cave with a cow. As Roux remarks, cows do not live in caves and there seems to be confusion with a myth of a wolf.[18]

The inscriptions also show, from the mid-ninth century, a god called Erklik, who is responsible for death and reappears in modern folklore. This god did not claim the dead man's widow: he is made to lament her loss. According to the Chinese the body would be burnt and the bones gathered and buried after a year, or at the year's end. The mourners did not cut their faces, but howled while circling the remains three times.[19]

Ninth and tenth-century evidence from the Middle East and north-west China

A small amount of evidence for the study of Turkic religion has been collected from the Middle East and north-west China. This is because of the political changes which had occurred since the Arab conquests of the seventh and eighth centuries. The Muslims used Turks as soldiers, and so Turkic motifs appeared in the decorations of buildings in the Middle East, while some Muslim writers began to record the Turks' beliefs and practices. Some Turks were forced out of their homeland on the steppes into north-west China, where they started to compose written literature evoking their past traditions.

One important element in the evidence from the Islamic world is the representation of fighting between a man and a bull. This is found in a fresco of the royal palace of Samarra, in Iraq, in the middle of the ninth century, and also, in the same period, in a bas relief at the Church of the Holy Cross of Aght'amar in eastern Turkey. Art historians have seen this as the result of a distinctively Turkic influence: we shall encounter the theme again, in Turkic epic. The link between human and animal is also reflected in the work of the Iraqi historian Mada'ini (752–843): he reports that the Turks demand of a good general that he have the qualities of various animals: the heart of a lion, the chastity of a hen, the craftiness of a fox and so on. Scholars have noted that these animals must correspond to the heraldic emblems of the Turks, already known to the Arabs about 730: each animal would have been the totem of a clan.[20]

The Muslim Arabic writer Ibn Fadlan, who took part in a diplomatic mission to the Bulghars, gives us useful information about one important branch of the Turks, the Oghuz, whom he visited in the course of his journey in 921–2. When one of them suffers a misfortune he looks to the sky and says, 'Bir Tengri (One God)'. The Oghuz never wash, and always wear the same clothes until these disintegrate. They kill sheep by hitting them on the head, not by slitting their throats. The Oghuz consider pederasty to be a very great sin. If one of them falls ill he is isolated from his family in a special tent. When he dies he is buried sitting, in a large tomb like a house, wearing his tunic and belt and holding is bow and a cup of wine together with his possessions. Then the mourners kill and eat all his horses and hang up the head, feet, skin and tail, to bear him to paradise. They put stone monuments (*balbals*) representing his fallen enemies on his tomb, so that they will serve him in the hereafter. After the horse sacrifice an old man will report that the deceased has appeared to him in a dream and said that he has now caught up with his predecessors on his tiring journey, after wearing his feet out. Later food and milk may be buried in the ground for him.[21]

Ibn Fadlan also gives us information about another Turkic people, the Bashkirs, situated between the Urals and the Volga. Each of them wears a wooden phallus and worships it as a god. Some of them have twelve lower gods, responsible respectively for winter, summer, rain, wind, 'the tree', men, horses, water, night, day, death and the earth. Above these is the great Lord in the sky, united with and in agreement with the twelve, each of whom approve of what the others do. One group of the Bashkirs worships snakes, another fish and another cranes.[22]

The list of twelve gods is extremely valuable for our purposes. It seems to fall into a typically Inner Eurasian tripartite pattern. At the top we find the sky [1]: winter, summer, rain and wind are precisely the four aspects of the heavens that we encountered in a Türk legend of ancestral kings, the first king being closely associated with all four. In the middle we find the space between the sky and the earth [2], which in the Türk legend was represented by the second generation of rulers and four sons, corresponding to a swan, rivers and the slopes of a mountain. Here we have 'the tree', stretching from the earth's surface to the sky, men, horses and water. At the bottom we find the space stretching from the earth's surface downwards [3]: night and day both disappear to beneath the horizon, and death and the earth are joined together in the grave. In the Türk myth, it will be recalled, sons in the third generation have to try to succeed their father by jumping up from the earth's surface and the foot of a tree against the tree's trunk, which presumably symbolizes the generation that they endeavour to emulate.

There is one important Turkic source from the ninth or tenth century, the *Fortune-Book* (*Irq Bitig*), a collection of short sibylline texts to which one is supposed to refer after throwing dice. The dice are taken to indicate that one particular text is to be read as an omen: the texts usually end with the words 'This is good' or 'This is bad'. It seems that the book was written in north-west China, after the Uighurs had fled there. However, it certainly reflects their earlier life on the steppes and their original Turkic religion. We find Tengri and his force (*küch*) intervening to save an exhausted horse ('This is good'). However, there is also a 'god of the road on a dappled horse' who gives 'good fortune (*qut*)' and says, 'I am the old god of the road. I fix your broken parts and I join together your torn things. I have organized the kingdom.'[23]

Animals loom large in the *Fortune-Book*. A man whose horse is tired is rescued by a swan which flies up into the air and carries him to his parents. 'The slave's words are a request to his master; the raven's words are a prayer to Tengri. Tengri above heard it; men below understood it.' There is a reference to the typically Altaic custom of hunting animals by surrounding them, with the result that the ruler kills the prey with his own hands: 'The kingdom's army went out to hunt. A roebuck came inside the circle. The ruler caught it with his hand. All his followers rejoice.' Animals and humans are joined together in a very common Altaic threefold pattern of (i) first animal, (ii) second animal and (iii) human. 'The young birds lost their way (i.e. died) flying; the young deer lost their way running; and the children lost their way walking. And again, by the 'good fortune' of Tengri they all met in the third year, safe and sound. They all rejoiced and were glad.' A prince finds that his white mare and white she-camel have both given birth to colts, and his wife to a son. Sometimes animals are shown fighting each other. A bear and a white boar wound one another: this is a bad omen, as when a falcon encounters an eagle or fails to catch a hare, or when a camel is eaten by a fox. A good omen is when a white-spotted cow gives birth to a white-spotted male calf: this will be a consecrated animal which must not be exploited for any purpose. Finally, at the end of the *Fortune-Book* we are told its purpose: 'In this way everyone is master of his own fate.'[24]

The eleventh and twelfth centuries

In the eleventh century there was an enormous expansion of Turkic military power and political domination. Turks moved out of Inner Eurasia into South Asia and the Middle East, and began to take over what is now Turkey. As a result we have a lot of evidence concerning Turkic religion from both Muslim and Christian eleventh and twelfth-century sources. Leading writers tell us of the Turks' myths and rituals, and we find the beginnings of the Turks' own antiquarianism, as they started to collect examples of their own folklore.

Our first eleventh-century Islamic source is the famous Iranian polymath Biruni, who was born to the south of the Aral Sea in 973 and died after 1050. He relates that the Hindus used to have Turkic kings residing in Kabul. The first of these, called Barhatakin, came to a cave there, which had to be entered by crawling on hands and knees and had its own supply of water. He hid in the cave while his associates arranged for peasants to work outside, and then emerged from it as if the product of a miracle. The peasants saw him as a newborn baby of supernaturally endowed size and hailed him as their king.[25]

The next source is the great philosopher Avicenna who was born in 980 near Bukhara in present-day Uzbekistan and died in 1037. He gives us the first known account of a shamanic seance, observed by him among a tribe of Turkomans (nomadic Turks): 'When they go to consult the shaman to get a prophecy from him he starts running very fast in all directions, gasping until he goes into a trance. In this state he utters what his imagination represents to him, and those present collect his words in order to make their arrangements accordingly.'[26]

After Avicenna one must note the evidence of the Iranian historian Gardizi who came from near Ghazna in what is now Afghanistan and wrote in the middle of the eleventh century. He relates that an ancestor of the Turks was given wolf's milk during a childhood illness, and the Turks are bad tempered for this reason. In a similar story the wolf is replaced by a dog. The Kirghiz, says Gardizi, practise cremation, because fire is the purest of things and makes everything else pure: notably, it purifies the dead of filth and sin. Some of the Kirghiz worship the cow, some the wind,

some the porcupine, some the magpie and others beautiful trees
Among them is a shaman, and every year on a special day, when
musicians begin to play, he goes into a trance: then people ask
him what will happen in the following year and he replies to all
their questions.[27]

These sources are less important than the extraordinary *Compendium of the Turkic Dialects* (*Diwan lughat al-Türk*), composed in
the 1070s by a Turk called Kashghari, after the city of Kashghar,
the capital of East Turkistan (now north-west China). The *Compendium* is written in Arabic, and is mainly a Turkic-Arabic
dictionary, but it also includes a lot of illustrative sentences, proverbs and verses and plenty of information about folklore. Here,
apart from Roux' work, we shall refer to the detailed studies of
the text made by the American Turcologist Robert Dankoff.

The usual Turkic word for 'shaman', *qam*, occurs four times in
the *Compendium*. Kashghari explains that it means 'diviner' (in
Arabic *kahin*). He gives three examples of its use: 'The shamans
murmured magical phrases'; 'The shaman prepared a spell', 'The
shaman drew an omen'. Roux considers that this, along with the
other Islamic evidence, is enough to demonstrate the strength of
Turkic 'shamanism' around 1000 CE. Dankoff takes the view that
there is no evidence to indicate that the *qam* is a shaman: there
are no initiatory sicknesses, techniques of producing ecstasy or
magical flights. He translates the word as 'diviner'. We may object
that Avicenna and Gardizi present running and listening to music as techniques of producing trances. However, Roux points out
that rainmaking with the help of a special stone is described by
Kashghari in terms which, as elsewhere, indicate that the practi-
tioner is often not a shaman.[28]

God (Tengri) is shown by Kashghari as making plants grow and
the lightning flash. The adjective *tengri*, 'divine', is, he says, used
by the Turks to designate everything that is imposing to their eyes,
such as a great mountain or a tree, and they bow down to such
things. Thus a knowledgeable or pious man is called a *tengriken*.
Kashghari also mentions a proverb referring to the goddess Umay:
'One who worships Umay will get a child.' He explains that her
name means 'placenta': this is said to be the companion of the
child in the womb. It is God, however, who is credited with granting 'good fortune' (*qut*).[29]

This 'good fortune' is of course most apparent in abundant
ossession of livestock. It appears from Kashghari and other
ources that the early Turks' clans mark their horses, camels and
attle with a distinctive sign, the famous *tamga*, which is the emblem of the clan itself. Kashghari also tells us what happens when
an animal is consecrated (*iduq*): 'One does not burden, milk or
shear it, because of a vow made by its owner.' The Oghuz taboo
the word for 'wolf' (*böri*) and replace it with that for 'worm' (*qurt*).
Kashghari often mentions that the name of an animal is also taken
by men – this is indeed extremely common among the Turks. The
Kipchak Turks call the bear 'father'. Of particular interest is a
belief about the vulture: when it grows old it lays and hatches two
eggs, from one of which emerges the last of its chicks, while from
the other emerges a shaggy dog (*baraq* – the name, as we shall
soon see, of a Muslim mystic who wears a shaman's costume).[30]

Animals naturally occur in proverbs about the inevitability of
fate and death: 'The mouse that is condemned to die scratches
the cat's testicles.' However, the ambassadors of kings must not
be killed: 'Fresh grass does not burn, the king's ambassador does
not die.' Another proverb denies return or rebirth of the dead:
'Man does not live for ever: when he goes down into the tomb he
does not come back.' Kashghari also gives us fragments of the
ancient Turkic dirges, in which the warriors' achievements are
celebrated at the funeral feast: this, he says, is held three or seven
days after the burial. Food is also prepared for the deceased. Other
feasts show off booty: a table is set up to display this, 'like a mina-
ret, 30 cubits high'. Here Dankoff compares the Khitans' use of a
platform over 10 feet high for sacrificing at festivals.[31]

As we move from the eleventh century to the twelfth we come
to the famous Iranian Muslim writer Muhammad Ghazali (1058–
1111). He tells us that the 'furthermost Turks believe that they
have a Lord, who is the most beautiful of things; and if they see a
person of the greatest beauty, or a tree or horse or something
else, they fall before it, praying, and say, "It is our Lord!"' Scholars
have disagreed about whether this 'worship of beauty' is
Manichaean or Turkic. It has been noted that earlier Islamic
sources had attributed the habit of falling down in veneration of
one's friends and physicians to the Khazars, the Bulghars and the
Turks.[32]

Two other twelfth-century sources present animals as guiding the Turks on their migrations from their Inner Eurasian mountain homeland. The first of these is the Arab geographer Idris (1100–65), who says that the Turks were led by a fish. We are told by the second source, the Christian writer known as 'Michael the Syrian', who was the Jacobite patriarch of Antioch from 1166 to 1199, that the Turks' guide was a white dog. Michael also informs us that the migrating Turks used staffs for divinatory purposes. He says that they divided themselves into three camps, and consulted destiny by throwing three staffs into the air: the Turks of each camp then followed the direction in which each staff fell. Michael further adds that the Turks 'were commanded by 70 chiefs: these chiefs drew a circle and stood around it, each holding a staff in his hand. Then they all threw the staffs into the air, having previously agreed that those whose staffs fell inside the circle would be kings.' As Roux observes, each staff seems to represent one man, like an arrow among the Mongols. An anonymous Italian historian of the Crusades, writing in the second half of the fifteenth century, says that the Turks, after coming to Iran, chose their king by lot. First they made 100 tribes each send an arrow, and a child chose one at random. Then, in that tribe, 100 candidates were chosen and 100 arrows were marked with the name of each candidate: again, the child chose one at random.[33]

The Cumans

Other Christian writers give us useful information about the Cumans, a Turkic people who had previously remained at a distance from the great civilizations of Eurasia and consequently retained a lot of archaic customs. In the eleventh century the Cumans moved westwards from their original homeland, which may have been in East Turkistan (now north-west China), and attacked the Russians, Byzantines and Hungarians. They established themselves on the steppes to the north of the Black Sea, but in the thirteenth century were defeated by the Mongols, so that some of them were absorbed into the Mongol empire while others had to take refuge in Bulgaria and Hungary where they gradually lost their separate identity.

The Italian Franciscan monk, traveller and historian John of

'lano Carpini, who visited the Mongols as an envoy in 1245, has
provided us with a valuable piece of evidence concerning the
Cumans. He says that when the son of the king of Hungary married the daughter of the Cuman king ten Cumans swore over a
dog, cut in half with a sword, that they would defend the Hungarians' country. We find this Cuman custom echoed in the reports
of another Christian writer, Jean de Joinville (c.1224–c.1317), a
French historian of the Crusades. Joinville says that when the
Cumans and the Byzantines made an alliance the former made a
dog pass between both sides and cut it up with a sword, obliging
the Byzantine representatives to do likewise: the Cumans said that
both they and the Byzantines should be cut in pieces as well if
they failed each other. He also provides a description of a Cuman
notable's funeral. The dead man was buried seated in a chair, and
his best horse and best 'sergeant' were put in the grave alive. Just
before this the Cuman leaders gave the 'sergeant' lots of money
to hand back to them when they too came into the 'other world',
and the Cuman king gave him a letter of recommendation addressed to the first king of their people. Afterwards a huge mound
was raised above the tomb.[34]

More details of Cuman customs are furnished by another
Franciscan traveller, Friar William of Rubruck in French Flanders,
who visited the Mongols in 1253–5. Rubruck says that the Cumans
erect a statue to a dead notable, facing east and holding a cup.
(This statue is not to be confused with the *balbals* representing
the enemies killed by him.) For richer notables the Cumans build
tombs in the form of houses. Rubruck himself saw that, for a man
who had recently died, the Cumans had hung up, between high
poles, sixteen horses' hides in groups of four, facing the four points
of the compass. The mourners had also placed meat and *qumis*
(the famous fermented mares' milk drink of Inner Eurasia) for
the dead man to consume. Other graves were adorned with plenty
of stones (here evidently *balbals*), four tall ones being set standing up and also facing the points of the compass.[35]

Another source for the study of Cuman religion is the *Cuman
Codex*, a book compiled between 1294 and 1356 by anonymous
Italian and German authors, which consists of a Latin-Persian-
Cuman glossary and a collection of Cuman texts. The glossary
has been studied by Roux, who notes that it mentions the activities

of shamans (*qams*): *qamlyqet-* is explained as meaning 'to proph esy'. (We may add that the glossary has an expression fo 'shamaness': *qam qatun*, 'sorceress'.) Like other Turkic languages, Cuman uses an Iranian word, *tamuk*, to designate the underworld – this suggests that the idea has been borrowed by the Turks at a later date. The *Cuman Codex* explains the usual Turkic word for 'blue', *kök*, as 'heaven', and Tengri as 'God'. In the glossary we also encounter the ideas of 'the person itself' (*öz*), and the soul or spirit (*tin*). Again like other Turkic languages, Cuman confuses the Turkic word *uchmak*, 'fly away, die', with an identical Iranian word meaning 'paradise': thus the verb acquires the meaning 'go to paradise'. To designate the tomb Cuman borrows yet another Iranian word, *keshene*, meaning 'nest': as in other Turkic languages, the idea is that the human soul has the form of a bird. The Cuman word for 'tree', *terak*, acquires the meaning 'pole' in other Turkic languages: perhaps, one may conclude, the poles seen by Rubruck represented trees.[36]

The historian Juwayni on the Uighurs

Much light on Uighur myth and religion is shed by the Iranian historian Juwayni (1226–83). He says that in the past the religion of the Uighurs had been that of the shamans (*qams*). Juwayni gives us the Uighurs' myth of a ruler called Buqu Khan. In this myth we are told that at the junction of two rivers there were two trees. A great mound arose between these trees, and a light shone down on it from the sky. The Uighurs heard a sound like singing com- ing from the mound. Eventually a door opened in the mound and revealed five tent-like cells, each of which contained a baby boy. In front of each boy there hung a tube, which provided him with milk. When the wind blew the boys gathered strength and came out. After they had grown up they were told by the Uighurs that their parents were the two trees. The boys paid due respect to the trees and the ground in which the latter grew, and the trees broke into speech to acknowledge this respect. Then the young- est of the boys, Buqu, was chosen by the Uighurs to be their king.[37]

    This story is also found in Chinese sources, where, however, we find, instead of the two trees and the mound, a single tree giving birth to the five boys. Marco Polo says that the Uighurs' first king

arose from a sort of tuber generated by the sap of trees.' The
myth, Roux observes, is echoed among the Kipchak Turks, who
explain that their name means 'hollow tree', because it was inside
a hollow tree that their original, human ancestress gave birth to
her son.[38]

Juwayni continues by informing us that one night, when Buqu
was asleep, the form of a maiden came down through his tent's
smoke hole and woke him up. He was frightened and pretended
to be still asleep. Two nights later, however, Buqu and the maiden
went together to a mountain called Aq Tagh ('White Mountain'),
and for seven years, six months and 22 days they would go there
every night. (Presumably the significance of these figures is that
they produce a period seven days short of seven years and seven
months.) Then the maiden bade Buqu farewell and said, 'From
East to West will be your domain. Be diligent and zealous in this
work, and care for the people.' Buqu immediately assembled four
armies: he and three of his brothers led these against four na-
tions, while the remaining brother was left behind to replace him.
The four generals returned in triumph. After this Buqu had a
dream in which he saw an old man, dressed in white and holding
a white staff, who gave him a jasper stone shaped like a cone and
told him that if he could keep this stone he would rule the four
corners of the world. Buqu duly conquered the whole world. He
confronted his shamans with Buddhist monks in a contest, and
the monks' readings from their scriptures dumbfounded the shamans and brought about the Uighurs' conversion to Buddhism.
Buqu lived happily until his death, after which he was succeeded
by one of his sons. Subsequently the Uighurs heard, in the sounds
made by animals, birds and children, the cry 'Köch, köch'! (Move,
move!)' and migrated to East Turkistan, where the cry stopped.[39]

Late thirteenth and early fourteenth-century sources

Juwayni's successor as the main Iranian historian of Inner Eurasian nomads is the famous statesman Rashid al-Din Tabib
(c.1247–1318). Rashid al-Din provides valuable information about
a Turkic word for 'totem', *ongon*. He says that this word means
'the blessed and happy sign', and also the special animal of a Turkic
tribe. The animal of a given tribe, says Rashid al-Din, cannot be

hunted by the members of that tribe: they cannot harm it in any
way or eat its flesh. Roux explains that an *ongon* can also mean the
image of a totem animal, but it is wrong to imagine, as some scholars have, that the word just means an 'idol'.[40]

Other Muslim historians of this period describe the appearance, at the end of the thirteenth century and the beginning of
the fourteenth, of a Turkic Muslim mystic who dressed like a shaman, Baraq Baba ('Father Shaggy Dog'). We are told that Baraq
Baba and his followers were beardless, but with long moustaches
and wore felt hats with two horns. Around their necks hung cows'
knuckle bones painted with henna, crooked sticks and little bells.
They would beat drums and play other instruments as they moved
along, thereby producing, with the sound of their ornaments, a
horrible and terrifying cacophony.[41]

The animal symbolism of Baraq Baba's name and appearance
is also found in the Islamic art of this period, as Roux has noted.
Here the dragon is particularly important, owing to the belief that
in April it comes out of the earth to go up into the sky. Thus it
represents both death (being buried in the earth) and resurrection. One of Baraq Baba's teachers is supposed to have chased it
out of a cave into the sky. Turco-Islamic art portrays it with a forked
tongue and sharp, frightening teeth. In architecture it is depicted
as beneath the surface of the earth, supporting the tree of life,
and also as curving up into the air, underlining the sinuosity of
arches and vaults.[42]

The Story of Oghuz

Animal symbolism is also prevalent in the earliest Turkic traditional narrative to have been preserved, the *Story of Oghuz*
(*Oghuz-name*), which was composed around 1300 in East Turkistan.
This *Story* is of immense importance for the study of Inner Eurasian myth and religion. It gives us the legend of the eponymous
ancestor of the Oghuz Turks, and also provides stories which explain the names of other Turkic peoples. The name 'Oghuz' itself
means 'Young Bull', and in the legend Oghuz himself is of partly
bovine origin. Unfortunately, the beginning of the unique manuscript of the work has been destroyed. It is clear that Oghuz has a
bovine as one of his parents, but it is not clear which. Moreover,

THE TURKS 57

Oghuz has the traits of other animals, the wolf, the sable and the bear, and it is possible that in the legend they were also involved in his conception. Oghuz was born in human form, but his face was 'blue' (*kök*), that is, celestial and thus divine. He was more handsome than 'the good spirits' (*yaqshi nabsikilär*). These 'spirits', explains the great French orientalist Paul Pelliot, are of Indian origin, the Sanskrit *naivasika*s, literally 'inhabitants' of, for example trees: they are 'protective divinities of a region', who have come into East Turkistan as a result of Buddhist influence.[43]

The baby Oghuz, as soon as he was born, demanded cooked meat and wine, and started to talk. After 40 days he grew up and walked. His feet were like those of a bull, his loins like those of a wolf, his shoulders like those of a sable and his chest like that of a bear: his whole body was covered in hair. Soon he hunted a unicorn, luring it first with a stag, secondly with a bear and thirdly with himself. One day, when he was praying to God, a blue light came down from the sky, with a beautiful maiden in its middle. Oghuz fathered three sons on her, called Sun, Moon and Star. Then, one day, he went hunting, and found another beautiful maiden in a hollow tree in the middle of a lake. Oghuz fathered three more sons on this maiden, called Sky, Mountain and Sea.[44]

Afterwards Oghuz invited his people for a feast and announced his intention to assert his rule over the whole world, making 'the blue wolf' his people's war cry. One neighbouring ruler refused to submit to Oghuz, who marched out to fight him. Oghuz reached the foot of the holy mountain of Muztagh, in the west of East Turkistan. There, at dawn, a light entered his tent, and from the light emerged a great male wolf, with a blue coat and mane. This wolf then led Oghuz's army onwards. Oghuz defeated the enemy ruler and conquered his kingdom. Then he defeated one extremely rich ruler, and finally another, whose resistance resulted in a terrible battle. (Thus the three enemy rulers seem to form an Indo-European triad, representing in turn sovereignty, wealth and warlike force.)[45]

Subsequently Oghuz's chief minister had a dream, in which he saw a golden bow, reaching from the east to the west, and three silver arrows, flying to the north. Oghuz, on being told of the dream, sent his sons Sun, Moon and Star hunting to the east and his sons Sky, Mountain and Sea hunting to the west. The first trio

found a golden bow, which Oghuz divided into three pieces, gi
ing these to the three brothers and telling them to shoot arrov
right up to the sky. Then the second trio found three silver a
rows, which Oghuz duly distributed among them, telling them t
be like arrows. He summoned a great assembly, to the right c
which he had a tree erected, topped by a golden hen, with a whit
sheep at its foot; to the left he had erected a tree topped by ;
silver hen, with a black sheep at its foot. To the right sat the firs
trio, to the left the second. Oghuz then divided his kingdom be
tween them. (The hens and sheep of course symbolize the sur
and the moon and day and night: we shall find extremely similar
materials below, along with other data reflecting the rest of the
Story of Oghuz).⁴⁶

The Book of Grandfather Korkut

After the *Story of Oghuz* the most important monument of Turkic
legend is the *Book of Grandfather Korkut* (*Kitab-i Dede Korkut*). This
is a collection of twelve stories about the early Oghuz Turks, and
clearly reflects their life in Inner Eurasia, but the collection seems
to have been put together in eastern Turkey in the early fourteenth century and re-edited there in the sixteenth: thus it presents
Islamicized Turks fighting against Georgians and other Christians
along the Black Sea coast. Beneath the Islamic overlay, however,
plenty of ancient Turkic myth and religion can be discerned.
'Grandfather Korkut' is presented by the historian Rashid al-Din
as living for 295 years and giving advice to the ruler of the Oghuz.
In the collection of stories Korkut appears at the end of each story
as a storyteller himself, and in an additional section appended to
the collection he provides pieces of 'wisdom' or wise advice. Thus
he seems to me to be very like a typical Indo-European 'frame-
figure' [represented by zero in my notation], a figure who, in
epics in Indo-European languages, lives before and after everyone else, gives wise advice, notably to kings, and appears in the
narrative to serve as a 'frame' to the action – for example, the
figure of Nestor in the Homeric epics.⁴⁷

In one of the stories a prince competes, successfully, with a
maiden of noble birth in an archery competition, a horse race
and a wrestling match. Afterwards their marriage is arranged, but

e prince is captured by a Christian king. Sixteen years later his
ancée is about to be married to a villain, but the prince is al-
wed to escape by his captor's daughter in exchange for his
romise to marry her. He disguises himself as a minstrel and comes
o the villain's wedding feast. There the prince finds his old bow
nd, in another archery competition, uses it to strike the bride-
room's ring, which is being used as a target. His fiancée and his
parents recognize him. Then the prince takes his Christian cap-
or's castle, destroys its church, kills the priests there and builds a
mosque instead. He keeps his bargain with his captor's daughter
(though in one version he marries his fiancée as well).[48]

Here there is an obvious parallel with the *Odyssey*. The most
probable explanation, as has been argued before, is that an ancient Inner Eurasian folk tale has gone into both the Greek epic
and the Turkish story. A typically Inner Eurasian pattern is found
in the wedding competitions: archery involves firing arrows into
the sky [1], and horse racing belongs to the space between the
sky and the earth's surface [2], while wrestling is closely linked to
the earth's surface itself [3]. The captor's daughter corresponds
to Nausicaa in the *Odyssey*, a king's daughter who enables Odysseus
to return home.

Another story has the theme of a man who is faced with death.
He fights the Angel of Death, but loses. God nonetheless gives
him the possibility of finding someone else to die in his place. His
wife offers to do so, but God decides to spare them both. There is
a clear parallel with the Greek myth of Admetus, a man whose
wife offers to die in his stead but is rescued when Heracles wres-
tles successfully with Death personified. However, the idea that a
sick and dying person can have his life saved by someone else
dying in his place is well attested among the Turks and Mongols.[49]

The next story is about a young hero who wants to find an
Amazon to marry. A suitable girl is the daughter of the Christian
king of Trebizond in north-east Turkey. The king insists that any
candidate for his daughter's hand must kill three strong beasts: a
lion, a black bull and a black male camel. All three are monsters.
The young hero kills them all. Now the king wants to prepare the
wedding, but the hero insists on seeing his own parents first, and
rides back to his country's border with the princess. Then he falls
asleep. The princess's family repents of having given her away and

gives chase to the couple. She wakes the hero up and routs he
family single-handed. The hero himself falls wounded, and sees
warrior chasing the enemy away. He is ashamed and then realize
that the warrior is his bride. Even more embarrassed, he quarrel
with her, and it comes to a fight. She shoots a headless arrow
which hits him, and then they are reconciled. (In this story, then
we find a typically Turkic tradition of triple fights with animals in
a wedding ceremony, reflected in materials studied below, along
with an equally Turkic custom of fighting with the bride, also echoed in later evidence.)[50]

In the following story a son has to rescue his captured father,
who is a prisoner of a Christian king for sixteen years. A champion tries but fails to rescue him. The prisoner's son is only one
year old when his father is captured. When he grows up he goes
to find his father, accompanied by various heroes, one of whom,
we are told, has captured 57 castles. The father is duly freed and
recites verses in which he asks if his she-camel, ewe and wife have
had male or female offspring. His son replies that they have given
birth to a stallion, a ram and a lion. Then the Muslim warriors
destroy the Christian king's church and kill its priests. (We may
remark that the son is evidently 17, and that rescuing a captive
father is a standard Inner Eurasian Turkic epic theme.)[51]

After this we are given a story about a one-eyed giant, who, as
he grows up, kills his wet-nurse, mutilates little boys and finally
becomes an outlaw. As an adult he eats two men a day. A hero
comes to kill the giant, but the latter catches him and imprisons
him in his cave. The hero succeeds in blinding the giant by driving a red-hot spit into his eye. Then he escapes by killing the giant's
favourite ram and covering himself with its skin when the giant
lets his flock of sheep out. He identifies himself to the giant, who
curses him, and then he cuts off the giant's head with the latter's
own sword. (Here there is, of course, a close resemblance with
the story of the Cyclops in the *Odyssey*. However, the story is a very
widespread one, found from Ireland to Korea, and from Iceland
to Africa.)[52]

The penultimate story again has a son rescuing his captive father, who has been put in a pit. This pit appears to be a shaft
leading to a crypt, since the father claims to be riding the dead
Christians there, who are presented as being given food by the

ving. Here we seem to have a Turkic rather than a Christian cus-
om. One undoubtedly Turkic practice appears at the start of the
1st story: a ruler allows his tent to be pillaged by the Oghuz nobles,
fter he has led his wife out of it. The Oxford orientalist Geoffrey
Lewis comments that in 1106–7, after a banquet given in honour
of a sultan belonging to the great royal family of the Seljuq Turks,
who ruled from East Turkistan to Turkey and Arabia, the guests
were allowed to loot the gold and silver plate, and the same was
done after the wedding feast of another Seljuq sultan in the early
thirteenth century. In this story some nobles who are left out of
the pillaging rebel, and kill one great hero, whose funeral is char-
acterized by another archaic Turkic custom: his horse's tail is cut
off. Lewis comments that when an Ottoman prince died in 1513
his horses were paraded with their tails cut off and their saddles
upside down, while his bows were broken and placed on his bier.[53]

The Romance of Abu Muslim

Another important monument of fourteenth-century Turkish literature is the anonymous *Romance of Abu Muslim* (*Abu
Muslim-name*), which gives us the legend of a historical figure in-
strumental in the fall of the first dynasty of Islam, the Umayyads
of Damascus (661–750). Abu Muslim, who was probably of Iranian origin, led a successful insurrection against this dynasty in
northern Iran in 747. Seen as dangerous by the dynasty which
replaced it, that of the 'Abbasids, he was murdered by them in
755. Since then he has been venerated by both Iranians and Turks
as a popular hero and supporter of Muhammad's family against
tyrannical usurpers. The Turkish prose *Romance* in which his exploits are celebrated is based on a Persian original of the eleventh
century, but is mainly a text of the fourteenth. Thus it devotes
much attention to firearms and to the Islamic institutions prominent in this period: brotherhoods of mystics and associations of
young men united by the tradition of 'young manliness' (*futuwwa*),
a tradition often compared to European chivalry and seen as being of Iranian origin.[54]

The *Romance of Abu Muslim* provides precious evidence about
the famous initiatory rituals of 'young manliness'. When Abu
Muslim was an adolescent, we are told, he had a vision in which

Muhammad crowned him with a diadem, clothed him in a shirt
and girded him with a belt. Then Muhammad said, 'The diadem
which I have given you is the Tiara of Good Fortune, the shirt is
the Shirt of Benevolence and the belt is the Belt of Majesty.'[55]

Here the tripartition is clearly Indo-European, corresponding
to [1] the head, [2] the upper torso and arms and [3] the lower
torso. I have argued elsewhere that the initiatory rituals of 'young
manliness' are both Iranian and Indo-European, notably in their
central element: the girding of the initiate with a belt. The element of 'Good Fortune', represented by a diadem, would seem to
reflect the ancient Iranian concept of 'Royal Glory' (khwarenah),
the 'luck' of the shahs of Iran which vouchsafes kingship to them.[56]

We are informed that 17 unsuccessful insurrections have taken
place before Abu Muslim's. When he starts his insurrection the
regime lets buffaloes loose upon his followers, but the animals
turn round and charge the rulers' troops. However, Abu Muslim
is soon obliged to retreat into a desert. There his army is dying of
thirst when a gazelle leads him to a spring. Then an Iranian king
comes to his assistance and gives him various presents, including
'a throne which has 47 corners.' This king's principal commander
falls in love with Abu Muslim's sister, an Amazon who first appears dressed as an anonymous male warrior riding a camel and
puts the enemy to flight before being found to be a maiden. Eventually Abu Muslim completely defeats the Umayyads in Egypt,
helped by a gazelle which miraculously leads his army across the
Nile. In the end, just before the 'Abbasid ruler succeeds in mur-
dering Abu Muslim, an unsuccessful attempt is made by one of
the ruler's subordinates, who offers the hero a poisoned apple
and is forced by him to eat it himself. (As Roux remarks, the motif of the apple as an instrument of death is typically Turkic: in
Turkey today the Angel of Death is believed to offer apples to
children.)[57]

Ibn al-Dawadari: a Turkic origins myth

An extremely important Turkic myth is presented in another fourteenth-century source, the universal history completed in 1336
by the Egyptian historian Ibn al-Dawadari. The writer found the
myth in a book based on much older materials, dating from at

east 500 years before. The myth is set on a 'black mountain', which is situated 'on the furthest edges of the Chinese highlands, facing the east'. High up on the mountain there was a cave, and at the beginning of time a flood of rain flowed into it, forcing some earth into a mould like a human body. The sun and winds acted on this mould for nine months and created the Turks' original ancestor. His wife was produced in the same manner, and they had children. This cave, we are told, has the two parents buried in it and is still the object of veneration by the Turks of the region. The first parents' eldest son succeeded his father as king and built two cities beside a nearby river, the branches of which water a land of great fertility where illness is unknown. When this king died his son also reigned as king and put his father's body inside a golden statue in a temple. People would come to this temple and worship there every year and they enjoyed the most prosperous of lives.[58]

This myth closely resembles other data concerning Turkic myth and religion studied above and reflects both typically Inner Eurasian and Indo-European tripartition. At level 1 we have the top of a mountain and the sun, acting for nine months, along with the rain and the winds. Previously, on this level, we encountered winter, summer, rain and wind. This level also has the aspects of religion and sovereignty. At level 2 we have a river and energetic activity (building two cities). On level 3 we have, below the course of the river, a land of fertility and immunity from disease (which, in the Indo-European domain, belongs to fertility as concept 3).

An imaginary history of an Islamic mystical brotherhood

Further light on Inner Eurasian religions is cast by a most peculiar book, an imaginary history of a Muslim mystical brotherhood, composed around 1600 by one Ahmad of Uzgen in what is now Kyrgyzstan. This history is called 'The History of the Uwaysis' (*Tadhkira-yi Uwaysiyya*), the reason being that the term 'Uwaysi' designates a Muslim mystic who looks for instruction from the spirit of a dead or physically absent person. It is derived from the name of a legendary contemporary of Muhammad, Uways, who is supposed to have communicated with the Prophet by telepathy. Ahmad's *History* consists of a series of biographies, usually of people

who never existed. The subject of each biography is said to be 'on
the heart' or 'on the back' of a given prophet: the mystics must
resemble the prophets, whose miracles they reproduce, and the
resemblance is especially strong when a mystic is 'on the back' of
the prophet in question. Thus the biographies tend to reflect the
Islamic legends surrounding biblical figures who are venerated as
prophets in Islam. In spite of this, some elements of Inner Eurasian religion can be discerned beneath the surface.[59]

In Chapter 1 of the *History* the subject of the biography is 'on
the back of Moses'. Like Moses, he produces water by striking the
ground with his staff, though on another occasion he does so in
the Turkic manner of using a special stone. After dying, he tells
someone in a dream that God 'has accepted all his acts' and that
his tomb will be destroyed and disappear: thus we find the Inner
Eurasian motifs of the dream which reveals the dead man's posthumous state (encountered above) and the concealment of the
grave of an important person (combined with the biblical motif
of Moses' grave's being in an unknown place). Chapter 2 shows
us a mystic who is 'on the back of Jacob': in an initiatory experience he loses consciousness and is granted Jacob's vision of the
angels (this is like modern accounts of shamans who are initiated
by being made to lose consciousness and familiarize themselves
with spirits). He also obtains the shaman's gift of being able to
travel round the whole world in the night.[60]

Chapter 7, aptly, has a strong Turkic flavour: it presents a historical king of East Turkistan, Satuq Bughra Khan (d. 951), to
whom the *History* is dedicated. Satuq is converted to Islam by a
hare, which turns into human form. Here we see the dominant
feature of Inner Eurasian religion, the animal as man's instructor, and also the veneration (later transformed into dread) already
accorded by the Turks to the hare. The motif of the hare as guide
is already attested in the Middle Ages, and is echoed, as we saw, in
Herodotus. This chapter is (again aptly) echoed in Chapter 17,
in which a Turkic hunter and archer is criticized for killing lots of
wild animals by people who object that all animals praise God:
eventually he is made to repent by a reproachful deer. Chapter 27
presents a pharmacist of Turkmenistan who has visions of 'good
spirits', presumably to be identified with those encountered above
in the *Story of Oghuz*. This pharmacist is called 'Abbas, the root

ɔrm of which, it is explained, read backwards in the Arabic script
ɔecomes *sab'*, 'seven': thus he has to become like the angels of the
ɔeven heavens, travel like the seven planets, revolve like the seven
ɔleiades and eat once every seven days. In Chapter 37 we again
ɔncounter a hunter, who is made to repent by a parrot before
ɔeing guided by a snake who turns into human form. The hunter's
ɡuide initiates him into the mystical path by 'breathing' on him
(a typically Turkic practice), slitting his chest, washing what is inside and sewing it up again (this reflects a legend about
Muhammad and also Inner Eurasian shamanic initiations). Then
the converted hunter comes to East Turkistan, where he meets
another mystic called 'Arrow-Breath', because his 'breath' travels
like an arrow, faster than everything. The two mystics agree to
communicate by shooting arrows to each other.[61]

Accordingly, Chapters 7, 17, 27 and 37 bind the sequence of
the book's 40 chapters together, the motif of 'Turkicness' being
linked to that of the number seven as holy to the Turks. In addition to the 40 chapters, the book also has 30 'sections', devoted
to secondary figures and women. Thus there are 13 biographies
of female mystics at the end of the book. These biographies resemble the legends of early Muslim women mystics in Syria and
Iraq, which reflect the Eastern Christian contrast between the
asexual wife (symbolized above all by Mary the mother of Jesus)
and the penitent courtesan. However, the biographies also con-
tain some Inner Eurasian motifs.[62]

In Section 19 we find a woman whose husband dies on their
wedding night and who imitates the Mary of Islamic legend by
making a withered tree turn green and bear fruit. Interestingly,
trees prostrate themselves before her at night, and engage in re-
citing formulae of 'remembrance of God'. A willow which has
invited her to lie down beneath it tells the woman that it has been
looking after her. This seems to echo Mongol materials which we
shall meet below, notably with reference to women. In Section 23
a penitent courtesan, who closely resembles her Eastern Christian predecessors, establishes herself on the top of a mountain
where she engages in protracted devotions before crossing a river
and coming to the foot of a tree which has lost its leaves: there she
finds her alter ego, a woman born and living beneath the tree.
(Now we seem to have a typically Inner Eurasian tripartition: [1]

mountain top, [2] river, [3] foot of tree. In our survey of Mongo
religion we shall encounter, apparently in a cult observed by
women, the element of crossing a river in a pilgrimage to special
trees.) Section 27 corresponds to Chapter 27: it presents a woman
of Turkmenistan. From the age of seven the sound of 'remembrance of God' miraculously comes out of her chest, and when
she reaches the age of 17 she sets off for the desert. She dies at
the end of her 67th year.[63]

Other elements of Inner Eurasian religion are found reflected
in parts of the *History of the Uwaysis*. Flying through the air is a
common feature in both the *History* and modern accounts of shamans. An apple is used to kill someone, as in the *Romance of Abu
Muslim*. One mystic shows a disciple the whole world displayed in
a fingernail: similarly, modern Hungarian shamans are credited
with the gift of being able to find hidden treasures by looking
into their fingernails.[64]

Strahlenberg: a Swedish observer of Inner Eurasian Turks

More information about Turkic customs is given by the eighteenth-
century Swedish writer Strahlenberg whose work was first
mentioned in our first chapter. He notes various practices of the
Chuvash of the Volga and the Yakut of northern Siberia who are
both of particular interest in that they speak languages which seem
to have separated from other Turkic languages at an early date, so
that they appear to have retained a number of archaic elements
in their religions. The Chuvash have a great festival in October,
when they brew beer and drink to the Tsar's health. They offer all
their first fruits to their god (whom Strahlenberg identifies with
the Scandinavian god of war and thunder, Thor) and bake a special loaf to present as an offering for him. The Chuvash venerate
horses so much that they make no use of them at all, merely hanging their hides on trees. As regards the Yakut, Strahlenberg says
that they sacrifice to an invisible God in heaven, of whom they
have made an image, hung upon a tree and surrounded with furs.
There are also sacred trees among the Yakut, adorned with iron,
brass and copper ornaments. The Yakut shamans use drums and
wear a special costume, to which are attached bits of iron, rattles
and bells. At the New Year festival, in April, the Yakut sacrifice

horses and oxen and sprinkle *qumis* in the air and on a special fire. The Yakut funeral customs vary. Leading members of the community are buried beneath imposing trees, but most people are just abandoned in their huts when they die. Each Yakut tribe has a totem bird or animal which it must not eat.[65]

Gmelin: a German natural scientist

Valuable observations regarding Turkic religion were made by the German natural scientist Johann Georg Gmelin (1709–55) who travelled in Siberia from 1733 to 1743. Gmelin provides more details concerning the Yakut. He and his companions met a leading Yakut shamaness who was most impressive when imitating the leaps and cries of bears, lions, cats and dogs, and would summon up all the spirits of the air and the earth. However, when she tried to demonstrate her claim that, helped by the devil, she could insert a knife into her flesh without hurting herself she failed, and had to admit to Gmelin's party that they had observed her too attentively: normally she deceived her fellow countrymen by slipping the knife into her clothing.[66]

Gmelin also tells us of a rite in which two Yakut demonstrate their friendship: if one of them is going on a long journey the pair go into a wood, and the friend who is staying at home climbs a tree and cuts its branches. The tree remains as a lifelong monument of the friendship between the two.[67]

In Gmelin's account we are further told of the various beings venerated by the Yakut in one of their ceremonies: the shaman officiating prays to gods, demons, dead shamans, important places, rivers, lakes, woods, rocks, the earth and fire and invokes by name 22 beings in all.[68]

Elsewhere Gmelin makes a number of comments on the role of the shaman among the Turks, which have been summarized by Roux. The Tatars between the Ob and Yenisei rivers, says Gmelin, admit that the shamans' prophecies and treatments are not always reliable. Among the Chuvash it is sacrifice and prayer, as prescribed by the shaman, that are seen as the main means of recovering one's health: this is very different from the usual shamanic method of producing a cure by going into a trance. However, the Turks of Siberia have a typically shamanic view of illness: the devil has taken the sick person's soul and it must b restored at once. This is often effected by means of the shaman' magic drum, which is essential for communication with the devil The shaman also intervenes to consecrate a sacred horse, utter ing a formula and slapping it lightly.[69]

Georgi: another traveller in the Russian empire

A general survey of the peoples in the Russian empire was made by the St Petersburg traveller Johann Gottlieb Georgi (1738–1802), who journeyed in 1773 and 1774. He describes a peculiar rite performed at the vernal equinox at Khiva, in a Muslim shrine. Near the tomb of the dead holy man venerated in this shrine there are several tall poles with ropes attached to them and on top of the poles is a large cage. In the rite the dervishes attached to the shrine try to climb up the ropes and into the cage. Only one succeeds: he is said to see the holy man there and obtain the gift of prophecy. He throws his clothes down, and the people present tear them to pieces and take them home as charms. (Clearly this is an adaptation of a shamanic ritual, involving a symbolic ascent to heaven, and resembling anthropological data surveyed below.)[70]

Of particular interest is Georgi's information about the sacrifice of the hare practised by the Teleut Turks of southern Siberia: they always perform this when encountering a misfortune and hang the skin, with head and feet attached, in front of the doors of their huts. The Teleuts also sacrifice weasels and other small quadrupeds, but in the case of major disasters will substitute larger animals, again hanging up their skins.[71]

Levshin: a Russian administrator's view of the Kazakhs

In 1832 the Russian administrator Alexei Levshin published his study of the Kazakh Turks who have given their name to present-day Kazakhstan. This study contains useful data on shamans and feasts. Levshin says that one day he asked two Kazakhs, 'What is your religion?' They both replied, 'I don't know.' Most Kazakhs, comments Levshin, would say the same. Beneath a thin veneer of Islam the Kazakhs believe, for example, that the souls of ordinary people live on, after death, in the stars, and come down to earth when invoked. The Kazakhs have various types of diviners (inspectors of burnt sheep bones, observers of the colour of the flame produced by burning mutton fat, and astrologers) alongside their shamans. These shamans are often clothed in rags, and also engage in divination. One seen by Levshin sang to the accompaniment of his lute in a tent before making increasingly violent movements and foaming at the mouth. Then he started summoning spirits. Eventually, after regaining his senses, he prophesied on the basis of what he claimed to have had revealed to him. Another Kazakh shaman, sitting in the middle of a tent and holding a long staff decorated with banners and stones of various colours, invoked dead Muslim holy men and then started chasing a demon, going out and mounting a horse to pursue him. When he returned he went into a trance, fell down and made such violent movements that it took four men to restrain him. After 10 minutes he calmed down and transmitted the revelations made to him, saying that the next year would pass well, without war or any disaster.[72]

The Kazakh shaman, says Levshin, also practises a form of medicine. He sits in front of the patient, plays the lute, sings, screams and goes into extraordinary contortions. Then he gets up and whips the patient (to expel the evil spirits), licks and bites him, spits in his face and jumps on him with a knife. This goes on for nine days. European physicians comment that this treatment sometimes succeeds with illnesses of psychosomatic origin.[73]

Kazakh feasts accompany weddings, burials and memorial services. They include games: horse racing, archery contests and wrestling, in that order, reflecting their importance. In one form of horse racing men and women take part in mixed pairs. The man is required to catch up with the woman and touch her bosom with his hand. Kazakh women, comments Levshin, allow this to happen only in the case of men whom they find attractive and avoid the hands of others by their adroitness and use of the whip. In the archery contests some Kazakhs shoot at hats and rings thrown into the air. In the wrestling matches the Kazakh men show great skill at seizing each other by the belt.[74]

Verbitskii: a missionary's account of a shaman's performance

The best known account of a shaman's performance is that given by the Russian missionary, Vasilii Verbitskii, on the basis of observations made in 1840 among the Turks of the Altai. This performance took place as part of the main tribal sacrifice to the Altaian Turks' supreme god, Bai Ülgen, and was attended by a large audience. During the first evening of the performance the shaman erected a tent in a birch thicket, around a birch tree, in which nine notches were cut for him to stand in while climbing. A horse was chosen for the sacrifice, and a man was designated by the shaman to act as its groom.[75]

In the ceremony itself the shaman sits down by the fire, next to the tree. His drum is enveloped by the smoke and he summons the spirits to gather in the drum. Each spirit is summoned by a song, and as it arrives the shaman speaks for it to salute him. Then he goes out of the tent and mounts an image of a goose made of cloth stuffed with hay. He flaps his arms as if flying and tells the goose to fly up to the sky. The shaman also speaks for the goose, cackling away in reply to himself like a ventriloquist and his puppet. In the flight the shaman has to capture the soul of the sacrificial horse: eventually he neighs and kicks like a horse when this is done. The business of the first evening is concluded when the shaman performs the sacrifice itself.[76]

In the following evening the shaman makes offerings of food and drink to the spirits by the fire in the tent. He fumigates his drum and puts on his costume. Beating the drum, he summons a number of spirits. Then he begins his ascent to the various heavens, climbing up the notches in the tree and indicating that each notch represents one particular heaven. (The point is that he is supposed to be conducting the sacrificial horse to Bai Ülgen.) Thus in the sixth heaven he pays homage to the moon and in the seventh to the sun. Various comic episodes take place: the shaman makes a bird smoke tobacco, gives the horse water and tells its groom to chase a hare. Eventually he reaches Bai Ülgen, is told whether the sacrifice has been accepted, and is given revelations. Now the shaman collapses, and after a while returns to his senses.[77]

Köroğlu: the bandit-minstrel

n 1842 the Polish scholar Alexander Chodźko (1804–91) published a volume entitled *Specimens of the Popular Poetry of Persia, as Found in the Adventures and Improvisations of Kurroglou, the Bandit-Minstrel of Northern Persia, and in the Songs of the People Inhabiting the Shores of the Caspian Sea*. This contains an English translation of an Azerbaijanian version of a widespread epic tale, entitled *Köroglu* after its hero, who apparently was a historical figure, a singer and leader of rebels in Turkey and Azerbaijan at the end of the sixteenth century. Chodźko's translation is based on a version in which the prose sections are in Persian and the verse in Azerbaijanian.[78]

Köroğlu's father, we are told, was an equerry whose royal master blinded him in a fit of rage: hence the name 'Köroğlu (son of the blind man)'. When Köroğlu grows up he sets himself up as a brigand and acquires 777 followers. When he comes to Istanbul he stays in the house of an old woman, whom he greatly upsets by eating up all the food set before him so that there is none left for her. (This looks like one of the 'three sins of the warrior', a pattern found by Dumézil and his followers in various parts of the Indo-European domain and consisting of offences against the main concepts of religious sovereignty, warlike force and fertility: the sin against concept 3, fertility, is almost always committed with reference to a woman.) After this Köroğlu kills a religious scholar who forges a letter enabling him to enter the Sultan's palace. (This is a typical example of the sin against concept 1.) Köroğlu duly elopes with the princess, but they are pursued by her brother. The bandit tricks the prince into dismounting in order to fasten his saddle and fells him with his club while sparing his life. (This looks like one of the 'three tests of the warrior', also found by Dumézil and his followers throughout the Indo-European field, and again corresponding to the three main Indo-European concepts: here the warrior is tested with reference to sovereignty, in the form of a prince, and intelligence, which forms part of concept 1.) On the way back to Köroğlu's lair he and the princess encounter the son of a European prime minister, who has come to Turkey to win the princess. In the ensuing fight Köroğlu single-handedly defeats him and his servants. (This is a classic test on the level of concept 2.)

Then the bandit and princess come across a rich merchant who tries to buy the latter. Köroğlu frightens him into paying a huge indemnity for this insult. (Here the merchant and his wealth seem to represent a test on the level of concept 3.) Subsequently, however, Köroğlu meets another merchant, who is a better warrior than himself, and commits a cowardly murder upon him. (This flouting of the warrior's ethic is a typical example of the sin against concept 2.)[79]

Later, when venturing deep into Ottoman territory, Köroğlu is captured as a result of treachery and imprisoned in a pit at Scutari (near Istanbul). There the governor's daughter rescues him, and he gives her as a bride to a loyal follower. Eventually, however, Köroğlu's beloved horse is killed by a pair of murderers, and, refusing to live without him, he offers no resistance to them.[80]

These last two episodes show familiar Turkic motifs: the rescuing by a daughter of a local ruler and the bond between man and horse. We have already seen another motif found here: the bride's family giving chase to the couple. It must nonetheless be noted that this element, like the 'three sins' and the 'three tests', is also found in the Byzantine Greek epic entitled *The Two-Blood Border Lord* (*Digenes Akrites*) and preserved in manuscripts from the fourteenth century onwards. There too the hero is a historical person (of the eighth century), fighting, like Köroğlu, on the border of eastern Turkey, who elopes with a general's daughter and is pursued by her brothers and many soldiers. He fights the pursuers, but avoids killing the brothers. After this the Border Lord is tested in three threatening attacks made against him and his bride (by [1] a supernatural dragon, [2] soldiers and [3] a woman), and thwarts all three. Previously he has sinned by rebelling against an emperor and raping a girl: now he commits a cowardly murder upon a warrior. In both epics, then, Indo-European patterns seem to have been adapted to historical personalities.[81]

The Memorial Feast for Kökötöy

In 1856 a Kazakh princeling, Chokan Valikhanov (1835–65), transcribed a Kirghiz oral epic about a memorial feast for a legendary hero called Kökötöy. The transcription was edited and translated nto English, with copious notes, by the British scholar Arthur Hatto in 1977. One finds in it fascinating information about Kirghiz traditions, and in particular the role of women. In this epic we encounter the celebrated hero Manas, the blueness of whose appearance even affects the colour of his lice. Manas, we are told, has a magnificent whip, which

> Makes a snappish woman cringe
> Makes a neglectful woman say 'My hero'
> Makes a nagging woman dote on one's words
> Makes an unhelpful woman embrace one
> Makes a woman who does not come to meet one shake
> Makes a woman who disagrees smile sweetly
> Makes a woman who does not caress one say 'My love'
> Makes a woman who does not reveal secrets confide in one.

(We shall find this attitude to wife beating echoed in Finnish poetry.)[82]

One of the contestants in the games at the feast is an Amazon called Oronggu, a name which seems to be derived from a name for a species of antelope. She appears in an old entertainment of the Kirghiz nobility in which 'a naked woman, bending down, untied with her teeth a camel tethered to a peg driven into the ground, and if successful took the camel for herself.'[83] In the epic Oronggu comes forward to do this and the men laugh and mimic her. Manas says:

> Your cave is full of money O shrew
> Your pasture is full of cattle O shrew.

He proceeds to make obscene comments on her genitalia, and she replies that she is the mother of great heroes. Hatto remarks that Oronggu appears to be an earth-ancestress and a deer-goddess, and compares a Tunguz ritual in which a shaman, in front of a sacred cliff, would ask a clan-goddess called 'spirit-mistress of the earth' for assistance in hunting. She would send him to another goddess, who took the form of a deer.[84]

In the feast's great horse race, which goes on for several months, Manas damages his chances by sleeping for nine days at the start.

He still wins, but his prize is stolen. Manas decides to go and fight the thief and asks a sworn friend to help him. The friend is too frightened to do so and instead offers Manas, in order of rising importance, for his wife, daughter and son. Manas sends his 40 companions to a lame master armourer, who makes a splendid sword for him. Armed with this, he kills the thief. (One will naturally compare the arming of Achilles by the lame smith Hephaestus in the *Iliad*.)[85]

Radlov's version of *Manas*

The famous Kirghiz epic called *Manas*, after the hero just encountered, was transcribed by the great Russian linguist Vasilii Radlov (1837–1918). Radlov's transcription has been presented in a new edition, with English translation and commentary, by Hatto, published in 1990. In this epic Manas fights a duel with his maternal uncle, Kökčö. Manas' corselet is supposed to be impenetrable, but Kökčö's musket ball goes through it and kills him. The dead warrior goes to the underworld, but invokes his 40 companions, and they somehow bring him back to life. Hatto comments that this episode must reflect Manas' original function of shaman and the 40 companions' original character of spirits. Afterwards Manas dies a second time, poisoned. His horse, falcon and dog mourn at his tomb, and God sends his angels with the instruction to bring him back to life if these animals turn out to have a good master: this duly happens. Yet again, we see the animal as rescuer.[86]

Töshtük: animals and an elm tree

Another Kirghiz epic transcribed by Radlov, called Töshtük after its hero's name, also presents a return from the underworld. Töshtük meets a supernatural maiden who says that she will own him in the next world. Later, in the course of a struggle with an evil spirit, Töshtük sinks beneath the ground, riding his horse. After a long and eventful life in the underworld the horse insists on making Töshtük return. The hero finds an elm tree which reaches through the centre of the earth to heaven. He kills the dragon at its base, and a grateful eagle carries him up to the world of the living. We have already noted that in Islamic architecture of around 1300 the dragon is represented as buried in the earth and supporting the tree of life.[87]

An epic of two shamans

Shamanic elements are also prominent in yet another epic recorded by Radlov, this time among the Kachin Turks of the Abakan region around the Yenisei river banks in central Siberia. This poem is called *Kara Tygan and Suksagal* after its two main characters. In the first part of the epic the hero Kara Tygan and his brother-in-law Olanger set out to restore two men to life. They turn themselves into swallows and make their horses into swans. After flying to the Altai mountains they obtain a white herb from the top of a tree: this herb effects the resurrection required. In the second part of the poem Kara Tygan's black horse falls and breaks its neck. The hero makes his way to the home of a man called Suksagal, who, by magical means, has used the apparent death of the horse to steal it. Suksagal and Kara Tygan engage in a trial of shamanic powers: the former steals the latter's eyes, and the latter the former's tongue. Then Suksagal makes a fascinating suggestion to Kara Tygan. Neither of the two men, he says, will have children, and so they should make an agreement: when one of them dies the other will come and look at his bones. The British scholar Nora Chadwick points out that in Turkic epic the duty of coming to look at a dead man's bones is normally incumbent upon his son, and that the explicit statement that neither hero will have children is paralleled elsewhere when a Turkic hero is a shaman.[88]

Three marriages and a bear's skin

Further archaic elements are found in an epic recorded by Radlov from the Kysyl Türks, also of the Abakan region. In this poem a hero called Südäi Märgän is living a comfortable existence in a house full of possessions, owning plenty of cattle. His wife tries to have him killed because they have no children and he escapes with his faithful and vigilant horse. Then he kills a bear and clothes himself in its skin. Südäi Märgän comes to another country and acquires another wife. His horse brings him weapons, and he kills a great bird and a tiger. After this Südäi Märgän's brothers-in-law imprison him in a pit, and his new wife has to send his horse to find a rescuer: a maiden who lives on the edge of Heaven and has supernaturally long hair. Hanging on to her hair, Südäi Märgän is pulled out of the pit; he takes her as his third wife. Thus the triad of marriages is Indo-European, corresponding to the concepts of wealth [3], force [2] and religious sovereignty [1], like other triads of marriages analysed by Dumézil and his followers. We must further note that a hero who resembles a bear in his outward form is a familiar character in Inner Eurasian narratives.[89]

A Kazakh prose epic: winning a bride

Marriage also dominates a Kazakh prose epic published by Radlov, in which the hero, Shentäi, has to find a bride who lives behind a barrier of fire. Thus he has to win her in a double competition, consisting of a horse race and a wrestling contest. Shentäi is disguised as a beggar, and advised by a clever maiden called Synshy Sary Kus. At the end of the competition she reveals his identity (thereby also revealing her own powers of clairvoyance). In order to demonstrate that she is right she orders Shentäi to turn into first a blue dove, secondly a hawk, and thirdly a handsome hero. (One will naturally compare the role of Athena in disguising and transforming Odysseus at the end of the *Odyssey*, and note the ancient Turkic triad of first animal, second animal and human.) Afterwards Shentäi's bride is swallowed up by a demon who lives under the earth. Shentäi, thanks to his own supernatural gifts, realizes what has happened and descends beneath the earth's surface to rescue his wife and the demon's other victims. Finally, they all escape from the underworld, in the same way that, as we saw above, the Kirghiz hero Töshtük does, being carried up by a grateful eagle.[90]

A dragon and three wives

A prose epic of the Tatars of Tyumen in south-west Siberia, also translated by Radlov, again presents a pattern of three marriages. A prince's son is obliged to leave his bride and brothers and surrender himself to a dragon, who takes him down through a hole in the earth to the home of his own prince. There the hero is married to a snake, who turns into a maiden: she is the dragon-prince's daughter. Her father imposes a number of tasks upon the hero, who duly carries them out. One of these tasks is acquiring another wife, the daughter of a distant ruler. This mission is encumbered by obstacles produced by the ruler and his daughter, but the hero, aided by six companions, eventually triumphs, thanks to the princess's advice: her father is killed. In the end the hero is reunited with his first bride.[91]

This story resembles one found in the famous Indian epic, the *Mahabharata* (*The Great Poem of the Clan of the Bharatas*), the original version of which was probably composed in the eighth century BCE. In it a prince is forced to leave his wife and brothers and is pulled under the water of the Ganges by the daughter of the king of the snakes. They make love, and then the prince goes to a distant country and marries its ruler's daughter. Eventually he is reunited with his original wife. The Oxford anthropologist Nick Allen and I have both compared this narrative with the amatory adventures of Odysseus before his return to Penelope.[92]

Czaplicka: an overview of Yakut shamans

In 1914 the Polish anthropologist Marie Antoinette Czaplicka published her *Aboriginal Siberia*, an invaluable survey of Siberian society and religion, which incorporates the results of a lot of nineteenth and early twentieth-century fieldwork. It covers the tiny Palaeo-Siberian peoples of north-east Siberia, whose languages are neither Altaic nor Uralic, as well as Turks, Mongols, Tunguz, Samoyeds and Finns. In this chapter we shall confine ourselves to summarizing Czaplicka's overview of Yakut shamans.

According to Czaplicka Yakut shamans, like the other shamans of Siberia, have a vocation when young, which often takes the form of mental illness. They tend to remain nervous and excitable, with strange eyes. One does not become a shaman willingly, it is believed: the ancestor-spirit jumps upon a young man and strangles him. Later on shamanizing will make him feel better. Among the Yakut the shamans feel very ill once a year, when the snow melts. At this time a type of spirit called the *yekyna*, 'mother-animal', begins to wander. There are various types of *yekyna*, represented by the dog, the bull, the stallion, the elk, the black bear and so on. The dog in particular will gnaw and tear the sha man's heart and body, and the wolf and bear are also insatiable There is also another type of Yakut spirit called the *ämägyat*, usu ally the spirit of a dead shaman which comes to a living one b accident or fate.[93]

Among the Yakut most shamans are 'black shamans', that is tc say ones who deal with evil spirits, although they help human: just as much as 'white shamans' do. The latter officiate in spring festivals, weddings, fertility rites and the treatment of patients whose souls are not thought to have been stolen. 'Black shamans' foretell the future, summon up spirits and journey to visit them. They dress and wear their hair like women, and are treated as women in taboos relating to sleeping arrangements and child-birth. The Yakut smiths are also divided into 'black' and 'white', smiths being seen as closely resembling shamans: they too can heal, give advice and foretell the future. Added prestige is acquired by the smiths through manufacturing the metal ornaments of the shamans' costumes: discs, plates and bells. One special copper plate has the figure of a man on it: this plate is designated by the term just mentioned above, *ämägyat*, meaning a spirit, usually just that of a dead shaman. Thus this is the most important of the shaman's ornaments, and is given to him by his teacher in an initiation rite. Metal ornaments also adorn the Yakut shaman's drum, which is egg-shaped and called the *tünür*, a word which means 'kinship through marriage', perhaps because the shaman is united with both the community and the spirits. The shaman's costume is called his 'horse' because it bears him to heaven and the underworld.[94]

In a shamanic performance, done to treat a sick person, the shaman operates at night. He dons his coat and smokes tobacco. A white mare's skin is put in the centre of the room, and he sits on it. Then he begins beating his drum and imitating the calls of birds. After this he chants obscure fragments, such as:

> Horse of the steppes Appear Teach me
> Enchanted bull of the earth Appear Speak to me
> Powerful master Command me ...

The shaman continues by talking to the spirits, questioning

em and giving answers for them. When the spirit called the *mägyat* comes to him he dances furiously, often foaming at the mouth. Eventually, he knows the cause of the sick person's illness and expels this 'cause' by spitting and blowing. He finds out what sacrifices have to be made to the spirits. Finally, he prophesies or tells those present what he has seen during the journey corresponding to his dance. If he sits down in this dance this means that he has come to a resting place in his journey. When he gets up it means that he is rising further into the heavens, whereas if he falls it means that he is going beneath the earth's surface.[95]

Potapov: the Altaian shaman's drum

In 1968 the St Petersburg researcher Leonid Potapov published an important article on the drums of the Altaian shamans of southern Siberia, based on fieldwork done by him from 1925 to 1955. The drawings on these drums, he observes, generally represent the usual tripartite view of the universe: heaven, earth and underworld. In 1946 Potapov interviewed one Altaian shaman, Roman Kaidarakov, aged 67. Roman explained that a white line on his drum, called a 'bowstring', was supposed to orientate him when flying to the spirits. Dark stripes on the drum represented a cloud, needed for summoning rain. A horn on the drum's framework was used by Roman to sail upwards. Various drawings on the drum served other purposes. A representation of the Orion constellation was needed to help the shaman find his way, both on earth and in the sky. Birds, youths and girls were also represented: they assisted the shaman in his flight and trance. There was also a drawing of a birch tree, which he had to visit to find the origin of the illness which he was treating. Also shown were the sun and moon, which lit the shaman's path as he rose up, 'seven blue wolves', used to protect flocks from the ravages of terrestrial wolves, and 'nine black dogs', used to drive spirits out of a patient. A snake, a lizard and an earthworm were used to help cure women's diseases and a frog for venereal ones.[96]

Diószegi: Tofa shamans

The year 1968 also saw the publication of a long article by the leading Budapest expert on shamans, Vilmos Diószegi. In it he presented the results of his fieldwork, done in 1958, among the tiny Tofa people, Turkic-speakers of southern Siberia. He provides examples of how people become shamans: this is seen as due to the will of the spirits, intervening to make people ill and torment them when they are young. These spirits are masters of lakes, mountains and birds. On agreeing to become a shaman one has to have a special gown made. The ornaments on this gown symbolize the human skeleton, but leather plaits and ribbons sewn on to it are called the 'tails' and 'wings' of a bird. A shaman is consulted if someone is ill, if something is lost, and to find out what is going to happen (for example in the hunt). However, the shaman also practises his art for its own sake. He 'rides' his drum, calling it 'white horse' or 'reindeer bull', in order to visit the spirits. The various parts of the drum symbolize parts of a saddled animal – the deer whose skin is used to cover its frame.[97]

One shaman told Diószegi how he used to practise. Juniper branches were held in the fire in a tent in order to summon the spirits. Then the shaman journeyed on his drum to holy mountains, where he met such important spirits as 'the master of the earth' and 'the great shaman master' of his clan. As he was only a minor shaman he flew at a height of only 8 or 9 metres, whereas great shamans flew in the clouds. He had three headdresses, made from the feathers of different birds (wild geese, owls and cranes), corresponding to his need to fly at different times of the year and in different parts of the shaman's performance.[98]

Roux: the nomads of southern Turkey

In 1970 Roux published the results of his fieldwork among two groups of nomadic tribes in southern Turkey: the Yörük, who are pastoralists, and the Tahtaci, who are woodcutters. The Yörük belong to the mainstream Sunni grouping of Islam, so called because of its emphasis on the exemplary practice (*sunna*) of Muhammad. By contrast, the Tahtaci belong to the minority Shiite grouping, so called because it constitutes a Party (*shi'a*) devoted o Muhammad's family. The Tahtaci are influenced by the Bektashi mystical brotherhood, allegedly founded in Turkey around 1300 by a man called Bektash from north-east Iran: they have an initia-tion ceremony very similar to that of the Bektashis, with a triple oath, symbolized by a triple knotting of a girdle and correspond-ing to the triple command 'Be master of your hand, your loins and your tongue!' (This would seem to echo the Indo-European triad of [1] head, [2] upper torso and arms and [3] lower torso.) Like the Bektashis, the Tahtaci venerate the threshold: the piece of wood at the entrance to a Tahtaci home must not be trodden on, and it is kissed when the Tahtaci visit each other. They have a myth about Muhammad's daughter Fatima, in which she is sup-posed to have conceived a daughter of her own without male intervention. One of Muhammad's companions is believed to have eloped with this daughter to Mount Ida (in north-west Turkey), called by the Turks Kaz Daği (Goose Mountain). There she died and became known as the Yellow Girl (Sari Kiz). Here Roux finds Inner Eurasian antecedents: the miraculous conception, the elope-ment, the colour yellow symbolizing light and the sun, and the idea that holy places are frequented by female beings who are half human, half goose.[99]

The Tahtaci have also preserved the ancient Inner Eurasian taboo which forbids one to pollute water with spittle, urine or blood. They do not wash after excretion or sexual intercourse, as Islam demands. The Yörük, although they obey the obligation to perform the ritual ablutions of Islam, show immense veneration for water, covering their heads when turning a tap on. As regards fire, the Tahtaci preserve the medieval Inner Eurasian prohibi-tion on putting a metal blade in the flame. Moreover, as woodcutters, they are also particularly respectful towards very large or old trees, which they avoid cutting down. In contrast to their usual taboo on using water to remove dirt, they have a ritual bath before felling trees: five or six women bathe a naked man.[100]

Domestic animals are treated with great affection by the Tahtaci. The Yörük, as pastoralists, have many rituals corresponding to the annual cycle in the lives of their goats and sheep. Most impor-tant is the feast of mid-August, when the male and female animals are put together to mate: humans never fail to make love on this day, and licentious dances also take place. In the spring the Yörük

organize fights between animals: rams, camels, cocks, he-goats an
horses. Previously, at the same time, men would fight each othe
or rams and bulls. Victory over a ram or bull would make a youn,
man an adult and ready for marriage, whereas victory over ar
other young man would give the right to marry a girl in the latter'
family. Boys and girls compete together in rifle shooting. The
Tahtaci have a traditional fight between boys and girls: the former
have to try to touch the latter's breasts. Both the Tahtaci and the
Yörük have a 'crane dance' in which male dancers simulate the
intercourse of cranes. Among adolescent males bestiality is universal and tolerated until adulthood.[101]

Basilov: transvestism among Inner Eurasian shamans

The year 1978 saw the publication of a fascinating article by the
Moscow anthropologist Vladimir Basilov on transvestism among
Inner Eurasian shamans. He notes that among the 'Palaeo-Siberian' peoples the spirits have often demanded that a man should
make himself look like a woman in every respect, and even marry
another man. In 1909 a Turkmen male shaman had been seen
dressed as a woman, and later similar instances were noted in the
cases of Kazakh shamans and those of the Karakalpak Turks of
north-west Uzbekistan. One of the latter also acted as a woman in
domestic tasks and in women's traditional activities: his associates
saw him as a hermaphrodite. In 1968 Basilov met an old Uzbek
shaman in eastern Uzbekistan. This shaman, called Tašmat, was
born in 1886. The people of his village said that he had become a
shaman, 'touched by a spirit', when young: ill, he was taken to a
shamaness. It was his spirits that made him dress like a woman,
according to the villagers, but he himself gave the explanation 'I
like it.' The villagers said that the spirits who appeared to him
were female. Tašmat preferred to sit among women at feasts and
sing together with them. He sat, swore and greeted and took his
leave of people like a woman, and walked, gesticulated and talked
like one. However, he wore a beard and had wives and children.
The villagers did not consider his behaviour improper. Tašmat
was also a singer and musician.[102]

　　Basilov comments that the famous Scythian 'womanish male
diviners' (*enarees*) mentioned by Herodotus are also mentioned

y the great Greek physician Hippocrates (c.460–c.377 BCE), who
ays that they 'are occupied with womanish tasks and talk like
omen.' Hippocrates says that the Scythians attribute this behav-
our to a goddess and venerate the diviners. He himself attributes
their condition to horse riding. Basilov observes that the Pueblo
ndians of North America used riding exercises to emasculate
males who had to change sex for 'religious orgies'. He adds that a
enth-century Muslim historian of Bukhara records a local custom: every male, after puberty and before marriage, finds sexual
gratification with a certain man, and in exchange, on marrying,
gives him the 'right of the first night' over his bride.[103]

Zhornitskaya: Yakut shamans' dances

Basilov's Moscow colleague Mariya Zhornitskaya also published a
useful article in 1978, on Yakut shamans' dances, based on her
fieldwork done in the 1950s and the publications of earlier observers. In shamans' performances, she observes, their movements
often reproduced those of a galloping or trotting horse. Their
dances were frequently in practice horse dances, with neighing,
snorting and pretending to be caught: the shaman would wear a
horse's halter. Thus he would travel, as a horse, to a sea or mountain, where he would have to turn into a bird in order to dive in or
fly up. Old ex-shamans interviewed by Zhornitskaya showed how
they imitated the sounds and movements of reindeer and swans.
A shaman treating a sick woman would in effect become a reindeer in order to chase after the sick soul. Then he would turn
into a hawk, fly, alight, turn into a reindeer again and fight an evil
spirit's reindeer for the woman's life. Zhornitskaya concludes that
the Yakut shamans' dances could be divided into two groups,
dances in imitation of animals and ecstatic dances at the end of
the performance which brought the shaman into trance.[104]

A south Siberian parallel to the legend of Jason

In 1986 the Italian researcher Ugo Marazzi published an annotated English translation of an epic poem in Altaian Turkic called
Maday Qara after the name of its hero's father. This poem was
recorded in 1964 at Gorno-Altaysk in southern Siberia. It seems

to me to be extremely similar to the legend of the Greek her■
Jason, which is preserved in Greek and Latin sources from circ
700 BCE to the second century CE. I am inclined to attribute th■
resemblances between the two stories to the existence of an an■
cient Inner Eurasian folk tale which would have provided th■
prototype for them both.

At the start of the Turkic epic a ruler, Maday Qara, has his position usurped by a villain, Qara Qula. Similarly, in the Greek
legend the rightful heir to a throne, Jason's father, sees this taken
by a usurper. Maday Qara's son is exposed on a mountain and
brought up by a horse and an old woman, rather as Jason is brought
up in a cave by a foster father who is half horse, half human. The
son is called Kögüdäy Märgän. When he grows up he sets off to
attack the usurper. There are three obstacles before him, forming a typically Inner Eurasian pattern. First, there are two black
heroes from the underworld [3], standing at the foot of a mountain and having no joints in their limbs. Kögüdäy Märgän duly
kills them and proceeds to the second obstacle, a long yellow sea
[2]. (Jason and his companions have to kill men who are 'earth
born' and have hands fixed into their shoulders and sides, before
proceeding to the Black Sea.) Travelling along the shore of this
sea, he meets three heroes in succession and asks them in vain for
advice on how the sea may be crossed. Finally, he meets a hero
who is fishing in the sea, apparently pointlessly, since it is poison-
ous, and who tells Kögüdäy Märgän that dangerous birds will attack
his horse. (Similarly, Jason, when about to cross the Black Sea,
meets a hero who cannot advise him before he encounters a
prophet who is engaged in futile attempts to feed himself and
warns him that murderous birds will attack his crew.) Kögüdäy
Märgän cleverly kills the birds and his horse (which has the gift of
oracular speech, like Jason's ship) takes him over the sea in a huge
leap, rather as Jason cleverly wards off the birds that threaten his
ship and is taken by it across the Black Sea. The third obstacle
comes in the form of two black mountains which open and close,
providing access between the earth and the sky [1]. Kögüdäy
Märgän rides his horse between the mountains, and as they close
they clip the horse's tail, just as Jason's ship has its stern clipped
by the Clashing Rocks.[105]

After these obstacles Kögüdäy Märgän finds himself in the land

f his quest, that of the usurper Qara Qula. Here the usurper's
wife, a demoness, is aware that the hero has come. She does not
tell her husband, because she wants Kögüdäy Märgän to be victo-
ious so that she can marry him. (In the same way Jason, on arriving
at the far shore of the Black Sea, is assisted by the local king's
daughter, Medea, a witch who wants to be his wife.) Kögüdäy
Märgän is at once faced with a new test: he has to kill two huge
black animals, a bull and a camel, and does so just as Jason passes
his next test, that of yoking two huge bulls. Then Kögüdäy Märgän
has to obtain a golden coffer which contains the usurper's soul,
and is again successful, in the same way that Jason, by succeeding
in the task of obtaining the Golden Fleece, seals the Greek usurper's fate. Kögüdäy Märgän, disguised as a badly-dressed vagabond,
comes to the wicked Qara Qula, who is informed by a shaman
that his killer has arrived. (Similarly the Greek usurper is warned
by an oracle to beware of a man with one sandal, and realizes that
his killer has come when Jason turns up clad in this manner.)
Qara Qula is killed by Kögüdäy Märgän, just as the Greek usurper
is murdered by Medea on Jason's orders.[106]

The demoness now tells Kögüdäy Märgän that she wants to live
with him, but he rejects her and she embarks on a career of exceptional wickedness, as does Medea after Jason abandons her.
Kögüdäy Märgän decides that he wants to marry the daughter of
another ruler (as does Jason), and goes to win her. The demoness
tries to kill him with a poisoned drink, but the cup is broken.
(Medea tries to poison the Athenian hero Theseus, but the cup is
dashed from his lips.) Then she abducts his bride and turns her
outer appearance into that of an old woman. (Medea ensures that
Jason's bride is covered in a robe steeped in burning poison.)
Finally, the demoness succeeds in killing Kögüdäy Märgän's parents. (Medea kills Jason's bride, father-in-law and children.)[107]

Reichl: an overview of Turkic epic

The year 1992 saw the publication of an important book by the
German scholar Karl Reichl, entitled *Turkic Oral Epic Poetry*. This
draws on his own fieldwork in the former Soviet Union and north-
west China and on a huge amount of primary and secondary
literature. Noteworthy subjects in this book are the horse, as having

an importance equal to that of the Turkic epic's hero, and the shaman, as closely connected to the singer of the epic.

This connection between shaman and singer is reflected in an autobiographical account given by a Kirghiz singer: he began to sing after an initiatory dream in which an epic hero pierced him with a lance, on the point of which a fire was burning. Following this the singer was ill for a long time. In general, says Reichl, a singer enters a state of inspiration when performing and describes himself as galloping on his stringed instrument as a steed. Sometimes he sings with a tense and guttural articulation, like an Inner Eurasian shaman.[108]

Reichl gives considerable attention to the famous Turkic epic called *Alpamysh*, after the name of its hero. The story of *Alpamysh* exists in many versions, both in prose and in verse, but the best-known one is in Uzbek verse, transmitted by the singer Fazil Yoldaš-oġli near Samarqand in 1927–8. In this version a ruler's son, Alpamysh, leaves his wife to go and fight against the Kalmuck people. He is faced with three tests, in what seems to me to be the usual Indo-European pattern of 'the three tests of the warrior', corresponding to the three central Indo-European concepts, here occurring in the order 3–2–1: fertility is represented by women and seduction, force by a battle with an army, and religion by the duty to show intelligence by preserving the use of one's reason. First, a witch called Surkhayil arranges for 40 slave girls to try to seduce Alpamysh and his 40 companions. The men manage to resist the temptation and then encounter a second test: a Kalmuck army arrives, and they defeat it. In a third test Alpamysh and his companions are plied with brandy. They get drunk and the palace in which they are sleeping is set ablaze. The 40 companions die, but Alpamysh survives, albeit asleep, and is hurled into an underground dungeon. Thus the narrative closely resembles that of the *Odyssey*: Odysseus is tested by the seductive Sirens [3], the force of a monster, Scylla [2], and the religious imperative to avoid eating the cattle of the Sun [1] – his companions fail the last test and are killed. (I have argued elsewhere that this Homeric narrative is closely paralleled in the Iranian national epic and the *Mahabharata*.)[109]

Returning to the story of Alpamysh, we find that in the meantime a usurper has taken power over the hero's country. Alpamysh's

on tries to arrange for his father to be rescued by the latter's
blood brother, who is, however, unsuccessful. After seven years
Alpamysh is rescued by the Kalmuck ruler's daughter. He gets
home just before his wife is to be married to the usurper. From
this point the external similarities to the *Odyssey* are very strong.
Alpamysh is recognized by his family and a faithful herdsman,
disguises himself and is alone able to handle his great bow at the
marriage feast's archery contest. He has the usurper killed and
reunites his people.[110]

One passage of Alpamysh presents another striking tripartite
pattern, this time of a typically Inner Eurasian kind, in its description of the hero's riding:

> When he came to a mountain he made his horse jump over
> When he came to a river he made him jump across
> When he came to a slope he made him gallop.[111]

Reichl notes important qualities of the horse in Turkic epic. It
may be able to transform its appearance or talk like a human,
giving the hero advice. The horse grows miraculously, often rescues the hero and can even bring him back from the dead, turning
into an eagle and flying up into the heavens. It may be born at the
same moment as the hero and be his 'double'.[112]

Later Reichl gives more attention to the problems posed by
the various versions of Alpamysh and their chronology. He points
out that these versions closely resemble the tale of a prince who
competes in archery competitions in the *Book of Grandfather Korkut,*
which we have discussed above. The story is the same, and cannot
be later than the eleventh century when the Oghuz Turks began
to migrate from Inner Eurasia towards what is now Turkey. In one
Inner Eurasian version, in Bashkir, the resemblances with the *Odyssey* are even closer: Alpamysh's wife insists that any man who
wants to be her second husband has to draw his bow and shoot an
arrow through a ring. Alpamysh, after punishing two disloyal shepherds, finds the usurper sitting in apparent security, passes the
test and, with a second arrow, kills the usurper as he tries to run
away.[113]

The internal logic of Turkic religion

As we have repeatedly stressed, method demands that one shoul
examine the internal logic of a people's religion before makin
comparisons. For the Turkic peoples, however, we have not foun
sufficient evidence in the case of any one of them to reconstruct
religion in its entirety. Consequently it seems best to treat the Turk
as one single people: this seems reasonable enough, given th
fact that many Turkic peoples have been just new confederation
of old ones, and especially given the strong degree of unity an
consistency in the Turkic materials which we have surveyed.

Shamans have been prominent in these materials. Their 'frenzy
is attested among the Türks, along with their function of foretell
ing the future, and Avicenna tells of their use of hyperventilation
in order to induce a trance and utter prophecies. Among the Yakut
we have seen the impressive leaping and crying out of a shamaness,
imitating bears, lions, cats and dogs, and among the Turks of the
Altai we have heard how a shaman flies and cackles like a goose
before neighing and kicking like a horse. Again among the Yakut,
we have found the spirits of the dog, wolf and bear gnawing and
tearing the shaman's heart and body. We have also noted the transvestism of Uzbek shamans, and the connection between shamans
and singers: the Kirghiz singer's dream of being pierced by a hero
with a burning lance is of course suggestive. In these materials
concerning shamans, however, it is often the role of the animal
which is dominant, and it is the animal that is the most important
motif of Turkic religion in general.

This role of the animal is noteworthy in the case of the wolf,
seen as ancestor, rescuer, guide and heraldic emblem. Here there
is a link with the schema sky–intermediate space–earth: the Türk
king with the wolf-head's emblem belongs to the heavens, his sons
to the space below and his grandsons to the earth's surface. This
schema, as we have seen, is reflected among the Bashkir Turks,
along with the quartet of winter, summer, rain and wind at the
celestial level. The same schema reappears in Ibn al-Dawadari's
Turkic myth of the origins: a mountain summit is affected by the
seasons, rain and wind, before the first Turk's eldest son lives beside a river and his descendants live on the plain beneath. Similarly,
in the *History of the Uwaysis*, we encountered a woman who moved

om the top of a mountain, across a river and to the earth at the
ot of a tree. The hero Kögüdäy Märgän was put to the test on
he surface of the earth, at the foot of a mountain, by heroes from
he underworld, and then in a jump over a sea, before having to
ass through the gateway to the sky.

In order to move between these three levels humans must ei-
her be carried by animals and birds or turn into them, while
animals and birds must themselves undergo transformations. Thus
a shaggy dog emerges from a vulture's egg, and a variety of animals produce the hero Oghuz. The Yakut shaman turns into a
horse to travel to a sea or mountain, and then has to become a
bird in order to progress further; alternatively, he becomes a reindeer in order to chase a sick soul, but in one section of his journey
has to transform himself into a hawk. In Turkic epic a horse has to
turn into an eagle in order to bring a dead hero up into the sky.
Thus Turkic religion has a logic of transformations which enables
humans to travel to different parts of the universe, in order to
heal the sick and meet important spirits.

Turkic religion in a comparative perspective

In spite of this strong internal logic a lot of the materials set out
in this chapter make sense only in a wider comparative framework, when compared or contrasted with other evidence, which
they in turn bring into sharper focus. This is particularly the case
with the purificatory use of fire and smoke, which we noted among
the Scythians and then found among the Türks and the Kirghiz,
as well as in Verbitskii's account of a shaman's performance: purification must not be done with water, since that would defile it.
The symbolism of the colour blue, representing the celestial and
the holy, is also especially significant, as is that of yellow to indicate light and the sun. That is very different from the usual
Indo-European colour schema: white for religious sovereignty, red
for warlike force and a 'dark' colour, black, green or blue, to symbolize fertility. It is also different from the colour schema found
in the Afroasiatic language family (which includes the Semitic,
Egyptian, Berber and Hausa languages); there black represents
the supreme storm-god, red the young warrior who kills him and
white the sun-goddess for whom they compete.[114]

On the other hand, there are strong resemblances with Indo-European patterns when one looks at the Turkic myths of the origins and the Bashkir gods. As we have just recalled, the top level, that of religious sovereignty, is divided into four aspects: winter, summer, rain and wind. One is tempted to link these to the four aspects of Indo-European sovereignty found by Dumézil and his followers, which I have numbered 1.1a, 1.1b, 1.2 and 1.3: thus one could see winter as sinister, summer as friendly, rain as assuring survival and the wind as distributing what it wills. The second level in the Turkic materials is that of rivers and mountain slopes: here, as on Inner Eurasian mountains generally, the river rushes down violently, corresponding to the second Indo-European concept of force, whereas in the Indo-European domain itself rivers are usually calm, peacefully flowing embodiments of fertility. In the third Turkic level we have the earth, as often in Indo-European religions, but the issue is complicated by the appearance, in later materials, of an underworld. The specialists are agreed that the underworld is a medieval borrowing from the historical religions to the south of Inner Eurasia: the original Inner Eurasian belief was that the souls of the dead went to heaven or some other world (like our own), whose location was unknown. We have seen traces of this original belief among the Oghuz and the Cumans. The translation of the eighth-century Kirghiz epitaph as 'He wandered in the three storeys of the universe' is uncertain, and does not prove that the Kirghiz already believed in an underworld.[115]

Other elements of Turkic religion are paralleled in our Introduction and first chapter. Grand burials for royalty and nobility, with sacrifices of humans and horses, are again significant features. The eagle, soaring up to the sky to rescue a Kirghiz hero, evokes prehistoric cliff drawings and the eagle feathers on Hsiung-nu arrows. Similarly, the transvestite Turkic shamans recall the Scythians' feminized male diviners, and the Muslim mystics who agree to communicate by shooting arrows to each other are reminiscent of Scythian 'blood brothers'.

It is, however, the theme of 'becoming-animal' that is the most important Inner Eurasian aspect of Turkic religion. Here the radical 'becoming-animal' of the shaman in the performance is far more real, as Deleuze and Guattari have pointed out, than what is

und in ordinary myths of animal ancestors, or simple imitations
of animals made in order to hunt them. Moreover, in the story of
Oghuz there is not just a bovine as one parent of the hero, but the
reproduction of the traits of other animals as well: there is contami-
ation between the human and animal worlds, produced by
bestiality. Fighting, hunting and shamanic healing all require 'becoming-animal' for obtaining speed and the ability to be
everywhere at once. Thus the nomadic tribes of southern Turkey
have intercourse at the same time as animals, simulate the intercourse of cranes and tolerate bestiality.[116]

3

The Mongols

In our survey of Mongol religion we shall encounter many elements just mentioned in our conclusions regarding the Turks. When examining the *Secret History of the Mongols,* and its stories about Genghis Khan and his ancestors, we shall again see the importance accorded to the colours blue and yellow, along with a holy mountain and blood brotherhood. The rich evidence concerning Genghis Khan's successors, provided by Mongol, European, Iranian and Chinese writers, will show us the divinatory and healing role of the shamans, along with details of offerings and taboos. We shall find the ideas that shamans are sodomized by the spirits and given food by them. Animals are again most prominent in these early materials, appearing in tripartite patterns which reflect the order of the universe and link them to humans. The parallelism between animal and human is evident in Mongol hunting customs.

Fifteenth and sixteenth-century Mongolian texts will show us Iranian influences in lists of deities and fire worship, but also authentically Mongol traditions in the veneration of banners and the importance accorded to the number nine. Later Mongolian texts, relating to the seventeenth century, again put animals and humans together in the main function of the Mongol shamans: offering protection from illness and disaster. In the eighteenth century we shall see how the shamans of the Buryat Mongols dress in animal skins and consecrate horses. Nineteenth and twentieth-

entury evidence will give detailed descriptions of the Buryat shamans' rituals and deities and it will be seen that the latter present
markedly Indo-European pattern. Finally, recent anthropologi-
al studies will provide more information about the significance
of trees, the military character of Mongol shamanic activities and
he role of shamanesses.

The Secret History of the Mongols

Our most important early source for the study of Mongol religion
is the Mongolian work, *The Secret History of the Mongols* (*Mongqol-
un niucha tobcha'an*), which seems to have been written shortly
after Genghis Khan's death in 1227. It may have been composed
by an adopted son of Genghis. The book is in prose, with some
short passages, nearly always dialogue, in verse: it is rather like an
epic, incorporating imaginary conversations and folklore. Genghis'
life is the *Secret History*'s main subject, and the anonymous author
does not hide his disapproval of the conqueror's many breaks with
Mongol traditions. Here we shall refer to the annotated English
translation by the Mongol scholar Urgunge Onon and the comments by the German orientalist Paul Ratchnevsky in his own
biography of Genghis.[1]

The Secret History begins by telling us that Genghis and his original ancestor had their destiny ordained by Heaven (Tengri). This
ancestor was a blue wolf, whose wife was a doe. They crossed a
lake and settled at the head of a river, on Mount Burqan Qaldun
in northern Mongolia. There one of their descendants had just
one eye, in the centre of his forehead, with which he could see for
a huge distance. With this eye he spotted a maiden, Alan-qo'a,
whom he considered a suitable match for his younger brother.
Alan-qo'a bore the latter two sons, and then he died. Afterwards
she had three more sons and claimed that these were due to divine intervention. Every night, she said, a bright yellow man had
entered her tent through the smoke hole. His light had sunk into
her belly before he slipped out of the tent in the form of a yellow
dog. Thus these three sons were children of Heaven and would
rule over the common people. When Alan-qo'a died her first four
sons divided up their inheritance, not giving a share to the youngest one because they thought he was stupid (his name, Bodonchar,

meant 'The Fool'). From him Genghis was descended.[2]

When about 14 or 15 Genghis committed a cowardly murder of one of his half brothers. Later, when taking refuge from enemies of his family, he hid on Mount Burqan Qaldun. Afterwards we are told, he said,

> On Burqan Qaldun
> My life like a louse's
> Hunted I escaped
> My life my only one was spared

I was very frightened. Every morning I shall sacrifice to Mount Burqan Qaldun. Every day I shall pray to it. Let my descendants and theirs know this!

Then, the text informs us, Genghis hung his belt round his neck, facing the sun, and, hanging his hat from his arm, beat his breast. Kneeling to the sun nine times, he offered libations and prayers.[3]

After this period of concealment Genghis renewed his friendship with his 'sworn brother (*anda*)', Jamuqa. At the age of 11 they had entered into the 'sworn brotherhood' relationship, exchanging knucklebones, and shortly afterwards Jamuqa had reinforced this by giving Genghis a whistling arrowhead, Genghis giving him a horn-tipped arrow in return. This meant that they shared one life and protected each other for ever. Now they exchanged belts and horses, professing eternal love for each other. At night they would sleep beneath the same quilt. However, after a year and a half the two young men separated. Later some of Jamuqa's followers joined Genghis, and one of them said that he had had a vision in which Jamuqa was butted by a white cow, while a white ox bellowed: 'Heaven and Earth agree, Genghis should be the people's ruler!'[4]

More Mongols now united behind Genghis, designating him as their ruler (*khan*) and promising to bring him booty and game: beautiful women, geldings with fine rumps and wild animals from the steppes and cliffs. One of his followers, Sube'etei, who was going to be one of his great generals, is presented by the *Secret History* as saying that he would become a rat, gathering booty, a bird, scooping up glory and a covering of felt for Genghis himself.

Here of course we twice see a pattern familiar to us from Turkic materials: first animal, second animal and human.) Jamuqa, who was now Genghis' open rival for power, had some of the latter's supporters boiled in cauldrons. Ratchnevsky comments that this form of execution was intended to stop the victims' spirits surviving and taking revenge. Subsequently Genghis executed two of his own clansmen (in defiance of Mongol custom) for failing to support him: they were suffocated (this time in respect for Mongol custom, which forbade shedding the blood of nobles). Some tribes gathered to oppose Genghis, cutting up and jointing a stallion and a mare as they swore brotherhood to one another. Declaring their support for Jamuqa, they attacked Genghis and his forces. Two of their leaders, who knew how to use a magic stone to produce a storm, did so, but the storm turned on their own troops and routed them. In a subsequent battle Genghis was wounded and one of his supporters, called Jelme, rendered two services to him: he sucked the congealed blood from his wound and brought him water and curds from the enemy camp. Genghis said that Jelme had now performed three services for him: he had 'taken out' his life, removing him from danger when he had been hiding on Mount Burqan Qaldun, 'made empty' his life by freeing it from the congealed blood and 'entered' his life by giving it nourishment. (This tripartition looks Indo-European: concept 1 is represented [in a typically Inner Eurasian manner] by the holy mountain, concept 2, warlike force, by the wound sustained in battle, and concept 3, fertility, by nourishment.)[5]

At this time Genghis had trouble with other local leaders, notably the Christian ruler of the Kerait people, who bore the title 'Wang-khan' and was famous in Europe as 'Prester John', a champion of the true faith behind infidel lines. Wang-khan had been a 'sworn brother' of Genghis' father, and Genghis had become his protégé and adopted son, in another typically Mongol special relationship between two men. Now Wang-khan, siding with Jamuqa, fought against Genghis, but the latter appealed, successfully, to Wang-khan's sense of duty. Wang-khan swore not to harbour evil thoughts of Genghis, under pain of having his blood shed, just as he now symbolically shed a little, cutting his finger with a knife and pouring the blood into a little birch bark container, which he sent to Genghis. However, Genghis attacked Wang-khan when he was off his guard, and he was killed.[6]

Subsequently Genghis achieved more victories over other re
gional rivals. Of particular interest is one of his decrees, in whic,
he instructs Sube'etei to pursue a couple of his defeated enemies
Genghis tells Sube'etei that if they become birds and fly up to the
sky he must become a falcon to catch them; if they become mar
mots, burrowing into the earth, he is to become an iron bar to
strike into the ground and find them; if they become fish, swim
ming into the sea, he is to become a net to scoop them up. (Here
the tripartition is typically Inner Eurasian: in between the sky and
the earth the sea, as being upon the surface of the latter, has an
intermediate position.)[7]

Eventually Jamuqa, betrayed by his own companions, was
handed over to Genghis. The *Secret History* gives a romanticized
picture of the ensuing dialogue between the two 'sworn brothers'. Jamuqa is made to say, of their original oath taking, 'Together
we ate the food that is not to be digested.' Onon explains that this
is gold dust, mixed with some liquid and swallowed by the two
'brothers', who before this would have drunk a little of each other's blood. Jamuqa is then presented as asking Genghis to kill
him without shedding his blood, and bury his bones in high
ground: dead, Jamuqa will eternally protect Genghis' descendants. Genghis is shown as agreeing to this, but, as Ratchnevsky
points out, we hear from the Iranian historian Rashid al-Din that
Jamuqa was handed over to one of Genghis' cousins, who put
him to an agonizing death by dismemberment.[8]

The Mongols had been united. Genghis was enthroned as Khan
at a large gathering, after the Mongols' great white banner with
nine corners had been raised: the banner itself symbolized the
people's protective spirit, while its nine corners represented its
nine constituent tribes. The new ruler rewarded his supporters.
His youngest brother was singled out for particular generosity,
and was given immunity from punishment for up to nine offences.
In the enumeration of rewards granted to others we find the important term *jüldü*, which Onon translates as 'highest merit' (here
disputed by claimants for shares in credit for saving a boy's life).
Onon explains that elsewhere in the *Secret History* it means 'head,
heart and lungs', constituting the 'best part' of an animal, the
part consecrated to the spirits when it is killed and the rest is eaten,

hile in other contexts it means 'champion wrestler' or the first
nimal caught on a hunt, which is given to the hunters' leader.[9]
    Genghis was soon to face a significant challenge to his author-
ty, coming from a Mongol shaman with the title 'Teb-tengri (Most
Ieavenly)'. A lot of Genghis' followers deserted him for this sha-
nan, who was evidently trying to become supreme ruler himself.
Genghis laid a trap for Teb-tengri, who was killed by having his
spine broken.[10]
    The rest of the *Secret History*'s account of Genghis' life is not
particularly informative about Mongol religion. Shortly before his
death in 1227 Genghis was campaigning against the Tangut people whose empire's northern frontier was contiguous with the
Mongol homeland. After the surrender of the Tangut ruler
Genghis, according to the *Secret History*, gave him the name
Shidurqu, 'Loyal', in order to make him serve the Mongol sovereign's descendants after his execution, and then had him
suffocated. Genghis' own death (the cause of which is not clear)
was accompanied by the genocide of the Tangut people, females
as well as males being massacred.[11]
    In the *Secret History* we read of a striking episode concerning
Genghis' successor, his son Ögödei. When campaigning in China
Ögödei fell ill and was unable to speak. The Mongol shamans
consulted their spirits and found that the local spirits, those of
the ruling Jurchen people's lands and waters, were raging against
Ögödei, because their people were having their cities plundered
and lands and waters destroyed. In response the shamans offered
these spirits every possible sacrifice, but in vain. Finally the shamans suggested sacrificing one of Ögödei's own relatives, and
Ögödei opened his eyes and asked for water. His younger brother
Tolui volunteered to die in his place, pointing out that being tall
and handsome he was a suitable sacrifice. The shamans uttered
special formulae, Tolui killed himself by drinking poison and
Ögödei recovered.[12]
    Various materials for the study of Mongol religion are found
scattered throughout the *Secret History*. It is made clear that
Genghis, like his successors, attributes his success and that of his
entourage to heaven (Tengri), constantly qualified as 'Eternal
(Möngke)'. The Mongol leaders sometimes associated Earth or
the supreme ruler's fortune with Heaven as granting them success.

Wild beasts are also seen by Ögödei as having their destiny given
to them at birth by Heaven and Earth. Once Genghis is shown
making an offering to his banner on the sixteenth day of a month
(i.e. at the full moon), when setting off on a campaign. Jamuqa
also makes an offering to his banner: Onon explains that this
means sprinkling *qumis* or ordinary milk on it. When Genghis renews his 'sworn brotherhood' with Jamuqa he does so beneath a
'many-leaved' tree. We also hear of the use of a pole, on which
the skin, head and hooves of an ox, horse, or sheep would be
hung as an offering to the ancestors. These dead ancestors are
thought to live in the sky: Genghis is said to have 'gone up to
Heaven' when he died. A Mongol, when he dies, is buried with
his quiver and bow.[13]

Carpini: an overview of Mongol religion and customs

Plenty of information about Mongol religion and customs is provided by John of Plano Carpini (whom we encountered above
when examining Cuman religion), on the basis of his mission in
1245–7. The Mongol men, says Carpini, can have as many wives
as they can afford, and marry the widows of their fathers and elder
brothers. They believe in one God, the creator and giver of all
things. However, the Mongols also have felt images in human form,
beside the doors of their tents: these images are venerated as pro-
tectors of the flocks and guarantors of fertility. A sheep is sacrificed
when these images are made: this happens if a child is ill, when a
newly-made image is tied to the child's bed. The Mongols' leaders each have a special goatskin in the centre of their tents.
Offerings of the first milk of the people's animals are made to the
images, and also of the first part of every meal, along with the
heart of every animal killed. Many offerings are made to an image
of Genghis. Horses are dedicated to it, left unridden to their
deaths, and other animals are immolated to it, their bones left
unbroken. A visiting Russian prince, after being made to pass between two fires, was required to pay homage to this image and
when he refused was kicked to death. The Mongols also venerate
the sun, the moon, fire, water and the earth, offering food and
drink to them in the morning before eating and drinking
themselves.[14]

According to Carpini the Mongols have no law of worship, eth-
cs or righteousness, but they do have traditional prohibitions:
hey ban putting knives in fire (because this is tantamount to cutting the fire's head off), leaning on a whip or touching arrows
with one, catching or killing fledglings, hitting a horse with the
bridle, breaking a bone with another bone, pouring food or drink
on the ground and urinating in someone's tent. This last offence,
if committed voluntarily, is punished with death; if involuntarily,
with a huge payment to a shaman who purifies the offender, the
tent and everything in it, passing the lot between two fires. If someone spits out a bit of food given to him or treads on a threshold
he is buried alive beneath the tent.[15]

The Mongols, says Carpini, believe that after death they will
breed livestock, eat, drink and do everything else in another world
just as in this one. They are devoted to prophecies, magic and
incantations: when the demons reply to them the Mongols think
that the replies come from a god called Itoga. All their undertak-
ings are begun at the new or full moon: the sun, they say, is the
moon's mother, giving the moon its light. Ambassadors and their
presents, along with livestock and humans struck by lightning or
other disasters, all have to be passed between two fires by
shamans.[16]

As regards death, Carpini says that a dying man is quarantined,
a lance wrapped in black felt being planted in the ground. A nobleman is buried in secret, seated in a tent with meat and drink, a
mare, a foal and a saddled stallion. Another horse is eaten and its
skin stuffed and placed on pieces of wood: its bones are burnt, to
make it join the dead man's soul. A bush can also be grown for
the soul's sake, and gold and silver buried with the corpse: the
dead man's chariot and home are destroyed and for two generations his name must not be pronounced. Sometimes a nobleman
will have his favourite slave buried alive beneath him. Rulers are
buried in special cemeteries, the surroundings of which are strictly
guarded against intruders. The relatives of the dead have to be
purified by fire.[17]

As regards the Mongols' non-religious customs and attitudes,
Carpini says that they revere their rulers more than any other
nation. They eat anything, including lice and rats. Adultery and
fornication are punished by death. Some women are archers. The

Mongols believe that after 18 years they will conquer the rest of
the world and then another, unknown people will conquer them;
any survivors should adopt the laws of the victors.[18]

Rubruck: offerings, beliefs and shamans

Further information is provided by Rubruck following his journey of 1253–5. Some details of the Mongols' tents and images
and the offerings made to the latter resemble those given by
Carpini. When the Mongols gather to drink together they begin
by sprinkling some of the drink on the felt image which hangs
above the master of the tent's head. Then their steward goes out
of the tent and sprinkles some drink three times to the south in
honour of fire, then the same to the east for the air, to the west
for water and the north for the dead.[19]

Rich Mongol ladies, says Rubruck, wear peacock feathers in
their headdress. The Mongol women never wash clothes, as this is
thought to make God angry and to cause thunder, of which the
Mongols are extraordinarily frightened. Wives are obtained by
purchase, with a mock capture.[20]

Rubruck informs us, from his own experience, that the Mongols take it as a bad omen if somebody sits with his head bowed
and looks sad, especially if he has his cheek or chin resting on his
hand. They ask if it is true that the Pope is 500 years old, and are
unable to understand Rubruck's assertion that the ocean has no
limits or shores. The Mongols practise the usual Inner Eurasian
form of divination by inspecting the burnt shoulder blades of
sheep. Rubruck also finds signs of what he calls 'sorcery' in the
residence of one of the Mongol emperor Möngke's wives: four
swords half drawn from their scabbards, two at opposite ends of
the lady's couch and two at the sides of the entrance, along with a
chalice filled with ashes, surmounted by a black stone. The Mongols have a superstition which forbids them to go back by the same
way by which they have come, and nobody ever passes through
the site of one of their camps as long as there are any traces of its
fire.[21]

Möngke's own religious views are expressed in a conversation
with Rubruck. 'We Mongols,' he declares, 'believe that there is
only one God, through whom we have life and through whom we

ie, and towards him we direct our hearts.' A little later he con-
nues: 'But just as God has given the hand several fingers, so he
as given humankind several paths.' The Christians, Möngke explains, have been given the Scriptures by God but wickedly ignore
hem, whereas God has given the Mongols shamans, whose advice they follow, living in peace.[22]

Rubruck also describes the role of the Mongol shamans. They
have a chief, who, like some of his colleagues, has a knowledge of
astronomy and forecasts eclipses. In preparation for these the
Mongols all store up food, in order not to have to go outside.
During the eclipses themselves the people make a lot of noise
with other drums and other instruments, and afterwards have huge
feasts. The shamans prescribe auspicious days for all undertak-
ings, and the Mongols do not make war without their permission:
it was the shamans who stopped them from returning to Hungary. In May, on the ninth day of the fourth month of the Chinese
calendar, the shamans gather and consecrate all white mares, sprinkle *qumis* on the ground and hold a great feast, marking the
drinking of new *qumis* for the first time in the year. The shamans
are called in whenever a boy is born to foretell his destiny, and
whenever anyone falls ill, to say if the illness is natural or produced by witchcraft. Some shamans hold séances at night, and
put cooked meat in the centre of the tent. The shaman officiating
utters incantations, bangs a tambourine on the ground, falls into
a frenzy and has himself tied up: a demon appears and gives him
the meat to eat, and he utters oracles.[23]

Finally, Rubruck transmits to us the text of Möngke's letter to
the King of France. In this Möngke presents himself as speaking
in the name of 'the everlasting God', whose command was issued
to Genghis. The Franks are ordered to send envoys if they are
willing to obey the Mongol emperor, and are warned of the dangers of disobedience and war. God has made easy what was hard,
and near what was far distant.[24]

Juwayni: shamans and animals

Many glimpses of Mongol religion are found scattered throughout the work of the Iranian historian Juwayni (noted above in our
examination of Uighur myth). Juwayni tells us that the Mongols

have many shamans, who are overcome with desire to b
sodomized, talk nonsense and claim to be possessed by devils wh
tell them about everything. Mongol informants have told Juwayr
that devils come down into the shamans' tents through the smok
hole, talk to them and sodomize them: the shamans' powers ar
strongest just after this has happened. The leading shaman Teb
tengri used to walk naked in the desert and mountains during
extremely cold weather, and would return to report that God had
granted the whole face of the earth to Genghis and his children.[25]

Juwayni confirms European evidence about Mongol taboos concerning water and lightning. In spring and summer it is forbidden
to sit in water in the daytime, wash one's hands in a stream or put
washing out to dry, since all this attracts thunder. This is because
in the Mongols' homeland rain falls during most of these seasons. If someone is struck by lightning his tribe is banished for
three years and nobody eats for the rest of the month. The Mongols also insist upon killing animals by slitting open their breasts.[26]

In Juwayni's work we also find descriptions of the elections of
new emperors. For Ögödei's election there was a 40-day feast, the
participating nobles all wearing clothes of a different colour for
each day. Then they all removed their hats, slung their belts across
their backs, enthroned Ögödei and, in homage to him, knelt three
times facing the sun. Afterwards Ögödei ordered that 40 maidens
of noble birth be decked out in fine clothes and ornaments and
sacrificed with choice horses to join Genghis' soul. When Möngke
acceded to the throne he issued a decree that on that day people
should not quarrel, domestic animals should not be burdened or
slaughtered, the creatures of the wild should not be hunted and
the earth and water should not be disturbed. (Again, one notes
the triad animal–animal–human, in the same order (and with a
similar classification) as in Genghis's followers' promises of gifts –
women, horses and wild animals.)[27]

This decree is echoed in an anecdote about Ögödei: he feels a
weakness in his bowels and thinks that if he rescues an animal
from death God will spare his life. Accordingly, he orders that a
wolf, which has just been captured, be set free, but some dogs
tear it to pieces and Ögödei realizes that his own end is near.[28]

The parallelism between human and animal is found also in
that between war and hunting: a Mongol emperor's 'great hunt',

t the start of the winter season, is conducted like a military campaign. Troops make an enormous ring to surround the game, and commanders who let any animals through are often executed. When the wild animals have been forced together the emperor moves in person to begin the killing. Eventually a few old men intercede with him for the lives of the few animals that remain. Once, it is related, a lot of wild animals started wailing in supplication to Ögödei, and he ordered that they should be set free. The Mongol army, observes Juwayni, is run like a pack of hungry hunting dogs: when fighting, the soldiers are like wild beasts, and in peacetime they are like sheep, providing useful contributions in the form of taxes and post horses.[29]

Rashid al-Din: a royal funeral

Juwayni's successor Rashid al-Din provides unique evidence about some aspects of Mongol royal funerary arrangements. When Möngke died, says Rashid al-Din, his coffin was brought to his four camps (*ordos*), each one of which was named after one of the Mongol royal ladies. On four successive days there was mourning for Möngke in one of these camps, and on each day the coffin was put on a throne in a different camp. Then he was buried on Mount Burqan Qaldun, in the great inviolable burial ground, alongside Genghis and his son Tolui. (We have already noted that according to Herodotus a Scythian's body would be carried around in a waggon for 40 days after his death, as his family visited their friends, food being placed before the corpse.)[30]

Marco Polo: gods and feasts

Marco Polo gives us a large amount of evidence about Mongol beliefs and practices. He says that the Mongols do not care what god is worshipped in the countries which they have conquered: as long as people obey the emperor they can do as they wish in religious matters. However, when an emperor dies and his body is being carried to the burial grounds everyone encountered on the way is killed and told to serve the emperor in the next world: in the case of Möngke over 20,000 men were put to death in this manner. The Mongols believe in a High God, exalted and heavenly,

but they also have a god called Natigai, an earthly deity who protects their children, animals and crops. Felt images of this god
and his wife and children are kept in tents. Roux points out that
here Polo is confused: Natigai, like Carpini's 'Itoga', is the earth-
goddess of the Mongols, Itugen, whose name is doubtless derived
from that of the Turks' holy mountain, Ötükän.[31]

According to Polo the Mongols punish petty thefts with strokes
of the rod, in proportion to the gravity of the offence: 7, 17, 27
and so on up to 107. Stealing a horse is punished by being cut in
half with a sword. However, one can evade punishment by paying
nine times the value of the stolen object.[32]

Polo also reports that if one Mongol man loses a son in infancy,
and another man loses a daughter, a posthumous marriage between the two children is arranged. The marriage contract is burnt,
so that as smoke it goes to the other world and tells the children
that they are married. At the wedding feast food is scattered, again
being seen as sent to the children, and pictures of slaves, horses
and other possessions are burnt as well. The two fathers are now
firmly related by marriage.[33]

In August, on the 28th day of the month, the emperor pours a
libation of mare's milk, from his special herd of white horses. Their
milk may not be drunk by people outside the imperial family or
one tribe granted this privilege by Genghis in memory of one of
his victories. These horses are greatly revered. In the libation their
milk is flung into the air and on to the earth, for the spirits, so
that the latter may protect all the emperor's possessions.[34]

As regards the Mongols' shamans, Polo says that they produce
one astonishing marvel. When the emperor is sitting at his dining
table, eight cubits above the floor, while his cups are 10 paces
away on the floor itself, filled with drink, the shamans make the
cups rise up to him, without being touched, in front of a huge
audience.[35]

Polo further tells us that when Mongol armies are ready to engage in battle they play musical instruments and sing while waiting
for the sound of their commander's drums, which is the signal for
fighting to begin. When Khubilai wins a battle against his uncle,
who has rebelled against him, and this uncle is taken prisoner he
is wrapped in a carpet and dragged around violently until he dies:
the point is that noble blood should not be spilt on the earth, and

hat the sun and air should not witness the killing. Khubilai himself kisses the Gospels on the principal Christian feast days and
also pays respect to Judaism, Islam and Buddhism on the appropriate days of the year. He points out that his shamans make the
cups rise up to him, and perform other marvels, so that he cannot convert to Christianity. Khubilai tells Polo's father and uncles
to ask the pope to send learned Christians who will make the shamans powerless to perform these marvels: then he will be
baptized.[36]

At the New Year festival Khubilai and his subjects all dress in
white. Everyone bows down, touching the ground with their fore-
heads, to pay homage to Khubilai four times. A scarlet tablet
bearing his name is put on an altar and paid great reverence.
There are 13 feasts, one for each of the lunar months, and for
each one robes of a different colour are worn. Khubilai has lots of
trees planted, partly because his shamans say that someone who
causes trees to be planted will live long. He also gives a lot of alms,
contrary to Mongol custom: previously they would drive a poor
beggar away, saying, 'Go, with God's curse upon you! If God had
loved you as he loves me he would have blessed you with
prosperity!'[37]

The official Chinese *History of the Mongol Dynasty*

After the fall of the Mongol dynasty ruling in China, in 1368, the
Chinese administrators produced, as usual, a dynastic history covering the Mongol rulers' reigns. This history tells us that the
Mongol shamans would make predictions at the birth of children
of important families: thus Möngke had a great future predicted
for him, and for this reason was given his name, meaning 'Eternal'. According to the Chinese historians the Mongols would serve
their ghosts as if they were living beings. Every year, after the first
day of the twelfth month, army officers were ordered to take the
shamans with them and dig a ditch in which offerings were then
burnt: meat, liquor and milk. Scholars have pointed out that today some Mongols have a similar rite for their dead: they dig three
ditches and burn meat and flour, sprinkled with liquor, in them.
The Khitans, as we have seen, would also burn food for the dead,
and so would the Jurchens.[38]

The fifteenth century

There is hardly any evidence concerning Mongol religion in the
fifteenth century. Around 1431, although the Mongols had temporarily abandoned their interest in Buddhism, collections of
Buddhist mantras intended for them continued to be printed in
Mongolian in China. One such collection mentions a supreme
god called 'Qormusta Khan Tengri (Qormusta king of the gods)'.
The name Qormusta is seen by scholars as coming from that of
the chief ancient Iranian deity, Ahura Mazda, 'The Wise Lord'. As
the leading contemporary German Mongolist Walther Heissig
observes, it is not clear how and when this Iranian god reached
the Mongols. Qormusta appears in much later materials as chief
of a group of 33 gods, as well as king of the 99 gods seen as constituting the Mongol pantheon in popular religious belief. A
collection of Mongolian proverbs, which Heissig thinks may pre-
date the sixteenth century, says,

> The highest of the gods is Eternal Heaven (Möngke Tengri)
> Their king is Qormusta Tengri –

Heissig adds that Qormusta is particularly associated with the origin of fire: thus Mongol fire-hymns often say that whereas the
Buddha struck the original light it was Qormusta who lit the fire
itself.[39]

Another source for fifteenth-century Mongol customs is the
forged 'autobiography' of the founder of the Mogul empire in
India, Babur (reigned 1526–30), whose mother was a Mongol.
The 'autobiography' was certainly composed not long after Babur's
death and contains some genuine traditions concerning Babur's
Mongol maternal ancestors. Thus we read that his mother's father, himself a ruler, had himself lifted up on a piece of white felt
and presented to the sky at his coronation, in the ancient Altaic
manner. Babur's 'memoirs' also provide an account of the Mongol 'ceremony of the yak tail standards'. In this ceremony the ruler,
after dismounting, had nine standards put up in front of him. An
official tied a long piece of white cloth to a cow's tibia. Then he
tied three more long pieces round the standards. The ruler and
two princes stood on the other ends of these. Then the official,

holding the first piece, said something in Mongolian and, facing the standards, made a sign. Everyone sprinkled *qumis* towards the standards. Trumpets and drums were sounded, and the soldiers, standing in ranks, uttered the war cry. This was done three times. Then the soldiers mounted their horses, uttered the war cry and galloped round in a circle.[40]

A sixteenth-century Mongol code of law

A law code of the Mongol ruler Altan Khan (1507–82) has been studied and presented by the native Mongolian scholar Šagdarin Bira, who has compared it with later examples. Altan Khan's code refers throughout to fines called a 'Nine' and a 'Five'. A 'Nine' is explained in later codes as consisting of four cattle and five sheep, or two horses, two oxen, two cows, two sheep and one two-year-old calf, whereas a 'Five' consists of a three-year-old horse, a three-year-old bullock and three two-year-old sheep, or one ox, one cow, one sheep and two two-year-old calves. In Altan Khan's code, however, a 'Nine' is two horses, two bullocks and five sheep or goats, while a 'Five' is a bullock, a horse, and three sheep or goats. We are told that nine 'Nines' are the penalty for failing to make an offering of incense after touching the bones of a dead body. If somebody comes from a place where corpses have been put and then enters a house, then everyone in the house is entitled to take one horse from him. Stealing a horse which has been dedicated to a dead person is punished by three 'Nines'. (In a Mongol code of 1640 we read that the penalty for disturbing the grave of a person of high rank is one 'Nine'; in the case of a person of middle rank a 'Five'; in the case of a commoner, a beating on the soles of the feet.) Fines of one 'Five' are used to punish the killing of protected game, such as antelopes, wild boar, mountain goats and badgers. (In the 1640 code we are told that certain animals and birds may not be killed on the 8th, 15th, 20th and 30th of the month.) Further penalties are prescribed for the protection of messengers.[41]

A Chinese account of sixteenth-century Mongolia

The details of Altan Khan's law code are echoed in an account of

Mongol traditions provided by a late sixteenth-century Chinese administrator, Hsiao Ta-heng (1532–1612), who wrote in 1595 after spending almost 20 years on China's northern frontiers. His work is entitled *The Customs of the Northern Slaves* (*Pei-lu fung-su*), reflecting the fiction that all peoples were subservient to the Chinese Emperor. It gives an excellent survey of Mongol institutions: marriage, inheritance, law, funerals, hospitality, hunting, taboos and military organization.

Hsiao Ta-heng tells us that Mongol marriages are preceded by libations to Heaven and Earth and involve a mock abduction. In the case of nobles the groom stays at his wife's home until she bears a child. When this happens the midwife cuts the umbilical cord with an arrow. As regards inheritance, the greatest part goes to the eldest and the youngest sons. Adultery is punished very severely. If the wife of a chief is found guilty of adultery with a commoner the chief strangles her with a bowstring, and only one male in the commoner's family will be left alive, while his own wife will be enslaved and all his possessions will be confiscated.[42]

The *Customs* tells us that the Mongols disguise the locations of their kings and nobles' tombs by erecting tents for their guards and then pretending that these tents cover the graves themselves. Mourning lasts for only seven days. If a married man dies and his father is still alive the latter puts on armour, takes a sword and thrusts with it three times in the direction of his tent's door; then he marries his son's widow.[43]

According to Hsiao Ta-heng the Mongols understand very well that animals must be left alone to breed: thus in spring they do not hunt, and in summer they do so only in small groups. In autumn the hunt lasts 100 days and is done with thousands of men and horses taking part together. The meat of the game is shared in common, while the men who have actually killed the animal take its hide, horns and hooves. The stealing of lost arrows is severely punished. Since the men have no activity except hunting the women have complete control over everything else.[44]

The Mongols, we are informed, are terrified of smallpox. If a husband or wife catches it the couple will not live together until they have heard thunder. Mongols see the 1st, 10th and 15th days of the month as very holy, and propitious for travelling; on these days punishments are suspended. If an animal is struck by lightning they see this as a very bad omen, and react by erecting two poles to form a gate: the other animals are driven forward, and those who pass between the poles are considered to be protected by good fortune and are retained, while those who pass on either side are considered unlucky and are abandoned.[45]

In general, concludes Hsiao Ta-heng, the Mongols are naive and simple people. They support poverty easily, and respect above all straightforwardness and sincerity. Men are valued for outstanding courage and strength. The Mongols love their bows more than anything else, and have more affection for good dogs and horses than for humans. They do not appreciate rare birds or unusual animals. The boys learn to ride from the age of five and soon after can use a bow and hunt. Consequently, when they grow up, they are perfectly accurate archers. The Mongol warriors are quick to come to the aid of wounded and endangered comrades, who will reward their rescuers with their most valuable possessions, although these rescuers act solely in order to win fame: renown, for the Mongols, is more important than gain.[46]

Seventeenth-century evidence

In 1953 Heissig published a long article on the Buddhist suppression of shamans in the seventeenth century. His main source was a Mongolian biography (written by one Prajña Sagara, probably a Buddhist monk) of a Buddhist missionary to the East Mongolian tribes, Neyichi Toyin (1557–1653). Heissig also used nineteenth-century Mongolian chronicles and the work of anthropologists to construct a picture of indigenous Mongolian religion as it was before the triumph of Buddhism. Then, it appears, immense veneration was accorded to the spirit images, shamans and shamanesses. Alliances were confirmed by sacrificing a white horse and a black cow to Heaven and Earth respectively.[47]

One chronicle used by Heissig seems to present shamanic traditions of the early seventeenth century. It is called *The History of the Black Tutelary Spirit's Image*, and gives us a myth of the origins of shamanizing. Once, we are told, there was a man called Ingdaqai, whose father knew a lot about magic and, shortly before his death, offered to give his son posthumous protection in return for worship. When he died Ingdaqai buried his corpse on

a high place called the Red Cliff. On the first, seventh and nint
days of each month he made offerings to him of tea, water an
milk brandy. His father's spirit allied itself with the local spiri
and produced hail, thunder and 'terrible evil'. Then Ingdaqai'
mother also died, and he buried her in the same place: her spiri
also allied itself with the local ones, and became known as 'The
Very Old Grandmother'. She also produced a lot of evil, poison
ing the blood of men and animals. People made propitiatory
offerings, and the spirits of Ingdaqai's father and mother now
entered a man and a girl respectively. The man became known as
'Black Image', being possessed by the 'Black Tutelary Spirit', while
the girl took the name of the spirit that possessed her, 'The Very
Old Grandmother'. One day the man and the girl went into ecstasy and exorcized the evil. They flew to the Red Cliff, discovered
their special drums, and returned to the people, promising protection in return for offerings. The people made images named
after the two spirits. Heissig concludes that the primary function
of the shamans and shamanic activity is to protect humans and
livestock from illness and disaster.[48]

Neyichi Toyin, according to his biographer, gave Buddhism victory over the shamans by beating the latter at their own games.
He showed greater magical power when one Mongolian shaman
galloped on his white stallion round Neyichi Toyin's tent, producing thunder, which the Buddhist missionary duly brought to an
end. Neyichi Toyin also displayed superior medical proficiency,
healing a shamaness who had gone blind.[49]

Georgi on Buryat religion and customs

A brief but useful survey of eighteenth-century Buryat religion
and customs is provided by the traveller Georgi (encountered
above in our chapter on Turkic religion). Georgi tells us that previously proclamations were circulated among the Buryats by
fastening the paper to an arrow and shooting it from one little
camp to another. Even now, says Georgi, this is done with war-
rants for the arrest of fugitives from justice. The Buryats have the
greatest imaginable fear of death, and would never spend the night
with a dead body, since they believe it to be surrounded by evil
spirits. A dead man is immediately carried out of his tent with all

is possessions. When he is buried his finest horse is led round
his grave several times, hit on the head with a mallet, and put in
the grave with its master. The Buryat shamans usually wear leather
costumes, decorated with iron images and leather strips, and also
iron masks and horns. (Heissig observes that while the most obvious explanation of the leather strips is that they represent a bird's
feathers and tail, among the Buryats it is common to see them as
snakes.)[50] Some shamans, however, wear only rags and animal
skins. These shamans, instead of a drum, use two rods about 3
feet long with a number of images tied to them, and during their
performances wave a small flag.[51]

In general, the Buryat images (*ongons*) are about 8 inches long
and dressed in the usual shaman's costume. They are often made
of felt. One particular image represents the assembly of all the
gods: it is a piece of animal skin, 8 inches square, and cut at the
sides like a comb. Other images are painted to give the outline of
a human figure and coloured with blood, while the head is provided with glass eyes and decorated with owls' feathers. Huts are
built on the mountains for these images, and to serve as refuges
for the gods during thunderstorms. Prayers are addressed to the
images at the autumn festival, the feast of the White Moon. Then
horses, oxen, sheep and goats are sacrificed and their skeletons
carefully left unbroken in order that they may be covered with
their own skins and placed upon poles.[52]

Horses are consecrated by the shaman, who lights a fire, makes
an offering of milk, cheese and milk brandy and pours milk on
the horse chosen. He waves a little flag and sets fire to it, so that
the horse inhales the smoke, and then he plucks hairs from the
horse's mane and tail and throws them to the south. Finally, he
ties a red rope to the horse's mane and puts the bowl which has
held the milk on the animal's back, letting the latter run: depend-
ing on how the bowl then falls, a decision is taken as to whether
the gods accept the horse or not.[53]

A description of Buryat shamanic worship

In 1879 the Russian orientalist Alexander Pozdneyev obtained a
manuscript of a short Mongolian treatise, entitled *On Shamanic
Worship*, from a Buryat village. (The treatise constitutes an

appendix to a chronicle written in 1875 by one Wangda
Yumching.) The treatise was translated into English, with annota
tions, by the Finnish scholar Jorma Partanen in 1941. It gives
useful enumeration of Mongol gods and an account of how a sha
man is initiated and practises.

The author begins by explaining that the Buryat shamans have
never had any books: all instruction has been oral. They worship
99 gods, 55 in the west and 44 in the east. Five of the gods of the
west are given sacrifices: a benign 'protector of prosperity and
souls' who lives in the north-west and rides a light bay horse, and
is called 'Red Official God' (Ulaghan Kihan Tengri); a terrifying
'White God' (Chaghan Tengri) of thunder who lives in the south-
west and rides a white horse; a 'protector of all living beings' called
'Star-Fate God' (Odun Jayaghan Tengri); a 'giver of prosperity to
people and of "cattle-luck"'; and the 'God of Providence'
(Jayaghaghchi Tengri), who, as Heissig points out is in fact identical with 'Star-Fate God', and is above all asked to save people from
injuries, in particular crippling ones, and to take care of one's
parents, wife and children. Thus there are really four supreme
gods of the west who fit the Indo-European pattern found by
Dumézil and his followers as constituting their concept 1, religious sovereignty, and correspond to the sub-concepts 1.1a
(terrifyingness), 1.1b (benignity), 1.2 (protecting the community)
and 1.3 (distributing goods).[54]

Of the gods of the east four are worshipped with sacrifices: a
provider of 'food-luck', a protector from diseases, a red bestower
of 'horse-luck' and a red giver of 'cattle-luck'. Here again the
patterning is Indo-European, representing concept 3, fertility,
which includes food, medicine, horse breeding and cattle
breeding.[55]

We are told that, in addition to these gods, there are also the
'thirteen princes of the northern lands, the leader of whom is the
son of Qormusda'. Qormusda, as scholars have pointed out, is
clearly the supreme god of ancient Iranian religion, Ahura Mazda,
'The Wise Lord'. These 'princes' are sometimes associated with
the ideas of protection, notably from death: thus they may correspond to the Indo-European concept 2, warlike force. The author
does not know the names of the '44 princes of the southern lands'.
He tells us that there are also the 'masters of many regions', who

ive protection against smallpox and other diseases. They are
alled 'heavenly arrows'. Among them we may note 'the white old
Time Man (Chagchi) who lives in the south-west on the snow-
covered white mountain, with the white Lion of Time to ride'.
This is presumably the Iranian god Zurvan, 'Time', who is symbolized by a lion and reflected in epic by an old man with white
hair.[56]

The author continues with an account of how a shaman is initiated. A man who wishes to become a shaman begins by asking a
master shaman if he can be accepted. If this happens the candidate goes home and, on the south side of his house, erects an
arrangement of birch trees, called a *chinar*, literally 'nature', as
being a representation of Nature itself. This *chinar* consists of three
rows of nine trees, facing south, with two much larger trees placed
on the northern and southern sides. The tree on the northern
side, which is called 'Mother Tree', bears a white image of the
moon; that on the southern side, called 'Father Tree', bears a red
emblem called 'Sun'. (Partanen points out that in Japanese imperial ceremonies one standard shows a red sun, representing the
Emperor as 'father' of his people, while another has a white moon,
symbolizing the Empress as its 'mother'.) This arrangement of
trees is called the 'Mother-white Chinar'. To its west is placed another group of nine trees, and to its east one of 27; to the
north-west two groups of four trees are put, and a table is made in
the middle of each group, one table being called the 'Ablution
Bench of the Living Things (the shaman's instruments)', and the
other the 'Ablution Bench of the Candidate'. Animal skins and
ribbons are tied to all the trees so far mentioned. Seven trees are
placed between the Mother Tree and the house, and four more
on the four sides of the house itself. Inside the house, on a table,
are placed nine candles and nine bowls, containing spirits, milk
and tea, along with plates bearing cream, butter and cheese. A
cloth is suspended from the roof, and a birch tree is inserted
through the smoke hole.[57]

After these preparations the master shaman who has accepted
the candidate brings his instruments. These consist of: an iron
cap with two horns, with a spear hanging behind, along with ribbons representing snakes; an apron, consisting of an animal skin
with metal rings attached; a deerskin coat; two staffs, decorated

with ornaments to represent horses; a whip, adorned with min
ature weapons; two drums and a drumstick; two collars, wit
ribbons again representing snakes, one attached to a bell and th
other to a mirror. Nine young men, along with an old man and a
old woman, called the Father and the Mother, are chosen to a
sist. Twigs of juniper and thyme are boiled, and 12 black and whit
stones are heated in a fire. At dawn all the people so far men
tioned, along with various shamans and shamanesses, pray an
go into trance inside the house. Then they go outside. The stone
are placed on the Ablution Benches and the water in which th
juniper and thyme have been boiled is sprinkled on the shaman':
instruments and the participants. A reddish brown goat is killed
cooked and eaten. Then the candidate is invested with the instruments (except for the drums), and shamanizes under the direction
of his master, as do the other shamans present: leaping up and
falling down, he goes with the rest round each of the trees, all day
long. Shamanizing and feasting continue for the next two nights
and days before the proceedings end.[58]

Afterwards the candidate takes part in the monthly ceremonies held by other shamans. Three years later his initiation
ceremony is repeated, and six years after that he obtains his own
instruments. The trees are erected as before, and the candidate
and the other previous participants visit the houses of the neigh-
bourhood on horseback. People give him animal skins, bound up
in the form of snakes, to attach to his instruments: now he is fully
qualified.[59]

The shaman visits the sick and practises divination with regard
to a patient's illness by burning a sheep's shoulder blade or play-
ing a Jew's harp. Then he directs that a given spirit should be
appeased, since it has made the patient sick, by sacrificing a sheep
or goat. The image of the spirit is placed, for its protection, in a
miniature hut put on a table. Then the shaman goes into a trance
and the people present eat the meat of the sacrificed animal. If
the patient is in danger of dying the shaman may have to get his
soul back from the hands of the 'Master of Death'. This is done by
giving a substitute for the life in question: a human effigy is made
of hay and burnt on the steppe. A shaman also officiates in sacrifices performed to secure the peace and prosperity of a district:
in these a sheep is killed and its head and bones are burnt on a

ugh platform. Shamans take part in other sacrifices made to en-
ure fertility, notably one dedicated to the god of Fire.[60]

urtin, Czaplicka, Klementz and Sanzheyev: patterns of Buryat eities

In 1900 the American scholar Jeremiah Curtin visited the Buryats
and conducted investigations into their religion. The results were
published after his death in 1909 and give an interesting view of
Buryat deities. One of the titles of the supreme god, who is more
often called Esege Malan, is 'World White God'. In him there sub-
sist three other gods or spirits, the first of whom produced 55
tengris and the second 44, while the third has seven sons and seven
daughters. This third spirit is asked in particular for rain, good
crops and children.[61]

Curtin's information is echoed by Czaplicka in her survey of
Siberian religion and society mentioned above. She says that the
chief of the 55 *tengris* of the west, also called the 'white' *tengris*,
have as their chief one Zayan Sagan Tengri ('Creator White God')
among some of the Buryats. The 44 *tengris* of the east are 'black'
and mischievous, sending sickness and death to men. There are
also spirits called 'smiths', also divided into western or white ones
and eastern or black ones, and subordinate to the corresponding
tengris. When these smiths descended to earth the first white smith
remained in the sky.[62]

In 1910 the Russian scholar Demetrius Klementz published a
long article on Buryat religion in which he noted that the supreme
god, Esege Malan, was believed to have three shepherds. The first
of these, called Makita Mangri, operated as an intermediary between the gods and humankind and was also the patron of
shamans, protecting them against evil deities and spirits. As for
the second shepherd, Badshindai, we are told that he was present
at the original creation of man: consequently he had a continu-
ing function of protecting humans from the diseases sent against
them by the maleficent eastern gods. The third shepherd was
called Debetsoi and was the patron of flocks and herds. He rode a
horse, holding a bow, a quiver and a lasso. (Here the tripartition
is clearly Indo-European: the first shepherd represents religion,
the second symbolizes warlike force, offering protection against

outsiders, and the third embodies fertility.)[63]

In 1927–28 the Buryat researcher Garma Sanzheyev publishe
an overview of the religion of the northern Buryats, to whom h
himself belonged. He noted that here there were 99 western, be
neficent spirits called *khans* (rulers) – inferior to the *tengris* –, bu
only three of them were identified with names and distinct per
sonalities. These three were connected with the supreme goc
Esege Malan, who stood outside this grouping. One of the three
was Esege Malan's brother and was the ruler of the 99, called Khan
Shargay Hoyon, 'Ruler Light-Bay Prince'. He was seen above all
as a good dignitary and judge. The second figure was a son of
Esege Malan, called Shara Tekhe, 'The Yellow He-goat'. He was
the protector of boys. As for the third, he was also a son of Esege
Malan, called Bukha Noyon, 'Bull Prince', who was envisaged in
the form of a bull, venerated as an ancestor, and called 'the
preordainer of the birth of all Buryats'. Here again we find the
patterning to be Indo-European: within the first concept of religious sovereignty Esege Malan is the remote supreme sovereign
[1.1a], the 'Light-Bay Prince' is the benevolent symbol of law
[1.1b], the protector of boys represents the guardian of the community and its young fighting force [1.2], and the 'preordainer'
is the giver of everyone's lot, the distributor of goods [1.3].[64]

Heissig: an overview of religion in Mongolia

The problems involved in studying Mongol deities and spirits are
discussed at length by Heissig in his invaluable survey of religion
in Mongolia, published in 1970. Heissig takes the view that Mongolian shamanic activity arose out of ancestor worship: the living
felt the need for their ancestors' powerful protection. The shaman acts in order to help living beings in this life alone and is not
concerned with rewards after death: thus he looks to the past and
the present, not to the future.[65]

In this perspective ancient gods are worshipped together with
figures from history and epic. At the top is Eternal Heaven
(Möngke Tengri). In the prayers of folk religion and shamans'
songs Eternal Heaven is the chief of 99 *tengris*, who are divided
into 55 in the west and 44 in the east, while there are another
three (not 13 as in the Buryat treatise of the 1870s) in the north.

f particular interest are Heissig's observations about the eastern
d 'bestower of horse luck' (Atagha Tengri), whom we found in
he Buryat treatise. Heissig says that he has a number of functions
longside the protection of horses: he looks after cattle as well,
nd grants clothes, food and help against death's messengers. He
as a thundering voice, and in the range of his specialities closely
esembles Eternal Heaven, with whom he is often identified. Thus
o us he seems extremely similar to the Greek god Apollo, who is
a deity of horse breeding, but also corresponds to other aspects
of the Indo-European concept 3 (fertility): Apollo is a healer, with
a sonorous voice, and often takes the role of the king of the Greek
gods, Zeus.[66]

Heissig is also informative about the Mongols' fire-cult. The
fire-deity is worshipped on one of the last days of the year, with
hymns and the offering of a sheep's breast bone. At other times
of the year the deity is invoked in other ceremonies, for example
in spring, when it is asked to bless the camels, and when libations
are poured at the summer solstice, as well as in wedding rituals.
Originally, the fire deity was feminine, and called 'Fire-Queen
Mother' (Ghalakhan Eke); the name 'Hearth-Mother' (Gholumta
Eke) is also found. She arose when the gods of Heaven and Earth,
along with mountains, trees and animals, were still imperfectly
formed. Invocations to her stress in particular requests for fine
sons, daughters, brides and sons-in-law. Butter has traditionally
been offered to her, as in the fire-cult of the ancient Indians. (We
may observe that the Indian god of fire, Agni, also plays an important part in weddings and is seen, similarly, as the oldest of the
gods.)[67]

The Mongols, Heissig points out, have also worshipped various
protecting deities seen as armed heroes on horseback. Noteworthy here is the concept of *sülde*, used in Genghis' time to mean
'sign of good fortune' and also the leader's standard. The *sülde* is
the protective spirit embodied in the standard and has been worshipped until recent times. As well as giving protection to warriors
in battle, it guards families and herds from illness and wolves.
Thus the *sülde* of the ruler becomes a god, Sülde Tengri, armed
and equestrian. Prisoners of war have been sacrificed to the *sülde*,
in the form of the standard, up to 1911. Connected with it is a
war-deity, called Dayichin Tengri, 'Enemy God'.[68]

Chabros: the ritual of 'beckoning fortune'

In 1992 the London-based researcher Krystyna Chabros published an important book entitled *Beckoning Fortune: A study of the Mongol dalalgha ritual*. This book considers a procedure in which some one uses an arrow or other object to draw circles in the air, cries out 'Qurui' (the meaning of this cry is not clear) and recites a text enumerating the varieties of 'good fortune' hoped for. Chabros' study is based on examples of these texts, earlier accounts of this ritual and her own fieldwork in Mongolia (done in 1988–9).

The most significant occurrence of the ritual is in autumn. It is performed outside the tent, by the 'head of the tent', at sunset. A sheep is sacrificed, and the official rides his horse round the camp, waving a special arrow and declaiming the text loudly. This text is not a prayer, and does not invoke any god: it simply enumerates the 'benefits' expected, as in the following example:

> The stallion with his uncut mane and
> The horses with their flowing pace
> The ram with his curling horns and
> The sheep with sturdy bodies.

This autumn ritual takes place in the first month of autumn, corresponding roughly to August, which until the thirteenth century was also the first month of the Mongol year. It is the best time for feasts, owing to the surplus of milk products and the fatness of the sheep. By contrast, the spring is the worst time of year, when extremely cold winds and storms threaten the lives of newborn animals in herds weakened by hunger. In spring a special 'beckoning' is performed for the camels, which appear to be of particular significance to the Mongols for two reasons: first, they are 'cold-muzzled', and thus distant from humans, unlike the 'warm-muzzled' sheep and horses; secondly, a male camel in rut is seen as symbolizing heroic fury.[69]

'Beckoning' is also done after hunters kill an animal, with the explicit purpose of obtaining the replacement of the animal that has just been killed. Similarly, the ritual is performed after slaughtering cattle, with the same aim. Chabros takes the view that in

eneral Mongol rituals are intended to ensure the onward flow-
ng of life itself. Thus in Buryat invocations of a bull-ancestor the
naman, representing the spirit, butts the men present in the groin
presumably to symbolize the transmission of vital force down
he generations.[70]

The rite of 'beckoning' is also combined with the annual sacri-
ice to the deity of the hearth, performed by the western Mongols
n the last autumn month. This may echo a very ancient Turco-
Mongol new year festival, marking the start of the hunting season,
when the Pleiades appear (about 7 November). At this time, in
Siberia, hunting is rendered possible by the freezing of the swamps,
which enables the hunters to give chase over the frozen ground;
for herdsmen this freeze-up is also the signal for the annual slaughtering of livestock. An important Mongol sacrifice of meat to the
ancestors, recorded in the fourteenth century, has continued in
the form of the hearth sacrifice up to our own time. One of the
texts recited at this hearth sacrifice is of particular interest:

> From the western region
> I request the holy blessings of wisdom
> From the eastern region
> I request the blessings of horses multiplying
> From the northern region
> I request the blessings of camels of the black Kipchak
> From the southern region
> I request the blessings of the material possessions of the great
> Chinese Emperor.

Chabros takes these four regions to be representations of the
peoples conquered by the Mongols. It seems to me, however, that
the picture is Indo-European. Holy wisdom is in the west and fertility in the east. Physical strength appears, as often among the
Mongols, to be symbolized by the camels, here in the north. China,
in the south, would denote the great unknown, the 'other', alien
and threatening, but possessing the material wealth which the
Mongol nomadic economy could not provide for itself. The rest
of the text gives us striking images of this nomadic economy as
viewed by the 'master of the tent':

The holy benefits which enriching my poverty
Compensate me for my death...
A family as large as the open steppe
A womb as large as a bedcover...
Vital force and holy benefits of bull-camels with plentiful hair ..
Serfs and dogs by the threshold of the tent.[71]

Humphrey and Onon: shamans, trees and a goddess

In 1996 there appeared a long book entitled *Shamans and Elder*
by the Cambridge anthropologist Caroline Humphrey in collaboration with Urgunge Onon, the Daur Mongol scholar whom we
encountered above as a translator of the *Secret History*. This book
explores Onon's memories of his early life among his fellow Daurs
in northern Manchuria, and also draws on Humphrey's fieldwork
and recent studies by other researchers.

Some authorities take the view that the Daurs are not Mongols
and are descended from the Khitans. However, the Daurs see themselves as Mongols and speak a Mongolian language, although this
has a large number of Manchu words. They seem to have separated from other Mongols before the rise of Genghis. In the
seventeenth century they joined the Manchu empire.[72]

Onon was born in 1919. When about five he was consecrated
to the Sky, in order to preserve his health. As his family's youngest
son he was expected to inherit his father's farm. He recalls the
ritual cairn (*obo*) at the summit of a mountain near his village: at
this cairn the Sky, mountain and forests would be worshipped. A
storehouse in the village contained images of spirits: women were
not allowed in this storehouse, and the reason why the images
were kept there was that witnessing sexual intercourse in the main
house would provoke them to anger. Onon also recalls the respect accorded to shamans, who were set apart from society in
various ways: for example, they were not buried when they died,
but were exposed in the branches of trees, so that their souls could
come back to the world more quickly. Also, shamans were excluded
from hunting, because, Onon said, they were part of the sky and
consequently 'cousins' of wild animals.[73]

Shamans, however, were by no means the only important people in Daur society. There were also 'elders' (*utaachis*), literally

old men' who had stopped shaving and begun to prepare for
death. They would lead worship and oversee the offerings to the
spirit-images. An elder who was particularly involved in rituals was
called a *bagchi* ('ritualist'), and would consecrate horses and engage in divination from the burnt shoulder blades of sheep. It
was an 'old man' who presided over the rituals of hunting expedi-
tions. Thus, Onon thought, the shaman did not have much
influence in the Daurs' life: he was just like an ordinary English
physician in general practice. In general, Humphrey observed,
shamans engaged in rituals directed to animate beings (wild animals – though not in hunting – birds, fish and insects), and 'elders'
engaged in rituals directed to inanimate things (mountains, cliffs
and fire). Trees, ambiguous as being alive but unable to move
around, were worshipped in rituals performed by the whole community. (A Mongol friend of Humphrey said that his father, on
moving to a region which had only one tree, decided: 'That beautiful tree is worthy to be worshipped.')[74]

Daur attitudes to trees are further illustrated in a story about a
hunter who rested under an old elm tree. This, like a willow next
to it, began to sway, and the two trees started talking. The willow
wanted the elm, which was a shaman, to go and cure its mother,
but the elm refused, because it was looking after the hunter.[75]

Another narrative about trees is provided by a Daur woman
anthropologist called Odongowa, writing in 1991. She tells of a
special group of 12 trees, six growing beside a river and six on the
summit of a mountain. In the past the people would go to these
trees to take care of them since if the trees withered humans would
suffer hardships. Once some of the trees were found to be withered and needed to be nourished with animal blood. In order to
reach the trees on the mountain one had to go through the heavenly world and cross the river on a raft rowed by the ferryman of
the dead. (Humphrey observes that this was perhaps a women's
cult.)[76]

Awesome journeys of the kind just mentioned required that
shamans be extremely brave. Humphrey and Onon show shamans
as respected for courage and the ability to recover from the tem-
porary insanity brought on by frightening events – an ability due
to control over various spirits. Shamans had to have military equipment: the most prominent aspects of a shaman's costume were

weapons, armour and the symbols of a heavily defended citade
such as mirrors and bells, which represented the walls of a ci
Mirrors also provided intelligence of what was going on in th
world and frightened demons by reflecting light at them.[77]

Humphrey and Onon also provide information about the ar
cient goddess Umay, who reappears among the Daurs as Om
Barkan ('Womb Spirit'). If a child was ill his soul was thought t
have been lost, and a shaman would consecrate him to Ome b
putting some of his hair in a bag, into which his soul would als
be summoned: then the bag would be tied to a picture of Ome
The goddess was also credited with responsibility for the rebirtl
of one's soul. The cult of Ome was reserved almost entirely tc
women. In Daur epic a shamaness went to the underworld and
was shown round it by Ome, who explained that a green tree symbolized the flourishing of children, whereas a withered one
represented infertility, caused by people's thoughtless burning of
grass intended for herds. Another Daur text showed Ome, or a
shamaness united with her, returning from our world to the sky:
it is impossible to decide who is going on this journey to the sky,
since the sentences have no subjects.[78]

The difficulties presented by Daur materials are compounded
by apparent Chinese influences: thus the Daurs' belief that they
are descended from a union between a man and a female fox
seems to reflect the ancient Chinese belief that a fox turns into a
beautiful woman. Similarly, Onon's insistence on the prevalence
of dualism and 'balance' in Daur thought has been suspected by
Humphrey to represent a borrowing from the Chinese theory of
yin and yang.[79]

The internal logic of Mongol religion

Mongol religion seems to be based on the parallelism between
animals and humans in war and peace. The number nine is also
an important element, the nine tribes of the Mongol people being represented by the nine corners of its banner, which symbolizes
its protective spirit. This spirit guards both families and herds from
illnesses and wolves. Blood is similarly significant: one must not
shed the blood of nobles or sacrificed animals. The sharing of
blood produces one all-important Mongol relationship, that of

e blood brother, and in another, that of the adoptive father and
n, blood is sent as a token of loyalty. Just as one must avoid
illing blood, one must avoid depleting resources of animals,
hich, like humans, have to be replaced. One can prevent the
eath of another human by sacrificing oneself, and one can im-
gine that rescuing an animal from death will save one's own life.
fter killing an animal one 'beckons fortune' to obtain a replace-
nent for it: life has to go on. Thus plentiful children and camels
ompensate the 'master of the tent' for his death.

For the Mongols war, as we have seen, is like hunting, but not
n the simple sense of the transfer of hunting techniques to the
nilitary domain. Rather, as Deleuze and Guattari have pointed
out, warriors take on the qualities of animals – hunting dogs or
wild beasts. Thus sometimes they display an incomprehensible
cruelty, sometimes a strange form of mercy and pity (since the
warrior's fury breaks the usual bonds of society).[80] In general, the
Mongols show indifference to the religious beliefs of the peoples
whom they conquer (an indifference often mistaken for toler-
ance). To give alms is illogical, since the poor are destined to be
so by Heaven. The Mongols prefer good animals to humans. It is
desire for renown that causes them to risk their lives in rushing
immediately to the rescue of endangered comrades, displaying
their extraordinary bravery – a bravery also shown by the shaman.
For the shaman is required to rush at once to save a living being
in danger. His main role is to protect humans and livestock, and
thus, in a wider religious context, he may seem unimportant, since
he is concerned with the past and the present, not the future: his
area of operation is that of animate beings, not of mountains or
fire. The Mongol shaman is a sort of military flying doctor, and
his apparatus works like modern military technology.

Mongol religion in comparative perspective

Other elements of Mongol religion encountered in this chapter
are better understood in the light of Inner Eurasian and Indo-
European parallels. Among the ancestors of Genghis, the blue
wolf which mates with a doe and the woman who mates with a
yellow dog illustrate both an Altaic colour scheme and the breaking down of barriers between species. Some triads in Genghis'

biography are of a kind already familiar to us from Turkic mateals: the pattern of first animal, second animal and third human
found in the sequences rat–bird–Genghis and wild animals–gelings–women. One also sees the typically Inner Eurasian triad c
sky, sea and the space stretching from the earth's surface dowr
wards, counterpointed by the trio falcon–fish–marmot. This Inne
Eurasian patterning is transformed into an Indo-European onwith the triad holy mountain–wound in battle–nourishment.

The Mongol shamans, like the feminized Scythian diviners an
some Inner Eurasian Turkic counterparts, appear as homosexu
als, sodomized by the spirits. They make cups move up
miraculously, to the drinkers' mouths, like the magic cup of the
Ossetians and also, one imagines, the cups in the mysterious
'throwing back of the cups' ceremony observed by the Khitans. In
a Daur text it may be a shamaness who, united with a goddess,
travels into the sky like a Turkic shaman, or it may just be the
goddess alone. We cannot say which since the sentences have no
subjects. As Nietzsche remarked, the thought of Altaic and Uralic-
speaking peoples must have a specificity of its own since their
languages accord little importance to the subject of a verb.[81]

Indo-European patterns in the lists of Mongol deities and spirits are of particular interest for the comparatist. The benign rider
of the light bay horse who lives in the north-west (and presumably corresponds to 'Ruler Light-Bay Prince') looks like the friendly
Indian god Mitra, just as his terrifying white counterpart in the
south-west (who presumably corresponds to 'Creator White God')
looks like Mitra's partner, the remote and supreme Varuna. Similarly, the two red bestowers of 'horse luck' and 'cattle luck' in the
east seem to be the famous Indo-European or Indian 'Divine
Twins', one of whom is associated with horse breeding, the other
with cattle breeding. Here the points of the compass appear to be
of special significance, as in the Indo-European patterning of the
text recited at the hearth sacrifice which puts holy wisdom [1] in
the west, strength [2], symbolized by camels, in the north, fertility [3], represented by 'horses multiplying' in the east, and the
alien figure of the Chinese Emperor in the south. Now the Oxford anthropologist Nick Allen has argued that Indo-European
religion has a fourth concept, that of the 'other' or alien, and
that all four concepts correspond to the cardinal points, as in the

se of the four Indian gods who guard these: Varuna (religious
overeignty) in the west, Indra (force) in the north, Kubera
riches) in the east and Yama (the other world, that of the dead)
1 the south.[82] One wonders, then, if the Mongol deities are in
act Indian gods, perhaps brought in, along with Iranian ones, by
Buddhism. Here one recalls the similarities between Mongol and
apanese symbolism noted by Partanen with reference to the
Buryat treatise of the 1870s, and also the Indo-European patterns
which have been found in lists of Japanese deities.[83] Thus it seems
that the Mongol lists offer valuable evidence for the possible transmission of Indo-European, Indo-Iranian patterns to Japan.

The Daur materials relating to trees presented by Humphrey
are also of great interest, and closely resemble those found by me
in the Turkic domain, in the imaginary *History of the Uwaysis*. There
too we found the symbolism of withered and green trees, speaking trees and trees looking after a human, along with a strong
connection with women's piety. We also found a woman crossing
a river to come to a tree, and a typically Inner Eurasian pattern:
summit of a mountain–river–tree's foot.

4

The Tunguz and the Manchus

The various Tunguz-speaking peoples (along with the linguistically-related Manchus) will introduce us to a different range of animals: reindeer, elks, tigers and bears, as well as pike and salmon trout. When looking at the medieval evidence concerning the Jurchens, a proto-Tunguz people who, like the Khitans, emerged from the forest to conquer China, we shall be confronted with a new logic in 'mingling tears with blood', alongside important early materials for the study of shamans and an overwhelming emphasis on the colour white. In the eighteenth century we shall again find a tripartite structure, this time in Tunguz oaths. The twentieth century will yield us exceptionally detailed anthropological descriptions of Tunguz and Manchu religion which undermine academic fantasies about 'shamanism' and 'the sacred'. We shall consider the intricate symbolism of a Tunguz shaman's tent, with its elaborate representations of birds and fish. After examining myths about the elk we shall see that Tunguz funerary rituals resemble those of American Indians. Then we shall encounter reflections of animals in amulets, and the rich complex of taboos and ceremonies surrounding the hunt of the bear. Finally, we shall discuss a Manchu epic about a shamaness who journeys to the underworld.

he Jurchens

'he Chinese sources for the study of Jurchen customs and reli-
ion have been translated and analysed by the German orientalist
Ierbert Franke in the 1970s. One of these sources is a mono-
;raph on the Jurchens by Hsü Meng-hsin (1126–1207) who used
an earlier work by a long-term captive of the proto-Tunguz conquerors, Hung Hao (1088–1155).

Hsü Meng-hsin, like other Chinese writers, mentions the
Jurchens' fondness for hard drinking. We may note that according to a southern Chinese envoy sent to the Jurchens' court in
1125 they would pass the wine round three, five or nine times.[1]
Hsü Meng-hsin also tells us that the Jurchens fastened their gar-
ments on the left side (a barbarian custom in Chinese eyes, says
Franke). The Jurchens, like the Mongols, preferred to dress in
white. They would pray to the sun on the first day of the year and
shoot arrows at willow trees on the fifth day of the fifth month.
Franke comments that this shooting was a Khitan custom, intended
to obtain abundant rain. Hsü Meng-hsin proceeds to describe
Jurchen marriage customs: the rich would give oxen and horses
as betrothal presents, but the poor would just let their daughters
find husbands in the streets and go to the latter's homes without
ceremony. Men would ride around, drinking, and carry off what
future brides they chose.[2]

According to Hsü Meng-hsin, the Jurchens would not respond
to illnesses with physicians or drugs, but with shamans or prayers:
the shaman would sacrifice a pig or a dog. The patient might be
taken to the mountains and abandoned. After the death of a nobleman his favourite slaves and horses would be burned alive, along
with food.[3]

We are also told that the Jurchens, when cutting their fore-
heads after a death, aimed to mix tears with the blood, and called
this 'to take leave with bloody tears'. Franke comments that the
Jurchens did this on other occasions: one ruler 'gashed his forehead and wept to Heaven' before a battle, and Jurchen chieftains
mingled blood with tears after a victory. Another ruler did the
same, again praying to Heaven, before attacking a city and after
sacrificing a white horse and a woman.[4]

Hsü Meng-hsin tells us that the Jurchens had a leading law

maker in the early twelfth century who was called a *shan-ma*
meaning in Jurchen a shamaness. 'This was because he unde
stood changing conditions like a god.' Scholars have observe
that this is the first known text in which the original form of th
word 'shaman' is found, and that it evidently reflects the exis
ence of plenty of female shamans.[5]

Franke has also studied the official Chinese history of th
Jurchen dynasty, the *Chin shih*, which was compiled by a commi
tee in 1344–45. This history gives us the legend of the founder o
Jurchen institutions, Shih-tsu, who is presented as having settlec
a quarrel between two clans: he decreed that a quarrel following
a murder should be settled by paying compensation for it (3c
head of horses or oxen). The grateful clans rewarded Shih-tsu by
giving him a grey ox as a betrothal present and a 60-year-old woman
as a bride, and he had two sons by her.[6]

Information about Jurchen shamans is also found by Franke in
the dynastic history. A male or female shaman would be summoned
to curse a murderer by going to his family and singing:

> Take your ox with one horn pointing heavenwards and one earth-
> wards
> And a horse which has no name
> Seen from the front the face is mottled
> Seen from the back the tail is white
> Seen from the side there are right and left wings.

Then the shaman marked the ground with a blade and took
the murderer's livestock. We may observe that this account seems
to fit in with the legend of the origin of compensation for murder
just mentioned. As Franke says, the verses may mean that the
murderer is condemned to have only misshapen animals in the
future.[7]

Franke notes that a shaman might be consulted by the Jurchens
to foretell a child's future: such a shaman is described as being
able to 'speak the language of the gods'. The two main gods invoked were Heaven and Earth, to whom the Jurchens prayed with
wine-cups held facing east.

Apparently their custom of burning the horses of a dead man
went back to their ancestors, a people called the Mo-ho. At one

nerary ritual, it is recorded, a Jurchen emperor rode a white
orse. Franke connects this with Khitan practices, and points out
1at one twelfth-century Chinese scholar saw the Jurchen custom
f shooting at willows as a continuation of the Hsiung-nu ritual of
acing round forests on horseback in autumn (when the horses
vere fat). In conclusion, Franke takes the view that Jurchen cus-
oms were largely inherited from the Khitans, and that Khitan
:ulture thus probably had a strong Tunguz element in it.[8]

Gibert: the holy mountain of the Jurchens

In 1934 the French missionary Lucien Gibert presented valuable
Chinese evidence about the Jurchens' holy mountain. This had
already been venerated by their predecessors, the Mo-ho. It is the
Ch'ang-Pai-Shan in south-east Manchuria, and its name means
'Long White Mountain'. The Mo-ho regarded the animals living
on the mountain as sacred, and the people of Manchuria believed
that all the animals at its top were white. A special cult of the
mountain was observed by the Jurchen emperors who believed
that its spirit protected their dynasty. One emperor gave this spirit
the title 'King who ensures the prosperity of the nation and protects those who invoke it', and another that of 'Great and holy
Emperor who has created the Sky'. The Jurchen rulers also built
a temple to the mountain's spirit on its north slope, and there
they made sacrifices to the spirit on special days, informing it of
important events in the people's history.[9]

Stein: a Jurchen sacrifice

In 1940 Rolf Stein drew attention to a Jurchen ritual, described
by a Chinese observer, in which a white dog was impaled on a
long pole. Its head was raised on another pole and soaked in wine.
The purpose of this ritual, it was explained, was to sacrifice to
Heaven and drive illnesses away. Stein compares this sacrifice with
the Khitans' royal sacrifice of a white dog whose head is buried in
the ground and takes the view that here heaven represents the
home of the Jurchens' noble ancestors.[10]

Tao: Jurchen marriage and inheritance

Information about Jurchen marriage customs is provided by the Chinese researcher Jing-shen Tao in a study published in 1976. The Jurchens were polygamous, and on the death of a man a surviving wife could be given to one of his brothers, while a concubine could be given to one of his sons or nephews. Marriages required that the groom should go to the bride's home with presents (generally horses and cattle). Following the wedding the bridegroom was obliged to serve in the bride's home for a period which usually lasted three years. Inheritance was from brother to brother in preference to children and it was only with great difficulty that inheritance by the eldest son was later established.[11]

Roux: the Jurchens and animals

Roux has collected various pieces of evidence, preserved in the Chinese sources, about the role of the animal in Jurchen religion. Capturing a white stag during a hunting expedition was a good omen for the Jurchens (as was a white sparrow hawk for the Khitans). The Jurchen emperors would offer up to the gods, with prescribed invocations, the first game and fish caught in the season. Wild dances would simulate hunting and fighting at Jurchen festivals. Animals would be sacrificed in a drought, on a mountain and at royal command, in order to obtain rain. Before the main Jurchen sacrifices, performed twice a year, a pole would be erected, apparently to send the souls of the victims to heaven or the ancestors in the sky.[12]

The seventeenth century

With the Manchu conquest of China in the seventeenth century Manchu legends and religious practices were recorded by the Chinese. Gibert and Roux briefly note the legend of the origin of the Manchus. To the east of the 'Long White Mountain' was another mountain with a lake on it, and there three daughters of Heaven came to bathe. A magpie dropped a red fruit on the youngest who became miraculously pregnant and gave birth to the ancestor of the Manchu emperors. Gibert also notes that in 1677

ne Manchu emperor gave orders for the summit of the 'Long
White Mountain' to be explored, and subsequently had a temple
built to honour its spirit. This temple, constructed on a small
mountain to the south-west of the city of Kirin in southern Manchuria, was the scene of sacrifices made in spring and autumn.[13]

The eighteenth century: Gmelin and Georgi

Gmelin, in the 1730s, provides information about the Tunguz shamans. A shaman would have iron antlers on his shoulders, along
with many other iron ornaments, and would make noises like a
bear, dog or cat. One Tunguz shaman admitted using sleight of
hand in order to pretend that he passed an arrow through his
body. He nonetheless claimed to have many 'devils' at his command. The Tunguz shaman would engage in healing, by sacrificing
a lamb at the command of 'the Devil': he would make an incision
in the animal's breast and pull the heart out. Afterwards the skin,
head and feet would be placed on a pole, as an offering that 'the
Devil' demanded. Alternatively the shaman, when rescuing the
stolen soul of the patient, promised the spirit who had stolen it
that he would sacrifice a horse to him.[14]

We are also told by Gmelin that the Tunguz cover their faces
with blue designs, just like those of some American Indians. They
have idols of wood or copper, sometimes three feet long, which
provide them with their worldly goods. The Tunguz pray to them
in the morning and evening to have success in hunting and fishing. The first animal caught is offered 'to the Devil'. If the hunt is
successful the idol is fêted and anointed with blood, but if not it is
thrown on the ground or drowned. The dead are exposed on trees
or on the ground, unless they are to be specially honoured, in
which case they are put on a scaffold with their bow, arrows and
utensils. This is done well away from roads, and in areas not visited by strangers, because the utensils might be stolen by them.[15]

Georgi, in the 1770s, provides more details of Tunguz religion.
The Tunguz have three kinds of oath in their litigation. In the
least important variety, the accused person brandishes a knife in
the direction of the sun, calling on the sun, if he is guilty, to send
into his bowels diseases as deadly as a stab with the knife. More
solemn is the oath pronounced when climbing a sacred mountain,

when the accused says that if he is not innocent he should die c
lose his children and cattle, or lose all success in hunting an
fishing. The most serious oath is uttered when drinking the bloo
of a dog which is impaled, burnt or cut into pieces: the accuse
says that if he is guilty he should suffer the same fate. Here th
tripartition seems to me to be partly Indo-European, partly Inne
Eurasian: bowels correspond to concept 3 (fertility) in Indo-Eu
ropean schemas, while the slope of a mountain, hunting and
fishing belong to the Inner Eurasian level 2, and the impaling o
a dog is directed, as we have seen to level 1, Heaven, the sacrificing of the animal representing religion (concept 1 in the
Indo-European domain).[16]

According to Georgi the Tunguz hang small iron idols over
their children's cradles. Pious people wear such idols, representing a man, animal or bird, on their chests. Georgi also mentions
the Tunguz custom of tattooing the face and compares the similar Thracian custom mentioned by Herodotus: for the Thracians
this was a sign of nobility, says Herodotus (for a Greek it would
have betokened enslavement). The Tunguz, Georgi informs us,
have both shamans and shamanesses, who wear very striking costumes when performing their rites. These costumes are made
mainly of leather and covered with iron idols, bells, rings and trinkets, along with eagles' claws and stuffed snakeskins. At marriage
feasts the Tunguz sometimes eat a wolf or fox: if nothing else is
caught a dog is eaten. During these feasts there are foot races,
displays of equestrian skill and archery contests. The Tunguz have
many gods, including specialized deities for health, hunting, travellers, women, children and reindeer. Hunters hang up sacrificed
birds in bowers of branches and on crosses. Divination is practised by listening to the sounds made by flying arrows or vibrating
bowstrings.[17]

Czaplicka: a brief overview of Tunguz religion

The nineteenth and early twentieth-century sources for the study
of the Tunguz have been summarized by Czaplicka. According to
her sources, after death the corpse used to be sewn up in the skin
of a reindeer and hung on a tree, and a reindeer and a dog were
killed, their bones being tied to a tree or post. When the mourners

ent home they would cover their tracks so as not to be followed
by the dead person's spirit. By the twentieth century burial in the
ground had taken over: in the case of a shaman wooden figures of
a goat, horse or camel had to be placed on the grave. A young
shaman would be selected for his piety and sensitivity and taught
the secrets of the spirits by an older shaman. Chief among these
spirits were one in the form of a snake, with power over illnesses,
and one in human form with the wings of an eagle, who would
carry the shaman through the air. The shaman's costume and
equipment, in Czaplicka's view, combined representations of human faces and pieces of bearskin in such a way as to suggest the
joint worship of an ancestor and the bear. Czaplicka also noted
the great veneration accorded to the eagle, and the peculiar custom of cutting off the muzzle of a fox and preserving it carefully.[18]

Shirokogoroff: an exhaustive survey of the Tunguz and Manchus

In 1935 the brilliant Russian anthropologist Sergei Shirokogoroff
published his massive and extraordinary survey of Tunguz religion and culture entitled *Psychomental Complex of the Tungus*. This
incorporates the results of his fieldwork, done from 1912 to 1918,
in the course of which he himself became an assistant shaman. It
includes a vast amount of work on the Manchus, along with references, often polemical, to the publications of other writers, and
the author's extended theoretical analyses. One is left in wonder
at his command of his materials and of a variety of academic
disciplines.

The Tunguz and Manchus, says Shirokogoroff, draw a very sharp
distinction between 'true stories' and 'imaginative stories', but
this distinction depends very much on the attitude of given people. An epic about a shaman is seen as 'true' by Manchus who
keep their faith in shamans, whereas a historical account of a war
is dismissed as a fairy tale. A similar distinction is made between
the material and invisible parts of a human being: the latter are
called the soul (in Manchu *fajanga*), which consists of three parts:
(i) the 'true' soul, the principal component; (ii) the 'preceding'
soul, which represents the continuity of the human species and is
responsible for physiological functions, and which, after death,
returns to the spirit of childbirth (who corresponds to Omi, the

equivalent of Umay and Ome among some Tunguz) in order to be given to other children, and (iii) the 'external' soul which after death goes to the spirit of the underworld and may also be reincarnated.[19]

Shirokogoroff points out that the Tunguz are excellent and dedicated observers of animals. When one of the Tunguz has an opportunity to watch an animal without its noticing he will do so for hours, and then share his information with everybody. The Tunguz always insist on having accurate knowledge of animals as a prerequisite for hunting. When asked to draw animals from memory they do so well, but they themselves prefer geometrical designs in their art.[20]

The Tunguz, according to Shirokogoroff, recognize a supreme being, called Bugha, 'Sky', which does not have human form and is not one of the spirits. These spirits include notably the master spirit of hunting, Bajan Ami ('Rich Father'), an old man who sends the animals to the hunter. There is also Omi, the female spirit who distributes souls to the children. In addition, there are the spirits of the dead ancestors in the underworld, located in the north-west. They have been taken there by a lame ferryman in a canoe, crossing a river. Animals cannot be spirits (although spirits may take animal forms), and thus, Shirokogoroff insists, animals as such play no part in the activities of Tunguz shamans. Animals are seen by the Tunguz as superior to humans only in certain physical attributes, not in mental power. Thus it is only for the sake of specific physical attributes, such as the strength of the bear or the effectiveness of the eagle's swoop, that the shamans assume the forms of animals and birds.[21]

Spirits and animals are not really believed to be responsible for women's pregnancies. The Tunguz and Manchus are too good observers of nature to think this possible, though for diplomatic reasons a spirit is said to have intervened in the case of an unmarried mother. In folklore tigers and bears have intercourse with women, but this is not taken as literally true. However, Shirokogoroff states: 'Occurrence of intercourse with animals is known more or less among all [Tunguz] groups as practised, if not among themselves, then among the neighbouring or other ethnical groups.' Moreover, the Reindeer Tunguz of Manchuria say that the Tunguz are descended from a female dog and a spirit-

.ke man aged around 70 who came down from the sky. Nonethe-
ess, the Tunguz and Manchus do not venerate the dog as an
ancestor.[22]

The Tunguz believe that a spirit has to be 'placed' in a physical
body for them to deal with it, just as a guest has to be shown where
to sit. Shirokogoroff uses the term 'placing' for a physical body so
used, as opposed to 'idol' or 'fetish': such a 'placing' has nothing
sacred about it. An animal, person, rock or tree may become a
'placing', or one may be made out of wood, brass or straw, representing an animal, fish or human. The spirits also have some
reindeer and horses dedicated to them. Sacrifices are made to
the spirits in order to influence them: animals are killed and their
blood smeared on the mouths of the 'placings', or the spirits are
given cooked animals, plants, sweets, cakes, incense, ribbons and
flowers. In dealing with the spirits the Tunguz often see them as
stupid, cowardly, vain and greedy.[23]

Shirokogoroff also considers the cult of the 'clan spirits' or souls
of ancestors among the Manchus. He points out that the priests
responsible for this cult, although called *samans*, are not shamans,
but merely sacrificers and officials responsible for rituals. This is
particularly evident in the main ceremony of the year, the sacrifice to the clan spirits in the autumn. In other sacrifices
Shirokogoroff notes the use of five stones to form a hearth, as in
archaeological remains on the banks of the Amur.[24]

As regards the modern academic concept of 'shamanism',
Shirokogoroff begins by describing various examples of psychological 'dysfunction', which shamans regulate. These examples
include typical hysterical fits, and also manifestations of the 'imi-
tative mania' often observed in Siberia: people repeat the last word
or words that they have just heard, or imitate the movements of
others. Other examples involve the use of obscene language or
behaviour. From these Shirokogoroff turns to the word 'shamanism' itself and attacks the European tendency to use it in
generalizations unfounded in knowledge. He insists on concen-
trating on seeing how the Tunguz word *saman* and its various forms
are used. The term designates someone who has mastered spirits
and can introduce them into himself, so as to use his power over
them, notably to help other people who suffer from these spirits.
A shaman, in this capacity, may have a 'complex' of special methods

for dealing with the spirits. When he stops practising he is said
not to be a shaman any more. Certain paraphernalia are indis-
pensable, but also variable: at the very least the shaman needs a
drum and a brass mirror with pendants, along with a special costume. The drum is needed to bring the shaman to ecstasy, and
the mirror is needed as a 'placing' for the spirits. Among the
Manchus the costume is not absolutely necessary. What is necessary for all shamans is a general understanding of the existence of
spirits and how they can be made to move and be mastered. Also
necessary for a shaman is that he be recognized by a community
as having a special social position. Shirokogoroff takes the view
that shamanic activity was, in its origin, strongly influenced by
Buddhism, and, as evidenced among the Tunguz and Manchus, is
not very old.²⁵

   There are two types of costume used by the Tunguz shamans:
the duck costume and the reindeer costume. The former is used
for dealing with the spirits of the upper world, while the latter is
used for travelling to the underworld. (Tunguz shamanizing to
the upper world seems to represent a direct borrowing from the
Buryats, with arrangements of trees in groups of 27, as described
above.) As a reindeer the shaman feels that he is swift and vigilant. The mirror is used for different purposes by different Tunguz
groups: to see the world, to serve as a 'placing' for the spirits, and
to protect the shaman against the spirits' arrows. Shirokogoroff
attacks the European view that the shaman's paraphernalia are
'sacred'. He says that the attitude of the Tunguz towards the paraphernalia is determined by purely practical considerations
regarding the spirits. When wearing his costume the Tunguz shaman can produce a great variety of sounds, by rustling thin pieces
of metal and shaking heavy iron rattles, conical trinkets, bells and
mirrors, and his art lies in using these various elements as musical
instruments: here a good shaman differs from a bad one.²⁶

   The shaman operates by producing ecstasy in his patient and
his audience in order to influence them. In particular, he produces hallucinations. Thus the shamans are believed to be able to
fly through the air. The audience hears the spirits and may see
and smell them. In instances of mass hallucination those indi-
viduals who fail to perceive such phenomena attribute their failure
to their own physical defects. Shamans use drumming and singing

o hypnotize patients and effect treatment by suggestion. How-
ver, the shamans themselves are not conscious of using hypnotism
and suggestion, because their methods have been developed over
a long period of trial and error. In most cases of psychological
disturbance the shamans are very effective. Owing to their practical orientation, their rituals have nothing 'sacred' in them, and
are altered for specific aims. A shaman acts as a 'safety valve' for
his clan.[27]

Candidates for the position of shaman have in the past been
subjected to special tests, such as being required to walk on burning charcoal or dive repeatedly through holes in the ice and pass
beneath it before re-surfacing. When shamans reach old age the
ecstasy obtained in a performance gives them extraordinary
strength and youthfulness, with a feeling of extreme lightness of
the body, even when wearing a costume weighing 30 to 40 kilos: a
weak old shaman of 86 was seen by Shirokogoroff to jump and
dance like a young man. In their performances the shamans also
jump to the height of about a metre without a run-up. They feel
extremely hot, and sometimes a shamaness temporarily appears
to be pregnant.[28]

Sometimes, the Tunguz believe, the shamans fight wars against
each other, usually at night, in dreams. In these wars a shaman
may often take the form of various animals, both for fighting and
for spying. Thus a shaman may use a bear, a bird or an insect as a
'placing' for his own spirit. Such 'fighting shamans' use immate-
rial bows and arrows to attack men and animals. Shirokogoroff
observes that these 'wars' are representations of delusions of per-
secution among the shamans, and sometimes result from
alcoholism (although most Tunguz shamans drink only in mod-
eration).[29]

The belief that some shamans use tigers and bears as 'placings'
for their spirits makes other shamans abstain from hunting these
animals. One shaman met by Shirokogoroff could not kill large
animals such as the elk. Many shamans have difficulty using firearms. All this causes problems for maintaining shamans, since
hunting is the main economic activity of the Tunguz. The shamans cannot accept money or become rich. They are dependent
upon the charity shown by the Tunguz to all their fellow clansmen. Among the Manchus a shaman will exact payment from

clients outside his clan and may become relatively prosperous. A
Tunguz shaman, however, has a hard life, constantly tense because
of his work, tired after performances, unable to refuse to assist,
weighed down by responsibility, confronted by hostility, worrying
about involuntarily harming people and troubled about by the
fate of his soul (owing to the danger that spirits may imprison it
in this world when he dies). So he lacks the cheerfulness of tem-
perament which usually characterizes the Tunguz.[30]

Anisimov: the Evenk shaman's tent and ritual

In 1952 the Soviet Russian historian Arkadii Anisimov published
a long article on the shaman's tent and ritual among the Evenks,
a tiny nomadic hunting and fishing people of the middle of the
Central Siberian Plateau, now engaged in fur production and reindeer herding. This article is heavily imbued with Stalinist historical
theory, but presents some useful fieldwork done in the 1920s and
1930s.

The Evenk shaman's tent, Anisimov explains, is accompanied
by a tall young larch tree, which is placed in the tent's centre, so
that its top goes through the smoke hole. Members of the shaman's clan build the tent while he prepares for his performance
by fasting and constant smoking. It consists of the tent proper
(symbolizing the 'middle' world in which we live) and two 'galleries', one to the east and one to the west (symbolizing the upper
world and the underworld respectively). A small fire is kindled
next to the base of the larch tree. Also inside, opposite the entrance, is a raft, consisting of wooden images of salmon trout spirits.
To each side of this are further wooden images, representing
knives, spears and other fish. Outside the tent proper, and opposite the entrance, is the eastern gallery, consisting of a row of living
larch trees and images of spirits. By contrast, the western gallery,
as representing the world of the dead, is made from dead wood.
Both galleries are surrounded by more larch trees: those of the
eastern one have their roots at the top (like the tree of the upper
world in Evenk belief), while those of the western one have their
roots at the bottom. In the eastern one stand wooden images of
reindeer with figures of salmon trout on their backs: these are
thought to swim in a cosmic river which flows from the upper

world to the lower one. Giant figures of another fish, the pike, guard the entrance to the tent proper. Beside the western gallery images of birds guard the path to the underworld, and next to the tent two images representing human ancestors guard the entrance to the realm of the dead. These are reinforced by two images of eelpouts, while in the centre of the western gallery is a huge image of an elk, flanked by figures representing stags, bearing another large salmon trout. Next to this is a row of dried larch trees with figures of birds at their tops. The point is that the entire construction functions like a fish weir: evil spirits are to be placed in a trap. These evil spirits appear in the forms of stoats or wolves, and are sent by the shamans of other clans. To keep them out, at the far end of the western gallery stand charred images in human form, holding spears: these guard the mouth of the river.[31]

In the performance the shaman sits on the raft and beats his drum. He invokes his spirits in verses repeated by those present. Then he imitates their noises (those of animals and birds) before giving them their orders to act as guards or stay with him awaiting further instructions. He tells one important spirit, his *khargi* or animal double, to go to the underworld, accompanied by other spirits, to find the cause of the illness of the patient who is being treated. The shaman describes this journey with further imitations of spirits' voices, goes further into ecstasy and begins to dance. Finally he falls, foaming at the mouth: he is representing his *khargi* in the world of the dead. His assistant persuades him to return, and he begins to do so, babbling weakly. Eventually the shaman leaps up and dances again, representing the return of the *khargi* to the middle world. He relates what has happened and repeats the advice obtained from the ancestor spirits as to how the evil spirit who has caused the illness should be fought.[32]

After a rest the shaman tries to expel the evil spirit from the patient. He whirls round, dancing furiously, but fails. Advised by his *khargi*, he rubs the affected part of the patient with parts of various animals and birds. This also fails, and so he suggests to the evil spirit that it should pass into a sacrificed reindeer. The reindeer is brought, and a rope is put round its neck and in the patient's hand. An assistant kills it with a knife as the patient twists the rope, the idea being that the evil spirit runs along the rope into the reindeer. The shaman bites into the reindeer's heart, spits part of it into one of his spirit images and carries the latter into the western gallery and thus the underworld. Sometimes, however, the evil spirit stays in the patient, necessitating further interventions. When it has been brought out it may attack the onlookers and have to be caught: then, imprisoned in a spirit image, it is overwhelmed by the shaman's spirits, who even urinate and defecate upon it. The shaman dances frantically, crying out with the voices of the spirits persecuting the evil enemy. Finally, one of his bird-spirits swallows the latter, flies over the abyss of the underworld and expels the evil spirit into it through his anus. The shaman returns to his usual place and recounts his success. Then he identifies the clan whose shaman had sent the evil spirit, and, in revenge, sends his own spirits off to attack them.[33]

At the end of the performance another reindeer is sacrificed to the gods of the upper world. This is done at a larchwood pole to the south-east of the eastern gallery. The shaman climbs up this and thus through the various heavens to the supreme god, to whom he entrusts the patient's soul, in a small wooden image of a man. Then he returns to the tent and engages in divination, replying to his clansmen's questions after throwing his rattle in the air and seeing which way it falls, and examining the cracks in the burnt shoulder blade of the sacrificed reindeer.[34]

According to Anisimov the basic underlying idea is that the Evenks think that evil spirits are sent by other clans. To keep such spirits away each shaman fences off his clan's land with an imaginary fence of spirit-watchmen. This fence or stockade, in the shamans' stories, stretches from each ridge, mountain or rivulet to the next, while bird spirits and fish spirits guard the air and water. The shaman also sends his spirits in military detachments to attack another clan: his paraphernalia, while on the one hand presenting animal symbolism, on the other have manifestly military functions as weapons and armour.[35]

Vasilevich: Evenk myths

In 1959 the Russian anthropologist Glafira Vasilevich published summaries of a number of Evenk myths. She points out that the Tunguz word *nimngakan* means both 'myth' and 'to put on a shaman's performance'. Telling myths was, in the past, one of the

haman's functions. Both storytelling and shamans' performances
involved imitating the voices of animals.[36]

Some Evenk myths involve the constellation of the Great Bear,
seen as an elk. In one myth three hunters prepare to hunt an elk:
the first is a braggart, the second carries the pot in which the
meat is cooked, and the third, small and weak, trails behind. However, on seeing the elk the braggart runs behind the others and
the pot carrier runs behind the small hunter. In the constellation
four stars make up the elk and three are the hunters. Vasilevich
points out that the idea of the Great Bear's being an elk chased by
three hunters is found among the Finns and the Khanty (one of
the branches of the Hungarians' Siberian cousins). Other Evenk
myths show a hero hunting a heavenly elk on skis: his ski track
becomes the Milky Way. More myths speak of the origin of the
sun and the moon. Originally, we are told, they were humans, but
they went up into the sky because of romantic adventures which
turned out badly. Sometimes the sun is female in these stories,
sometimes male.[37]

The Evenks also have the widespread 'earth diver' myth about
the creation of the world: in the beginning, they say, there were
two brothers, one of whom sent a bird to dive down into water
and bring up earth. Sometimes, as often, the two brothers appear
as God and the Devil. Also found among the Evenks is the myth of
man's being born from a tree. Another myth is that of the miracu-
lously-born boy who avenges his people: the Evenks are attacked
and swallowed up by a monstrous bird, Kerendo, but one old
woman survives. She looks after some goose eggs, and from them
a boy is born, Unyany, who attacks Kerendo and his family and
frees many Evenks.[38]

Lopatin: death among the Golds

Another important observer of the Tunguz was the Russian anthropologist Ivan Lopatin, who did his fieldwork between 1913
and 1924 among the Golds, a Tunguz-speaking people who live
to the north of the river Amur in eastern Siberia. After leaving
the Soviet Union he did more fieldwork in 1930 among the Kitinat
Indians of British Columbia. In 1960 he published a book called
The Cult of the Dead among the Natives of the Amur Basin. This provides

plenty of information about the Golds, along with comparison
with American Indian customs.

Among the Golds a person who has recently died is considered
to be still alive until the holding of a final funerary feast (*kaza*)
which may take place three or four years later. Such a person con
tinues to be given food and tobacco. At the actual moment of
death a man's soul is transformed into a 'shadow' (*fania*), which
goes out of him and has to be found by an experienced shaman
and imprisoned in a special cushion. The origin of death is attributed to the first woman, who saw that the world had become too
crowded. Nowadays the cause of death is attributed to the gods,
evil spirits, and the witchcraft of wicked shamans. The Tunguz
put aged fathers to death, but not mothers. Killing their fathers
does not show lack of esteem, because the afterlife is a happy one.
The land of the dead, called Buni by the Golds, is far beneath the
earth's surface, a place of peace abounding in fish and game. A
dead person's soul has to be taken there by a shaman at the final
feast.[39]

The Golds are frightened of the spirits of unburied dead people and of people who have committed suicide. In order to prevent
the return of a dead person his corpse has to be removed from
his hut by a route other than the ordinary door – thus usually the
window is used. (This rite is paralleled among the ancient Norsemen, the early Russians, the Eskimos and the Kuruk Indians of
California.) A dead person is told to stay away and not frighten
the living in exhortations uttered during the initial feast which
precedes a burial. After this the corpse is placed in a shallow grave
with drawings of animals on paper. The deceased's favourite dog
is killed by the grave, and his personal belongings are placed upon
it.[40]

Seven days later the special cushion for the man's 'shadow' is
prepared: this cushion, like the 'shadow' itself, is called a *fania*. It
is white (the colour of mourning), with multi-coloured designs at
each end. The shaman searches for the soul, finds it and 'places'
it in the cushion, in the course of another feast. (The Miskito
Indians of Central America have a similar custom: a sorcerer has
to catch and recover the 'shadow' of a dead person.) Further com-
memorations take place once a month, until eventually the final
feast for the deceased is held. This is extremely expensive, and

onsequently is often delayed until five or six years after the death. At the high point of the feast the shaman makes his spirits come to him, and then imitates the wild animals and birds who represent them. After this he climbs a ladder and peers at the land around him, looking for the road to the land of the dead. People ask him about the prospects for hunting and fishing and he replies. On descending he calls on a spirit named Buchu to come and guide him and bring a magic bird, Koori, to carry him as he takes the 'shadow' to its new home. After dancing wildly he takes the cushion on to a long board, to which he harnesses imaginary dogs. He performs his journey, returns and tells people how they are going to hunt in the coming year. Then he throws the cushion into a great fire. From then on the dead person is forgotten: the Golds never engage in ancestor worship.[41]

Lopatin concludes that the Golds' funerary customs are very similar to those of American Indians, the similarities being greatest when one compares the Eskimos of Alaska, and then, in descending order, the Indians of British Columbia, Washington, Oregon and California. There are also close similarities with the mortuary customs of the Turks and Finns.[42]

Diószegi: animal amulets among the Golds

In 1968 Diószegi published a brilliant article on the amulets used by the Golds against lung diseases. These, he observes, are of three types, in an ascending order of strength and efficacy, and in the forms of three corresponding animals: the bear; the tiger and the panther. The Golds pay great respect to the bear, whom they see as an ancestor who once united himself with a woman. The Golds' closest relatives among the Tunguz have similar legends. Even greater respect is accorded by the Golds to the tiger. They and their neighbours present sacrifices to it, and in the past would even offer human victims, tied to trees. The Golds do not hunt tigers, and if they kill one by accident are extremely upset: expensive offerings have to be made in atonement. One must not kill animals wounded or hunted by tigers. The tiger is seen as a friend. Some clans claim descent from it, either as an ancestor or (as sometimes with the bear) as an ancestress. The panther is seen as a healing animal because of its name, *iarga*, which is phonetically interchangeable with *erga*, 'life spirit'. Illness, for the Golds, i caused by the kidnapping and torturing of the *erga* by an evil spiri from which it must be rescued by a shaman. As for the ascending order bear–tiger–panther, this reflects the increasing degrees of danger and terrifyingness represented by these three animals.[43]

Paproth: bear rituals

The Uppsala-based researcher Hans-Joachim Paproth produced an important study of Tunguz bear rituals in 1976. This deals with Tunguz beliefs about the bear, the rituals involved in hunting it and the ceremonies surrounding the killing of bears and eating their flesh. A lot of materials gathered from other peoples are adduced for comparative purposes, since, as Paproth observes, similar rituals involving the bear are found in the region stretching from Lapland across northern Eurasia and North America to Greenland.[44]

It is believed by the Tunguz, like other Siberian peoples, that the bear has telepathic powers and can hear everything that people say about it. Thus they swear by the bear, calling on it to devour them if they are guilty. It has a huge number of euphemisms used to avoid mentioning it or the process of hunting it. A bear also has a special area marked out for itself. Stories depict the bear as both clever and stupid.[45]

The northern Tunguz (like other peoples) hunt the bear mainly in late autumn or early spring. Then the bear is hibernating. When the hunter discovers the bear's den he marks the spot and goes to his home where he makes preparations in the strictest silence. Returning with his companions, he kills the bear, and then they all pretend to the bear's soul that it has been killed by foreigners or ravens. A Yakut informant relates that once he was accompanying two Evenks, and one of the latter killed a bear. The victorious hunter went up to the bear and began to simulate a sexual act. Then he told the other Evenk and the Yakut to do likewise. The Yakut felt obliged to demur, this conduct striking him as quite extraordinary. Thereupon the Evenks forcibly dragged him to the animal and he complied. When the bear was taken home an old Evenk woman started to cry out: 'Why has grandfather been killed?' She pretended to wipe away tears, while really rejoicing inwardly in the informant's view, her appearance of grief being demanded by ritual). Paproth is doubtful about this report, since the sexual rite is not evidenced elsewhere for the Evenks, but is well evidenced for the Yakut. When Yakut hunters kill a bear the older hunters force the young ones who are on their first bear hunt to simulate a sexual act on the animal. This is intended to make them coura-geous and strong in subsequent bear hunts (as are the rites of tasting the bear's blood and imitating ravens' cries when eating its flesh). Among some Yakut an older hunter puts himself be-hind the youth and pushes him with a branch held against his own penis. This, we are told, is done so that the youth's legs should not buckle in fear. Similar rites are found among other Siberian Turks (apparently to win the bear's sympathy, because he was once a woman), with a parallel ritual observed in horse sacrificing.[46]

Among the Tunguz the skinning of the bear must be done by someone unrelated to the killer. A further taboo concerns the eating of the bear's flesh: the upper part of the animal is reserved for the men, the lower for the women. In addition to hunting bears, the southern Tunguz have a ritual killing of a bear who has grown up in captivity: this ritual involves a symbolic firing of an arrow in the direction of the animal before it is shot. The ritual also includes music making on the part of the women. This has not been described in detail as regards the Tunguz; among the Gilyaks (one of the 'Palaeoasiatic' peoples of north-eastern Sibe-ria) part of this music making consists of the singing of highly erotic ditties. (The Gilyaks are also noteworthy for bringing bears up as tame household pets.)[47]

A Manchu epic

Further information about the activities of shamans is provided by a Manchu folk epic entitled *The Tale of the Nishan Shamaness*, which was presented in English by Margaret Nowak and Stephen Durrant in 1977. In this epic a youth falls ill and dies and a sha-man is sought to bring him back to life. The youth's father denounces bogus shamans who live off cheating people out of food and cannot prove their competence by correctly giving the time of someone's death. Then he goes to see a powerful shamaness, called 'the Nishan shamaness' because she lives on

the banks of the Nisihai River in southern Manchuria. She du[.]
engages in divination to find out the circumstances of the deatl
Inhaling incense and beating a tambourine, she is possessed by
spirit and mutters an account of how the youth has died: in add[:]
tion to establishing her credentials by correctly describing th[e]
circumstances, she explains that the Lord of the Underworl[c]
(called Ilmun Han) has sent an evil spirit which has abducted hi[s]
soul. After reviving, the shamaness comes to the youth's house
and prepares for the soul's rescue. The spirit-images are set up,
incense is burnt and a competent assistant is brought to beat the
tambourine. Then the shamaness puts on her costume, adorned
with bells, and her cap, decorated with images of nine birds. She
again becomes possessed by a spirit, and instructs that a rooster
be fastened to her head and a dog to one of her feet, and that
bean paste and coarse paper be placed beside her (to be used for
paying the spirits which she will encounter).[48]

The shamaness now proceeds on her supernatural journey. She
comes to the bank of a river, and a lame ferryman takes her across.
Then she comes to a second river, and animal spirits help her to
cross it. She goes on to two gates, each guarded by two harmful
spirits, and is allowed through. At a third gate she meets the evil
spirit who has taken the youth's soul. This spirit explains that he
and his colleagues have subjected the youth to three tests. First,
they have hung a gold coin on a tall pole and made him shoot an
arrow at a hole in this coin; secondly, they have made him grapple with a 'blue wrestler'; thirdly, they have made him grapple
with a 'lion wrestler'. The youth has been victorious and so the
Lord of the Underworld has adopted him as his son. On hearing
this the shamaness goes on to the Lord of the Underworld's city.
Unable to enter it, she calls on birds and animals to go in and
rescue the youth and their spirits duly fly up: one great bird
snatches him and brings him to her. On their way back she encounters her dead husband, refuses to bring him back to life, and
gets a great crane to throw him into a city from which he can
never be reincarnated. After this she pays her respects to the goddess of childbirth, Omosi-mama, who arranges for her to see the
punishments inflicted on the wicked. Then the shamaness and
the youth return to the land of the living. The assistant starts to
apply water and incense to revive the shamaness, and calls on birds

nd animals to effect this. She recounts what has happened, and
.akes up. The youth's dead body comes back to life.[49]

The internal logic of Tunguz and Manchu religion

'et again, the materials surveyed have a very strong logic of their
)wn. The colour white is dominant, preferred for clothing by the
jurchens and appearing in the sacrifices of horses and dogs. A
white horse is ridden by a Jurchen emperor at a funerary ritual,
and it is believed that all animals at the top of a white mountain
(also venerated by the Manchus) are themselves white. The head
of a white dog is raised on a pole when sacrifices are made to
Heaven, apparently here seen as the home of the Jurchens' noble
ancestors. Similarly, the Golds use the colour white for mourning
and the special cushion into which a dead person's soul is
transferred.

A Jurchen ruler sacrifices a white horse and a woman before
praying to Heaven. This pairing corresponds to that of the grey
ox and woman given to the founder of the Jurchens' institutions.
Perhaps it corresponds also to Heaven and Earth, the two main
deities of the Jurchens. Two poles are used when sacrificing the
white dog, one for its head, one for its body. Among the eighteenth-century Tunguz, a dog is impaled in the most serious of
oaths: presumably Heaven itself is being invoked. In the eighteenth century a dog is used as a substitute for a wolf or fox in
marriage feasts, and in Czaplicka's nineteenth and early twentieth-century materials a dog is sacrificed along with a reindeer in
funerary rituals. Perhaps the custom of preserving a fox's muzzle
is a survival of the importance accorded to a dog's head. The head–
body dualism is reflected in the taboo which reserves the upper
part of a bear for men and the lower part for women.

Dogs also appear in the sacrifices made by Jurchen shamans in
order to treat the sick. The eighteenth-century Tunguz shamans
wear iron antlers and make noises like those of a bear, dog or cat.
Tunguz shamans, Shirokogoroff explains, assume the forms of
animals and birds for purely practical reasons, in order to exploit
their specific physical attributes. Thus, as Anisimov observes, enemy shamans send diseases through evil spirits in the forms of
stoats or wolves. Before fighting them a healing shaman tells his

animal double to go to the underworld to find out what has hap
pened. In his performance the shaman becomes his anima
double, travelling and returning. Accordingly, as Vasilevich point
out, the same word may be used to mean 'myth' and 'to put on
shaman's performance'. As we have seen in the *Tale of the Nisha*
Shamaness, the shaman's performance, the journey, the story o
the journey and the telling of the story are all united. A number
of wild animals and birds are invoked on the journey and to bring
the shamaness back to consciousness, just as, among the Golds, a
variety of animal spirits are invoked in order to prophesy success
in hunting and fishing, and to get rid of the souls of the dead. For
the Golds, there is a hierarchy among animals: the panther, as
corresponding to the 'life spirit' itself, is seen as a healing animal,
because illness is due to the kidnapping of the 'life spirit.'

Tunguz and Manchu religion in comparative perspective

The study of Tunguz and Manchu religions calls for a very wide
range of materials to be adduced for comparative purposes. The
use of the colour white to denote religious sovereignty, noteworthy among the Jurchens, is characteristic of the Indo-European
field. On the other hand, the dualism of male and female is typical of other linguistic domains, the Chinese and the Afroasiatic
(the latter stretching from Nigeria to Arabia and Iraq). The obligation of the Jurchen bridegroom to serve in his bride's home for
three years looks like an archaic reminiscence of 'uxorilocal'
marriage, that is to say the incorporation of the groom into the
bride's household, found in early or undeveloped societies. Using a pair of poles for worship is also an archaic practice, evidenced
in Egypt and Arabia.[50]

Other elements of Tunguz and Manchu religion are already
familiar to us. Exposing the body of a specially honoured person
in a hidden place corresponds to the secret royal burials of Inner
Eurasia. The marriage feasts have a typically Inner Eurasian pattern in their games: [1] archery contests belong to the sky, into
which arrows are fired, [2] displays of equestrian skill belong to
the space between the sky and the earth, and [3] foot races belong to the earth's surface. Here there is a close parallel with the
Turkic marriage contests noted above, as with the three tests

nposed on the youth in the *Tale of the Nishan Shamaness:* shoot-
ng an arrow at a hole in a gold coin on a tall pole, followed by two
vrestling matches. On the other hand, many aspects of Tunguz
ife point to links with the American Indians: the pattern of the
attoos, the constant observation of animals, the myths of the hu-
nan origins of the sun and the moon, and the taboos and rituals
surrounding the dead and the hunting of the bear.[51]

Shirokogoroff's work is particularly rich from the standpoint
of a comparatist. He points out that shamans are often not involved in sacrifices: we have seen this among the Mongols.
Shirokogoroff shows how the shaman produces mass hallucinations: these are of course the stock-in-trade of the modern stage
hypnotist, and may well account for the Mongol shamans' miraculous raising of the cups. When rejecting the idea that the shamans'
paraphenalia are 'sacred', Shirokogoroff anticipates contemporary historians of religions who find their predecessors' constant
evocation of 'the sacred and the profane' to be unsupported by
the evidence.[52]

Anisimov's description of the shaman's tent and performance
is also exceptionally valuable. The idea (symbolized by the inverted
larch trees in the tent's eastern gallery) that a tree has roots in the
upper world is one that we find echoed in Finnish epic poetry. As
for the shaman's performance itself, it is a striking example of
'becoming-animal'. This, as Deleuze and Guattari have observed,
requires that someone should enter into a combination with an
object or objects: here a drum and a raft; elsewhere, iron antlers
or a special cap. This combination results in the noises of animals
or birds: a human being takes on animal aspects, crying out, ex-
creting and flying in his battle with the evil spirit.[53]

Conclusions

In this concluding section I intend to look first of all at Inner Eurasian parallels to the Altaic materials which I have already surveyed. Thus we shall begin by examining the Samoyeds of the shores of the Arctic and the plot of one Samoyed epic. Then we shall consider the Hungarians and their Siberian cousins, while also noting similarities with American Indians. After that we shall move to Finnic evidence, and produce new interpretations of the Finnish and Estonian national epics. Finally, we shall discuss the significance of the Inner Eurasian religious inheritance for world literature in general, before ending with a broad overview of this inheritance's defining characteristics and its relationship to the legacies of other domains.

The Samoyeds

The tiny Samoyed peoples live in between the White Sea (to the north of Finland) and the River Khatanga in northern Siberia. They are either semi-nomadic reindeer hunters or sedentary fishermen, and are seen as being linguistically closest to the Finns and Hungarians, but perhaps not unrelated to the Tunguz. Their shamans appear in descriptions of performances and stories which will help us to reach general conclusions about various epics.

An English navigator, Stephen Borough (1525–84), has left us a description of a Samoyed shaman's performance which he

itnessed in 1556. The shaman beat a large drum, crying out
ildly, until he lost consciousness. It was explained by the Samoyeds
resent that a spirit was telling him what to do. When they called
ut to the shaman he got up and continued with his perform-
nce. Five reindeer were sacrificed, and the shaman demonstrated
. number of tricks. He stabbed himself with a sword without be-
ng wounded, heated the sword and passed it through his body,
and finally covered himself with a large cloth and pretended to
cut off his head, shoulders and left hand behind it.[1]

In the eighteenth century Georgi noted that the Samoyeds con-
sumed a hallucinogenic mushroom, fly agaric (*Amanita Muscaria*).
A man chose a wife from another clan and after paying the bride
price carried her off by force. Wives were treated with the greatest
cruelty. A dead person had to be taken out of his tent through a
hole in the wall, and after his burial a shaman had to appease his
spirit in case he troubled the living, who tried to forget him as
soon as possible.[2]

The year 1913 saw the publication of a summary of a Samoyed
epic, made by the Finnish linguist Kai Donner. In this epic a hero
called Itte is orphaned by a man-eating giant and brought up by
an old woman. When he grows up he goes to a strange lake where
he steals a fish from a blind shaman. This shaman sends his spirits
to carry away Itte, his dog and the old woman, and swallows them
up. Itte cuts a hole through his stomach while he is asleep, escapes, kills him and rescues the old woman and his dog.
Subsequently Itte allies himself with a great bird in order to hunt
an enormous fish. To catch the latter he constructs a musical instrument with seven strings and plays so beautifully that all the
creatures of the forest, sea and air come to him. The huge fish
offers Itte his daughter as a wife, and he accepts. Later Itte meets
the seven sons of the spirit of the forest and retrieves their three
lost sisters who have been abducted by warriors. He marries all
three and one of them gives birth to a son, called the bear spirit,
from whom the Samoyeds on the river Ket claim descent. Finally,
Itte finds the man-eating giant who devoured his parents. Itte takes
advantage of this giant's illness to trick him into taking off his
armour: then he gets the giant's neighbours to kill him. The giant
rises from the dead, but Itte again lures him into a trap, kills him
and burns up his body. Afterwards Itte rules his people happily

until the Devil and Christ come to plague him. He leaves his cou
try to wander off and sleep (this element of sleeping is give
particular emphasis), promising to return.[3]

In the years following World War I further studies present i
teresting details of Samoyed religion. Czaplicka notes that th
sacrificing of reindeer has to be done by strangulation, so as t
avoid the spilling of blood. She further records that in Samoye
belief people can turn into bears by leaping over fallen trees an
uttering specific formulae. Another Finnish linguist, Toiv
Lehtisalo, observes that the Samoyeds have a tripartite colou
scheme, white–green–black, for the shaman's spirits, represent
ing spirits who come respectively from heaven, earth and th
underworld. A shaman, Lehtisalo points out, is somebody whc
knows the origins of things (such as fire or iron), and thus ha
control over them and can summon them to support him.[4]

One of the most interesting texts for the study of Samoyed shamans was presented in 1968 in a posthumously published paper
by the St Petersburg researcher Andrei Popov. Popov notes that
Siberian shamans are often initiated by spirits who take them on
journeys, in which they meet other spirits whom they will subsequently invoke. In the text published by Popov a shaman of the
Nganasan branch of the Samoyeds, named Sereptie Djaruoskin,
recounts his journey with a spirit in the form of a man who has
jumped out of a tree. Together they descend through a hole in
the earth and come first to a river, and then to nine tents. The
second tent is a Tunguz one, with a black rope round its middle,
which, Djaruoskin's companion explains, will help him to heal
diseases of the stomach, while red stuff on the top of the tent will
cure madness caused by headaches. Another rope, in between,
will counter epidemics. The third tent has inside it an old woman,
who is the spirit of the placenta. Subsequently they come to another river, and a hill with two tents, representing the origins of
diseases. Here another woman breathes on Djaruoskin three times
and gives him advice.[5]

A brief overview of Samoyed religion was published in 1987 by
the American scholar Robert Austerlitz. He points out that the
Samoyeds' chief god, Num, is usually not involved in human af-
fairs. By contrast, such involvement is prominent in the case of a
spirit called Ilibemberti, 'the spirit that gives riches or sustenance

in reindeer or game)'. Spirits are divided into a hierarchy of three classes: those of the elements and hunting; those in human form and those of the shaman (usually in animal form). Special reverence is accorded to reindeer, the bear and the pike.[6]

Hungarian and Ob-Ugrian religion

Useful information about the religion of the Hungarians and their 'Ob-Ugrian' cousins (so called after the river Ob in western Siberia, on the banks of which they live, 'Ugrian' being from the Latin for 'Hungarian') was provided by the Finnish researcher Uno Harva in 1927. One aspect is eating the hearts and livers of slain enemies. A chronicle of 889 tells us that the Hungarians would cut up the hearts of prisoners-of-war and eat them. The same practice is recorded in the cases of the early Ob-Ugrians and Finns: evidently the aim is to take over the enemies' strength and prevent them from rising from the dead. Among the Ob-Ugrians a widow makes a memorial doll representing her dead husband and gives it food for some years after his death. A man who is killed by a wild animal or in battle goes straight to heaven, but one who dies a natural death goes to the underworld. The Ob-Ugrians hold special feasts when a bear is killed: the bear's life is recounted in a kind of drama. They also keep family gods in a special box. Other gods are believed by the Ob-Ugrians to exist within specific boundaries, which constitute sacrosanct domains. A goddess of childbirth, identified with the placenta, is also found among the Ob-Ugrians. They possess typical Siberian shamans, who use drums to go into trance and have animal spirits to help them journey to another world.[7]

The year 1954 saw the posthumous publication of a book called *Hungarian and Vogul Mythology* (Vogul is the old name for what is now called the Mansi branch of the Ob-Ugrians) by the leading Hungarian anthropologist and psychoanalyst Géza Róheim (1891–1953). Róheim points out that one medieval Hungarian chief is said to have been born after his mother had a dream about a falcon making her pregnant. He also observes that in Ob-Ugrian myth two hunters pursue a pregnant elk along the Milky Way, and that the Milky Way is supposed, in Hungarian legend, to have led the original Hungarian invaders from Asia into Europe. These invaders, we are informed, believed that the people whom the killed had to be their slaves in the other world. In Ob-Ugrian Finnic and Turkic beliefs the Milky Way is also associated wit migratory birds: in Estonian folklore these have to fly through narrow passage between two hills, where two men try to stop then (just as in Amerindian myth birds have to fly between clashing rocks).[8]

In 1959 the Russian anthropologist and archaeologist Valeri Chernetsov published an article on Ob-Ugrian concepts of the soul. He notes that the Ob-Ugrians believe that men have five souls and women four: these numbers are often connected with the two sexes. One soul lives on in the graveyard. Another has the form of a bird, and in order to keep it in the body tattooing of figures of birds is practised (while a different kind of tattooing is done for the purpose of relieving pain). Bird tattoos are also executed when someone is about to die, in order to assist the soul in its journey to the next world. A third soul is also in the form of a bird, but specifically in that of a grouse: it comes to a person during sleep. The fourth soul is that of reincarnation, and is located in the scalp: thus the Ob-Ugrians have scalped enemies to prevent their rebirth (this is recorded by a Christian traveller of 1235–6). As for the fifth soul, possessed by men but not women, this is something explained by the Ob-Ugrians as being a second soul of reincarnation, sometimes as being 'strength'.[9]

The Hungarian scholar Béla Gunda published an interesting article in 1968 on a peculiar type of person found in modern Hungary and designated by the term *táltos*. A *táltos*, usually male, has superhuman strength or other striking attributes. Sad in his childhood, he is a loner, living mainly on milk, prophesies, heals and can control the weather. He can find hidden treasures by looking at one of his fingernails. The *táltos* falls into trances and has visions. When aged seven he has to fight a stronger *táltos* in the form of a bull or stallion, and while being initiated he has to climb a tree or ladder. Using a drum, he conjures up spirits and turns into various animals. Thus some scholars have argued that he is a shaman. He is believed to have an animal as one of his parents, and is often mentally disturbed.[10]

Another Hungarian researcher, the folklorist Tekla Dömötör, has produced a number of studies of Hungarian folk customs, as videnced from the Middle Ages to today. One of her books, which appeared in 1977, mentions medieval documents which refer in particular to a variety of games involving horses, along with the sacrificing of a white horse. Horse bones have been found in graves dating from the Hungarians' conquest of their present territory, along with swords. Even in the twentieth century the Hungarians have continued the Inner Eurasian tradition of providing a dead young bachelor or maiden with a bride or groom in a ceremonial wedding. The singing of dirges has also survived, with relatives recounting the merits of the deceased. In the Middle Ages this would be done in the first person in the case of a leading warrior, who would be made to recount his heroic exploits.[11]

A linguist based in California, Otto Sadovszky, has produced a number of studies arguing for a relationship between Ob-Ugrian languages and the Californian Penutian language family. In 1989 he published an article on religious terms, such as the words for 'shaman', 'healing' and 'praying', suggesting that the terms in both language families are related. Sadovszky also points out that both Ob-Ugrian and Penutian speakers talk of the drumming sound made by the grouse in its mating season, when it dances as if possessed. Ob-Ugrian hunters are fond of depicting a dancing grouse on the backs of their hands (where Californian Indians also have tattoos). Sadovsky further notes that among Penutian speakers the shamans use angelica root for magical purposes, and this root is also important in Ob-Ugrian myth, in which a she-bear becomes pregnant after eating it and gives birth to human ancestors.[12]

Finnic religion

The term 'Finnic' is used to designate all the Finns, including the Lapps and the Estonians, whereas 'Finnish' is used to designate the Finns of Finland. Literary sources refer to Finnic shamans as early as 1071 CE, when a Russian chronicle speaks of a shaman's 'lying dumb' on the ground while invoking spirits. From the thirteenth century we hear of the prodigious feats performed by the shamans of the Lapps in divination and healing. Norwegian merchants tell of a shaman who uses a drum resembling a sieve, on which is portrayed a whale. The shaman turns into a whale to

cross a lake and rescue the soul of someone who has apparentl
died. Medieval sources also relate that Finnic shamans knew wha
was happening at the same time in distant places.[13]

In 1551 the Finnish bishop Michael Agricola compiled lists o
his country's indigenous gods. These fall naturally into a tripar
tite schema: [1] at the top are gods of the heavens and the weather
[2] in the middle are gods of the forest and water, who provide
game and fish; [3] at the bottom are gods of the crops.[14] This
schema, we may remark, contains both the Inner Eurasian triad
sky–intervening space–earth and the Indo-European triad religious
sovereignty–forceful activity (here hunting and fishing)–fertility.
In 1672 the Swedish traveller Johannes Scheffer provides more
information about the Lapp shamans: they are famous, he says,
for their ability to stop a ship in its course. The Lapps, according
to Scheffer, use angelica as a panacea.[15]

Twentieth-century scholars have added more important evidence. The Estonian researcher Ivar Paulson (1922–66) rightly
pointed to the religious significance of his country's sauna, used
for consecration, healing of all sorts of sicknesses and life cycle
rituals. A sauna was personified and seen as vouchsafing strength
through its steam. It had its own spirits and was thought to be
visited by those of famous Christian figures.[16] The Finnish folklorist Anna-Leena Siikala has examined Finland's prehistoric rock
paintings, which date from c.3000 to c.100 BCE. In this connection she has echoed the widespread scepticism expressed about
'shamanistic' interpretations of Palaeolithic art. However, she
thinks that the Finnish rock paintings which depict elks may have
shown the sacred abode of a spirit-keeper of this animal: hunting
elks on skis is a very early form of hunting in Finland, and is found
in a Finnish version of the Greek myth of Orion, a hunter who
incurred divine anger and was turned into a constellation. Siikala
takes the view that Finnish rock paintings depicting humans with
horns or owl masks may represent shamanizing. She also thinks
that representations of a fish, a snake, a bear and birds and lizards undoubtedly show the shaman's spirits, since these are the
most common spirit-helpers of northern Eurasian shamans.[17]

The *Kalevala*: a reinterpretation

The name of the Finnish national epic, the *Kalevala*, means 'the land of a gigantic ancestor called Kaleva'. In the epic this land is identified with Finland itself. It was compiled by Elias Lönnrot, a district health officer who later became a university professor. He published a first version in 1835 and an expanded edition, the one familiar today and examined here, in 1849. Lönnrot took considerable liberties with his materials as he combined folk poems into a connected narrative. He would adapt poems, add lines of his own and attribute the exploits of one hero to another.

Cantos 1–10 of the *Kalevala* are dominated by a shaman called Väinämöinen, the main hero of the epic, whose mother gives birth to him after being made pregnant by the wind (Canto 1). As an old man Väinämöinen cuts down trees in order to sow barley, but leaves one birch tree standing for birds to perch on (2). He is approached by a young rival shaman, who challenges him to a singing contest: Väinämöinen 'sings' him into the ground, so that he is obliged to offer his sister to the old man (3). However, when Väinämöinen goes to collect her she drowns herself (4). He catches her in the form of a salmon, but she disappears (5). Väinämöinen, in search of a new bride, rides to the North (Lapland) on a mysterious mount, variously described as a 'stallion of straw' and a 'blue elk', but his young rival shoots this from under him, so that he falls into the sea (6). An eagle carries Väinämöinen to the north, where he encounters the Mistress of Northland. She offers him her daughter in exchange for his forging the mysterious Sampo, an object which will guarantee fertility. Väinämöinen cannot do this, but says that he will go home and send a smith called Ilmarinen (7). On his way home he meets a maiden and proposes marriage to her. She sets him tasks in a threefold sequence: first, splitting a hair and pulling an egg into a knot; second, peeling a stone and cutting ice without bits falling off; third, carving a boat out of a spindle. Väinämöinen clears the first two hurdles, but then cuts himself badly and has to rush off and find an old man who can heal him (8). He gives the old man his own knowledge of iron's origin, and this knowledge enables the wound, caused by iron, to be healed (9). Arriving in his homeland, he 'sings' a magic tree into existence, persuades Ilmarinen to climb it and

makes the wind take him to the North. There Ilmarinen forge
the Sampo, which is given three 'roots', in the earth, a river banl
and a mountain (10).[18] (Here we see the familiar Inner Eurasiar
pattern of [1] mountain, [2] river and [3] earth: the root in the
mountain is paralleled in the Evenk shaman's tent, where the inverted larches' roots symbolize the idea of a tree's having its roots
in the sky.)

In Cantos 11–15 a rogue, Lemminkäinen, is involved in various exploits. He seduces a lot of maidens and then abducts one,
who agrees to marry him (11). Then Lemminkäinen goes to
Northland and 'sings' all the men into humiliating defeat, with
the exception of an old herdsman, whom he accuses of raping his
own sister and having intercourse with horses (12). After this the
rogue asks the Mistress of Northland for her daughter, but is told
that to qualify he must hunt the Demon's elk on skis (13). (This is
the first of three tests, in the Inner Eurasian pattern of [1] mountain, [2] space between sky and earth and [3] space extending
from the earth's surface downwards.) He catches the elk after ski-
ing in the mountains [1], and is then informed that he must also
bridle the Demon's horse, which he sees beneath the sun in the
east [2]. After succeeding in this second task Lemminkäinen is
required to shoot the swan of Tuonela (the underworld land of
the dead) [3]. When he goes to do this he is killed and cut into
pieces by the old herdsman whom he has insulted (14).
Lemminkäinen's mother searches for him frantically, and eventually drags the pieces of his body out of the river of Tuonela and
sews them together. She sends a bee to get honey, in three journeys (in the Inner Eurasian pattern [1] sky, [2] sea and [3] earth).
The bee has to fetch honey first from flowers and grasses [3],
then from a cabin on an island in the sea [2], and finally from
heaven [1]. With the help of the honey Lemminkäinen is brought
back to life (15). (Scholars have shown that this story has come,
via the Byzantine Empire, from Egypt: it is a version of the famous
myth in which Osiris is killed and dismembered by Seth before
being found, reconstituted and revived by Isis. In the materials
available to Lönnrot, Lemminkäinen's killer is Väinämöinen, who
as a perpetual bachelor is a figure of irregular sexuality, like Seth,
who is a bisexual rapist.)[19]

After this Cantos 16–25 take us back to Väinämöinen. The old

haman has himself ferried across Tuonela's river in order to en-
er the land of the dead and obtain spells for making a boat, but
returns after failing to get them (16). Still in search of these spells,
Väinämöinen visits the grave of another shaman and is swallowed
up by him. After causing a lot of trouble inside his predecessor's
belly he learns the spells and comes out of his mouth (17).
Väinämöinen finishes his boat and sails off to woo the Mistress of
Northland's daughter, but she prefers to marry Ilmarinen (18).
The latter is made to perform three tasks (in the Inner Eurasian
pattern [1] sky, [2] river and [3] earth): ploughing a field full of
vipers [3], capturing a bear and a wolf, which he does by forging
a metal bridle in a river [2], and catching a pike – this last task he
performs by flying on the back of an eagle through the sky [1]
(19). In the preparation for the ensuing wedding feast we are
told of the origins of beer: its ingredients were fetched from three
places (which again form an Inner Eurasian pattern): a tree top,
in the sky [1], a bear's underground cave [3] and an island in the
sea [2] (20). At the feast itself Väinämöinen sings, evoking God's
use of song to produce fertility (21). The women sing of the mis-
ery endured by a wife in another family's house (22). Advice is
given to the bride: she must work hard and respect the holy row-
ans in the yard, the berries of which will teach her to please her
husband (23). The bridegroom is advised to counsel and instruct
his wife, and, if she takes no notice, to whip her on the shoulders
and buttocks: beating her will make her affectionate (24).
Ilmarinen brings his bride to his home, and Väinämöinen, after
singing at the welcoming ceremony there, breaks his sleigh and
has to go to Tuonela to bring a spike and a drill for making a new
one (25).[20]

In Cantos 26–30 Lemminkäinen is again the principal character. Angry at not being invited to the wedding feast, he decides to
go to it nonetheless. His mother warns him that on the way he will
encounter three obstacles (in the Inner Eurasian pattern of [1]
sky, [2] space between sky and earth and [3] earth): first an eagle
[1]; then a fiery ravine [2] and thirdly a wolf and a bear, blocking
the gateway into Northland [3]. In Northland itself he will find
an array of snakes, and in the Master of Northland's cabin men
will 'sing' him on to their swords. Lemminkäinen, using magic,
prayers and force, gets past the obstacles and enters the cabin

(26). Inside he quarrels with the Master, and they engage in
contest of shamanic 'singing', producing animals which attac
each other. Then they fight with swords and Lemminkäinen kil
the Master (27). Turning into an eagle, he flies home, where he i
told by his mother to go and hide on an island (28). On this i:
land he 'sings' riches into existence and seduces almost all th
women. Sailing homewards, he is shipwrecked and given a nev
boat by a kind-hearted woman. When he returns to his home h
finds that the people of Northland have destroyed it (29)
Lemminkäinen sets off by boat to wreak revenge, but the Mistress
of Northland immobilizes his boat by sending the frost to freeze
the sea (30).[21]

Cantos 31–6 present a fresh cycle. An eagle snatches up three
swan chicks, takes one to Russia, where it becomes a merchant,
brings one to the east of Finland, where it grows up to be a man
called Kalervo, and leaves one at home, where it grows up to be a
man called Untamo. Untamo massacres most of Kalervo's family,
but a son of his, called Kullervo, is born shortly afterwards and
shows abnormal strength from the cradle. Untamo tries in vain to
drown, incinerate and hang him. Kullervo proves to be a useless
serf, killing a child and ruining trees, a fence and rye, and Untamo
sells him to Ilmarinen (31). Ilmarinen's wife sends Kullervo out
to pasture her cows and recites verses to protect them, notably
from the bear (32). Kullervo, finding that she has put a stone in
his bread, kills the cows, makes wolves and bears take their place,
and murders her (33). Then, learning that his parents are still
alive, he goes to live with them (34). Travelling as a tax collector,
he forces a maiden into his sleigh. When she sees how much money
he has she willingly has intercourse with him, but then learns that
he is her brother and drowns herself (35). Kullervo goes on to
massacre Untamo's family, but comes home to find his own family dead. By chance he comes to the place where he has committed
incest, and there his sword wants to punish him: he kills himself
with it (36). (In order to understand the story of Kullervo it is
necessary to examine the Estonian national epic, which is analysed below.)[22]

In Cantos 37–8 we return to the bereaved Ilmarinen. He makes
himself a new bride out of gold, but, dissatisfied, offers her to
Väinämöinen, who rejects her and tells people not to bow down

ɔ gold because of its chilliness (37). Ilmarinen then forces the
꜀istress of Northland's other daughter into his sleigh, determined
ɔ marry her. She, in a typically Inner Eurasian pattern, threatens
ɔ turn herself into a fish in the sea [2], a stoat in a rock hole [3],
ɔr a lark in the sky [1]. Eventually Ilmarinen 'sings' her into a sea
ฐull (38).[23]

Cantos 39–49 give us the theft of the mysterious Sampo.
Väinämöinen, Ilmarinen and Lemminkäinen sail off to commit
the theft (39). Their boat gets stuck on the back of a huge pike,
which Väinämöinen kills before using its bones to make the Finnish national stringed instrument, the *kantele* (40). He plays it, and
animals, birds and fish come to listen (41). The trio reach
Northland, and Väinämöinen puts the people there to sleep.
Lemminkäinen uses an ox to plough the Sampo's roots, and the
thieves take it homewards, but the Mistress of Northland wakes
up and uses prayers to stop their boat (42). Turning into an eagle, she alights on the boat's mast and drops the Sampo into the
sea, from which its pieces come to give Finland fertility (43).
Väinämöinen, having lost his *kantele*, makes a new one out of birch
(44). The Mistress now puts Väinämöinen to three tests, in what
seems to be an Indo–European pattern, involving in turn [3]
medicine (an aspect of fertility), [2] strength and [1] religious
sovereignty. First she sends plagues (to which a woman of Tuonela
gives birth) to Finland, but Väinämöinen counters them by pre-
paring a sauna and inviting God into the steam (45). Secondly,
the Mistress sends a bear to attack Finland's livestock, but
Väinämöinen kills it and his people eat it with typical northern
Eurasian rituals. The hero sings of the bear's being born on the
Great Bear's shoulders, and denies having killed him (46). In a
third test the Mistress robs Finland of the sun, moon and fire, but
God sends fire down to a lake, where it is swallowed by a pike
(47). Väinämöinen catches the pike and restores fire to Finland
(48). Ilmarinen makes a moon out of gold and a sun out of silver
and puts them on two tree tops, but they fail to shine.
Väinämöinen, practising divination with slivers of alder, locates
the sun and moon in Northland and goes to rescue them with
such terrifying force that the Mistress has to let them go (49).[24]

Finally, in the last Canto we are given the birth of Jesus, after
his virgin mother has been made pregnant by eating a bilberry.

Väinämöinen, mocked by the newborn Jesus, sails off, vowing to return (50).[25]

Now we can see how Lönnrot has organized his materials into a superbly well structured work of literature. In Cantos 1 and 50 he has framed his epic with the Inner Eurasian theme of a heavenly-granted miraculous birth. The epic itself is based on the pattern of the triple testing of a hero. In Cantos 2–10 we see a man who is unmarried when old, Väinämöinen, try unsuccessfully to find a bride: he fails the third test. Cantos 11–15 show Lemminkäinen also trying in vain to obtain a wife and failing the last of the three tests (here in an Inner Eurasian pattern). In Cantos 16–25 Väinämöinen renews his unsuccessful wooing, while Ilmarinen passes the three tests (again in an Inner Eurasian structure) and succeeds. Cantos 26–30 present Lemminkäinen overcoming the triple testing (yet again in an Inner Eurasian configuration) and killing the Master of Northland, a sin which produces revenge. In Cantos 31–6 Kullervo commits more sins, which in the parallel Estonian version, as we shall see, constitute the 'three sins of the warrior', a well-known Indo-European triad sometimes put in parallel with the 'three tests of the warrior'.[26] Again, retribution ensues. Cantos 39–44 narrate another sin, the theft of an object which guarantees fertility. (Here scholars compare Norse legends which belong to an older Indo-European tradition involving the theft of a drink or cauldron which grants immortality. I should like to point to the parallel with the biblical story of the theft of the Ark of the Covenant.[27]) This sin also produces retribution, in the three new tests (now in an Indo-European pattern) imposed on Väinämöinen in Cantos 45–9.

The Estonian national epic

The Estonian national epic is called the *Kalevipoeg*, 'The Son of Kalev'. It was put together in the nineteenth century, in imitation of the Kalevala, by the Estonian scholar Friedrich Kreutzwald (1803–82), who published his work from 1857 to 1861. The epic's hero is clearly identical with the *Kalevala*'s Kullervo. Cantos 1–3 of the *Kalevipoeg* present the hero's parents. Three brothers leave the North in three different directions. (They do this in a clearly Indo-European triconceptual pattern, as in other epics in ndo-European languages.[28]) One brother goes to Russia and becomes a merchant [3]; one goes to Lapland and becomes a warrior [2]; the third, Kalev, is carried to Estonia by an eagle and becomes a king [1]. Kalev marries a maiden called Linda (Canto 1). They have several children, but Kalev foretells that his youngest son, Sohni, as yet unborn, will succeed him. Then Kalev dies, and Linda gives birth to Sohni, who is exceptionally strong from the cradle (2). A sorcerer tries to abduct Linda, but the gods turn her into a rock (3).[29]

In Cantos 4–6 Sohni commits the 'three sins of the warrior', sinning in turn against the three main Indo-European concepts, fertility, in its sexual aspect [3], religion [1] and the warrior's ethic [2]. He rapes a maiden [3], who, on learning his identity, is seized with terror and falls into the sea where she disappears (she is Sohni's sister) (4). Then he murders the sorcerer who had tried to abduct his mother, and now begs for mercy (as he is a religious specialist this is a crime against religion [1])(5). Finally he murders a young man in a quarrel, cutting his head off with a great sword without granting him a fair fight [2](6).[30]

Cantos 7–19 present Sohni's adventures. To begin with, he undergoes the 'three tests of the warrior', in an Indo-European pattern and in the 'canonical' order of the three main concepts, [1] sovereignty, [2] warlike force and [3] fertility (the last being represented by maidens in the underworld). First, he agrees with two of his brothers, who have stayed at home, to undergo a test to decide who will be king (7). Sohni succeeds in this test, a stone throwing competition (8). Secondly, he is tested by a war, when Estonia is attacked by a foreign army (9–10). His great sword is stolen by a second sorcerer, who drops it in a brook. Sohni, ambiguously, tells the sword that if the man who brought it there comes back it is to cut his legs off (11). Subsequently the sorcerer puts him into a deep sleep for seven weeks (12). After this, in his third test, Sohni visits the underworld where he meets three imprisoned maidens (13). He defeats the Lord of the Underworld and takes the maidens with him on his homeward journey (14). They marry relatives of Sohni (15). Sohni himself now sails on a great voyage to the far North (16). On his return he defeats Estonia's enemies (17). Then he revisits the underworld, where he meets his mother, and again defeats its Lord (18–19). Finally, after

more victories over invaders of his kingdom, Sohni abdicates. H
absent-mindedly returns to the brook where his great sword lie
and it decides to take vengeance for the murder of the youn
man in the quarrel. The sword mortally wounds Sohni, but on
day he will return (20).[31]

Thus the Estonian national epic gives us the 'three sins', bring
ing retribution, and the 'three tests'. It also gives us Inner Eurasian
motifs: the seven-week sleep of the hero seems to represent the
hibernation of the bear, and the visits to the underworld are echoed in Turkic epics. One will naturally compare the sleeping of
Odysseus on his homeward journey and his subterranean meeting with his mother.[32]

The Inner Eurasian heritage and world literature

These comparisons lead us to ask in more general terms how great
the indebtedness of world literature to Inner Eurasia may be. One
problem is that the idea of an underworld as the realm of the
dead is clearly a late addition to Inner Eurasian religions, coming
from the great 'historical' religions in the south, at some time or
times in the Middle Ages. Originally, the Inner Eurasian peoples
believed that the dead went to Heaven or some realm located at a
considerable distance, in some unknown region, but not beneath
the earth. However, Inner Eurasian narratives often appear to have
anticipated European stories about a subterranean realm of the
dead, either by placing this realm elsewhere or by having a hero
go beneath the earth's surface in various ways: entering a cave
(like a bear), a pit, a dungeon or indeed a tomb or complex of
tombs in a cemetery.[33]

In this perspective the *Odyssey* takes on more Inner Eurasian
tones. It would appear that the folk tale on which it is based came
from Central Asian Turkic nomads after about 3000 BCE, when
the reflex bow (of the type strung by Odysseus and the Turkic
hero Alpamysh) was invented by them. After that it probably went
through Indo-European or Indo-Iranian intermediaries to the
Greeks and the Indians.[34] When the folk tale reached the Greeks
it was apparently attached to a typically Inner Eurasian 'bear's
son' hero, Odysseus, who represents the barbarian, Thracian tradition to the north of Greece and its cult of the sleeping bear. For

non-Homeric data concerning Odysseus show him as coming from a Thracian enclave and surrounded by relatives with names meaning 'bearish' or 'bear cub'. Odysseus, we are told, became very sleepy in his old age, like the Samoyed's ancestor Itte, whose son is called the 'bear spirit'.[35] In this context Odysseus' shaman-like journey to the realm of the dead in order to obtain advice from the dead seer Teiresias seems more explicable.

The Inner Eurasian pattern of levels, [1] sky (or mountain top), [2] intermediate space and [3] earth's surface (with what lies below) is, as we have seen, bound up with the 'three tasks'. Now this patterning emerges in the temptations of Zarathushtra, the legendary or semi-legendary founder of Iran's national religion, Mazdaism, and of Jesus. In an Iranian text of the period stretching from the fourth century BCE to the early third century CE, Zarathushtra's spirit, before he is born, has a meeting with the Devil.

First, there is a confrontation on the Inner Eurasian level 3: Zarathushtra is asked why he is carrying huge stones across the surface of the earth. He replies that he is aiming to destroy the Devil's creatures (snakes, scorpions etc., as injurious to agriculture). Secondly, evoking the Indo-European concept 1, religious sovereignty, the Devil asks Zarathushtra to renounce his religion and be rewarded with lordship over the world. He refuses. Thirdly, evoking the Indo-European concept 2, warlike force, the Devil demands to know what weapon Zarathushtra will use to fight him. Zarathushtra replies that his weapons are the objects used in sacrifice and a prayer which has been created by the archangels.[36]

This order is also that found in Luke's account of Jesus' testing by the Devil. There, on level 3, stones on the surface of the earth are designated by the Devil as suitable for transformation into bread. Then, on level 1, the summit of a high mountain, the Devil calls on Jesus to worship him and be rewarded with sovereignty. Finally, on level 2, the Devil takes him to the pinnacle of the Temple, and presents a test of force: Jesus can be saved from physical destruction, he suggests, by the strength of the angels. The Gospel story, I suggest, has an Iranian and Inner Eurasian origin.[37]

The triple testing of the hero reappears in *Beowulf*, the Old English epic thought to have been composed in the eighth century CE. Here scholars have long argued that the epic is a version

of a widespread folk tale, labelled 'The Bear's Son'. The very name
of the poem's hero means 'Bee-Wolf', a euphemism for the bear
employed to avoid breaking the taboo on mentioning it.[38] It seems
to me, however, that what is most significant is the tripartite pattern of Beowulf's tests, which are located in a typically Inner
Eurasian structure. First, on level 2, he fights and mortally wounds
a strong monster in human form, in an imposing hall which fills
the space between sky and earth. Secondly, on level 3, he descends
into an underground cave to kill the same monster's mother.
Thirdly, on level 1, he kills a supernatural creature, a dragon which
occupies a raised position corresponding to a mountain top: on
'an upland heath', upon the top of a barrow.[39] However, the
patterning is also Indo-European, resembling the tripartition
found in the twelve labours of the Greek hero Heracles: [1] four
labours involving supernatural animals, symbolizing religion; [2]
four labours of pure force, and [3] four labours involving female
opponents and other symbols of fertility.[40]

A further example of Inner Eurasian influences on world literature has been found in the motif of the author's journey to
heaven, hell or both. Here we have already noted a Samoyed shaman's account of his initiatory journey beneath the earth's surface
in the company of his instructor: this account, Popov says, is typical of Siberian shamans' stories. Other scholars have argued that
'Uralic' or 'Finno-Ugric' shamans would have transmitted their
practices to the Indo-Iranians in their original Inner Eurasian
homeland, and have pointed to Iranian texts of the period stretching from the third century CE to the seventh, in which Mazdean
priests go on visits to heaven and hell. After taking a psychotropic
drug these priests go into a trance, and their souls leave their
bodies, fly to paradise and the underworld, and then return: on
regaining consciousness the priests describe their journeys. It has
been noted that these accounts have been reflected in medieval
Islamic narratives, as well as in the Divine Comedy (in which Islamic influences have been discerned).[41]

The Inner Eurasian religious heritage's defining characteristics

The defining characteristics of the Inner Eurasian heritage have
now become familiar to us. An emphasis on the opposition

etween summer and winter has been noted among early Inner
Eurasian peoples and in the Turkic domain: it is to be expected,
given the enormous variations in temperature in Inner Eurasia,
and is reflected in the Mongols' division of animals into 'cold-
muzzled' and 'warm-muzzled'.[42] Hunting rituals are prominent,
with humans taking on the characteristics of animals, as they do
in warfare. Horses are buried together with humans in royal graves,
which must be kept hidden, and after funerals purification has to
be made with fire and smoke. Dead enemies are scalped, or their
skulls are turned into cups, and they themselves are made to serve
the warriors who have killed them in the hereafter.

Central above all is the figure of the animal. When sacrificed
its blood, like that of a noble, must not be shed. Animals turn into
humans, have intercourse with them and become their ancestors.
It is necessary to ensure the continuity of animal as well as human
life: sometimes humans have to be eaten by animals, and sometimes humans have to refrain from killing them. In return, animals
grant, above all, guidance: they lead humans on their migrations,
and by being observed they grant vast amounts of knowledge.
Animals rescue humans and are their heraldic emblems and
totems.

The importance of animals is demonstrated in humans' need-
ing to turn into them in order to fly into the sky, move rapidly
through the world or descend beneath the earth's surface. Eagles
are necessary to reach Heaven, as the home of the ancestors, the
recipient of sacrifices and the supreme god. Heaven itself is reflected in groupings of animals or birds in sevens and nines,
corresponding to the number of visible planets. The sky is also
reflected in triads of birds, fish and burrowing animals, corresponding to heaven, sea and earth, or triads incorporating humans
(e.g. bird–rat–Genghis).

This tripartite vision of the universe provides the registers in
which the shaman displays his artistry. In his life the shaman, alongside his 'becoming-bird', 'becoming-fish' and 'becoming-animal',
may also engage in a 'becoming-woman', as among the Scythian
feminized diviners, the Turkic transvestite shamans of the twentieth century and the homosexual Mongol ones of the thirteenth.
Eventually, in what is evidently a highly developed form of
shamanic activity, the Tunguz shaman turns his spirits into invisible

barriers of spirit-watchmen: as Deleuze and Guattari have remarked, phenomena such as 'becoming-animal' and
'becoming-woman' tend towards a 'becoming-imperceptible'. The
shaman camouflages himself in all the aspects of nature in order
to defend his clan, and himself advances, invisibly, in the form of
his spirits, to attack others. Thus the shaman, as we have seen also
among the Mongols, is a warrior, a possessor of military secrets.[43]

The Inner Eurasian religious heritage in comparative perspective

Other distinctive elements of the Inner Eurasian religious heritage appear more clearly in a comparative perspective. We have
seen throughout that this heritage is closely bound up with the
Indo-European one: the Inner Eurasian triad of sky, intermediate
space and earth often merges into the Indo-European triad of
religious sovereignty, force and fertility. Here the Turkic materials show most clearly the difference between the two heritages. In
Inner Eurasia mountain tops and tree tops are typically used to
represent heaven and religious sovereignty. Mountain slopes are
the area of forceful activity, in particular hunting, which in Inner
Eurasia constitutes work, whereas in the Indo-European domain
it belongs to pleasure, part of concept 3, fertility. Rivers in Inner
Eurasia charge violently down mountain slopes, and thus symbolize force, whereas among Indo-European speakers they usually
flow along peacefully, making the soil fertile. In Inner Eurasia
fishing, like hunting, is part of work.

Here the Samoyed Djaruoskin is particularly instructive. He
sees a Tunguz tent with red stuff on its top, which will cure madness caused by headaches: this reflects the Indo-European concept
1, which includes reason and madness and corresponds to the
head. Below this is a rope, which will counter epidemics: doubtless this reflects the Inner Eurasian view of epidemics as biological
warfare conducted by enemies – an adaptation of the Indo-European concept 2, warlike force. Further down, round the middle
of the tent, is a black rope, which heals diseases of the stomach,
corresponding to the Indo-European concept 3, fertility as embodied in food consumption. The schema is Indo-European, but
given a particularly Inner Eurasian slant by the symbolism of the
tent and the shaman's activity.

While it is often difficult to distinguish the Inner Eurasian heritage from the Indo-European, it is easy to spot the differences which separate both from the Afroasiatic inheritance, found among Afroasiatic-speakers in the region stretching from Iraq and Arabia to Nigeria, and including the Horn of Africa, North Africa, Egypt and Syria. Here sacrifices are not bloodless but bloody. As opposed to tripartition, everything is dualistic. Although, to be sure, we have found some dualism in the Inner Eurasian domain, it is usually limited to the opposition between cold winters and hot summers, and when it is more extensive, in Onon's presentation of Daur thought or among the Jurchens, this may well be the result of Chinese influence. In the Afroasiatic field a male–female dualism is overwhelming, symbolizing the union of the forces of nature for the successful pursuit of agriculture. Thus water and fertility are all-important, especially given the precariousness of the water supply: the opposition of the dry and the wet is echoed by that of the light and the dark.[44]

On the other hand, there are marked similarities between Inner Eurasian shamans and African healers. An African 'seeress' will, like her Manchu counterpart, inhale incense and go into a light trance in order to learn from the spirits what has happened, before giving advice to her client; further trances will grant prophecies and healing. Initiation into a spirit-possession cult takes place when a candidate is ill (as often with Inner Eurasian shamans), and consists of learning about spirits while inhaling smoke and being given a hallucinogenic drug.[45] These similarities show that there is no such thing as 'shamanism' as opposed to 'spirit-possession': an African 'seeress' is not, as has been claimed, a slave to the spirits as opposed to the shaman's being their master. The term 'shamanism' is the product of a modern illusion about widespread techniques of healing and prophecy: its further abuse to designate the totality of Inner Eurasian religions is even more misleading, since, as we have seen, the shaman is often absent from central religious activities.

What, then, is the legacy of the Inner Eurasian shaman, viewed in a wider perspective? Surely it is in part the legacy of an artist, a performer. We should speak of 'shamanry' or 'shamanship', to indicate a relative command of a craft. In 'becoming-animal' and jangling metal accoutrements the shaman is like a composer,

following a creative line of development. Thus the shaman's legac
is partly found in twentieth-century music. The dark orchestra
tions of Sibelius, so often inspired by the *Kalevala*, echo the evi
spirits that the shamans have fought: the forests are full of hostil
and destructive forces, harsh and threatening gods who symbol
ize dangers that, for Sibelius, have to be confronted. Similarly, in
the work of Bartók, both as ethnomusicologist and composer, we
see a return to the Inner Eurasian past: in finding the original
Inner Eurasian stratum of Hungarian folk music Bartók also discovered the inspiration for his own breaking away from the
servitude of settled existence. This breaking away he expressed in
his *Cantata profana*: nine boys turn into stags and leave home for
the forest and the mountain. When their father begs them to return the eldest explains that now they can drink only from the
mountain's clear springs.[46]

A 'becoming-animal' of this kind is at odds with Christianity's
dogmatic insistence that a human cannot become an animal and
an animal cannot become a human. This insistence has been echoed in the severe penalties which Christianity has prescribed for
the wearing of animal disguises in survivals of earlier religions.
No such dogma is found in Islam, where the Qur'an explicitly
mentions human-into-animal transformations as having taken
place. Thus Islam has easily accepted and adapted the Inner Eurasian motif of the animal as guide, along with legends of humans
who turn into animals and take on their qualities. Consequently
the legacy of the shaman is seen most clearly in the fighting mystical brotherhoods of Islam: there his martial and military functions
have been preserved, along with his secrets and his self-transfor-
mations: from his endless acquisition of the characteristics of
animals the shaman has gone on to the endless acquisition of the
attributes of God.[47]

Notes

Introduction

1. Cf Denis Sinor, 'Introduction', in Denis Sinor (ed.), *The Cambridge History of Early Inner Asia* (Cambridge: Cambridge University Press, 1990), pp. 1–3.
2. Robert N. Taafe, 'The geographic setting', ibid., pp. 19–37.
3. Sinor, 'Introduction', pp. 7–10.
4. A. P. Okladnikov, 'Inner Asia at the dawn of history', ibid., p. 57; A. P. Derevyanko and Lu Zun-E, 'Upper Palaeolithic cultures', in A. H. Dani and V. M. Masson (eds), *History of Civilizations of Central Asia*, vol. 1 (Paris: Unesco Publishing, 1992), pp. 102–3.
5. Okladnikov, 'Inner Asia', pp. 64–6; V. Sarianidi, 'Food-producing and other Neolithic communities in Khorasan and Transoxania: eastern Iran, Soviet Central Asia and Afghanistan', in Dani and Masson (eds), *History*, vol. 1, p. 119.
6. Okladnikov, 'Inner Asia', pp. 66–7 and 87–9; A. Askarov, V. Volkov and N. Ser-Odjav, 'Pastoral and nomadic tribes at the beginning of the first millennium B. C.', in Dani and Masson (eds), *History*, vol. 1, pp. 467–71.
7. A. Abetekov and H. Yusupov, 'Ancient Iranian nomads in western Central Asia', in Janos Harmatta (ed.), *History of Civilizations of Central Asia*, vol. 2, (Paris: Unesco Publishing, 1994), p. 29.
8. N. Ishjamts, 'Nomads in eastern Central Asia', ibid., pp. 164–7.
9. Peter B. Golden, *An Introduction to The History of the Turkic Peoples* (Wiesbaden: Harrassowitz, 1992), p. 18.

10. Denis Sinor and S. G. Klyashtorny, 'The Türk empire', in B. A. Litvinsky (ed.), *History of Civilizations of Central Asia*, vol. 3 (Paris: Unesco Publishing, 1996), p. 331.

11. Golden, *An Introduction*, p. 18.

12. Cf Morris Rossabi, 'The reign of Khubilai Khan', in Herbert Franke and Denis Twitchett (eds), *The Cambridge History of China*, vol. 6 (Cambridge: Cambridge University Press, 1994), p. 463, n. 83.

13. Golden, An Introduction, p. 18.

14. Peter B. Golden, 'The peoples of the Russian forest belt', in Sinor (ed.), *The Cambridge History of China*, pp. 231–2.

15. Cf Julian Baldick, *Homer and the Indo-Europeans: Comparing Mythologies* (London: I. B. Tauris & Co, 1994), pp. 4–6.

16. Ibid., pp. 15–16.

17. Covington S. Littleton, *The New Comparative Mythology* (Berkeley: University of California Press, 1982), pp. 59–60.

Chapter 1: Early Inner Eurasia

1. Herodotus, *Le Storie*, Volume IV: Libro IV, La Scizia e la Libia, ed. Silvio M. Medaglia, tr. Augusto Fraschetti, with introduction and commentary by Aldo Corcella (Vicenza: Arnolo Mondadori, 1993), pp. IX-XXVII and 229–331.

2. Herodotus 4: 5–7.

3. Georges Dumézil (tr.), *Le Livre des Heros: Légendes sur les Nartes* (Paris: Gallimard, 1965), pp. 24–5; Littleton, *The New Comparative Mythology*, pp. 130–2.

4. Herodotus 4: 26; Corcella, 'Commentario', in Herodotus, *Le Storie*, Volume IV, pp. 254–5.

5. Herodotus 4.59.

6. Georges Charachidze, *La Mémoire indo-européenne du Caucase* (Paris: Hachette, 1987), pp. 22 and 48–54.

7. Cf George S. Robertson, *The Kafirs of the Hindu-Kush* (Karachi: Oxford University Press, 1974), pp. 400–1.

8. Herodotus 4: 60–2; Corcella, 'Commentario', pp. 283–5; Robertson, *The Kafirs*, pp. 401–5.

9. Herodotus 4: 64–6; Dumézil (tr.), *Le Livre*, pp. 81–3 and 207–8.

10. Herodotus 4: 67; Corcella, 'Commentario', pp. 287–8.

11. Herodotus 4: 70; Jean-Paul Roux, *La Religion des turcs et des mongols* (Paris: Payot, 1984), p. 228; cf below, pp. 65 and 94.

12. Herodotus 4: 71–2; Roux, *La Religion*, p. 281.

13. Herodotus 4: 73–5; Corcella, 'Commentario', pp. 292–3.

14. Herodotus 4: 93–6; Corcella, 'Commentario', p. 308; Rhys Carpenter, *Folk Tale, Fiction and Saga in the Homeric Epics* (Berkeley: University of California Press, 1946), pp. 112–19.

15. Herodotus 4: 127–32; Stephanie West, 'The Scythian ultimatum (Herodotus iv 131, 132)', *Journal of Hellenic Studies* 108 (1988) 207–11.

16. Philipp Johann von Strahlenberg, *An Historico-geographical Description of the North and Eastern Parts of Europe* (London: J. Brotherton et al., 1738), p. 98.

17. Herodotus 4: 134; Corcella, 'Commentario', pp. 328–9.

18. Roux, *La Religion*, pp. 65–7, 82–3, 104, 110–12, 150, 160, 164, 166 and 175.

19. Jean-Paul Roux, *Faune et flore sacrées dans les sociétés altaïques* (Paris: Adrien-Maisonneuve, 1966), pp. 70, 72, 104, 108, 190, 193, 199, 201–3 and 206.

20. Ibid., pp. 298, 311–18 and 383–4.

21. Roux, *La Religion*, p. 235.

22. Jean-Paul Roux, *La Mort chez les peuples altaïques anciens et médiévaux* (Paris: Adrien-Maisonneuve, 1963, pp. 47–9, 108–9, 170–2, 175 and 182.

23. Wolfram Eberhard, *Kultur und Siedlung der Randvölker Chinas* (Leiden: E. J. Brill, 1942), pp. 47–8.

24. Kao Ch'ü-hsün, 'The Ching lu shen shrines of Han sword worship in Hsiung Nu religion', *Central Asiatic Journal* 5 (1960) 221–32; Otto J. Maenchen-Helfen, *The World of the Huns* (Berkeley: University of California Press, 1973), pp. 280–8.

25. Wolfram Eberhard, *Das Toba-Reich Nordchinas* (Leiden: E. J. Brill, 1949), pp. 356–8; Roux, *La Mort*, pp. 110, 120 and 123–4.

26. Roux, *Faune*, pp. 140 and 268.

27. Maenchen-Helfen, *The World*, pp. 259–70.

28. Ibid., pp. 274–8.

29. Ibid., pp. 278–96.

30. Ibid., pp. 306–30.

31. Roux, *La Religion*, p. 208.

32. Denis Sinor, 'The establishment and dissolution of the Türk empire', in Sinor (ed.), *The Cambridge History*, p. 294; Roux, *La Religion*, p. 122 and *La Mort*, pp. 142 and 166.

33. Aḥmad Ibn 'Umar Ibn Rusta, *Les Atours précieux*, tr. Gaston Wiet

(Cairo: Société de Géographie d'Égypte, 1955), p. 166.

34. Ibid., pp. 165–6.

35. Samuel Szádeczky-Kardoss, 'The Avars', in Sinor (ed.), *The Cam bridge History*, pp. 226–8.

36. Roux, *La Religion*, pp. 143 and 163, *La Mort*, pp. 44, 49, 111, 113–114, 153 and 172 and *Faune*, p. 269; Ibn Faḍlān, *Voyage chez les Bulgares de la Volga*, tr. Marius Canard (Beirut: Éditions de la Méditerranée, 1981), pp. 67–8.

37. Movsês Kağankatouaçi, *The History of the Caucasian Albanians*, tr. Charles J. F. Dowsett (London: Oxford University Press, 1961), pp. 155–65.

38. Roux, *La Religion*, pp. 127 and 164, *Faune*, pp. 72, 200 and 208 and *La Mort*, pp. 61–2 and 170.

39. Rolf Stein, 'Leao-tche', *T'oung Pao* 35 (1940) 70 and 110; Karl Wittfogel and Feng Chia-Sheng, *History of Chinese Society. Liao* (907–1125) (Philadelphia: American Philosophical Society, 1949), pp. 201, 216, 256–8, 268 and 272–3.

40. Stein, 'Leao-tche', pp. 94–104, 127 and 141; Wittfogel and Feng, *History*, p. 271; Roux, *Faune*, p. 209.

41. Stein, 'Leao-tche', pp. 11–13, 20–7, 62 and 88; Wittfogel and Feng, *History*, pp. 238 and 272; cf Baldick, *Homer*, pp. 50–1.

42. Stein, 'Leao-tche', pp. 41–5 and 63–4.

43. Ibid., pp. 69–70; Wittfogel and Feng, *History*, pp. 222, 239, 258, 268 and 273–5.

44. Wittfogel and Feng, *History*, pp. 67, 214 and 219; Édouard Chavannes, 'Voyageurs chinois chez les Khitan et les Joutchen', *Journal Asiatique*, 9th series, 9 (1897) 401–2.

45. Stein, 'Leao-tche', pp. 121–5; Wittfogel and Feng, *History*, p. 269.

46. Herodotus 4. 75.

47. Roux, *La Religion*, p. 104.

48. Gilles Deleuze and Félix Guattari, *Mille Plateaux* (Paris: Éditions de Minuit, 1980), pp. 296–9.

Chapter 2: The Turks

1. Roux, *La Religion*, pp. 66–7; Édouard Chavannes, *Documents sur les Tou-kieue [turcs] occidentaux* (Paris: Adrien-Maisonneuve, 1903), pp. 235 and 248; Joseph de Guignes, *Histoire générale des Huns, des Turcs, et des autres Tartares occidentaux* (Paris: Desaint et Saillant, 1756–

), vol. 1, part 2, p. 386.

2. Roux, *La Religion*, p. 103; Chavannes, *Documents*, p. 248; Talât Tekin, *A Grammar of Orkhon Turkic* (Bloomington: Indiana University, 1968), p. 262.

3. Roux, *La Religion*, pp. 106 and 111–23; Tekin, *A Grammar*, p. 263.

4. Denis Sinor, article 'Umay' in Mircea Eliade (ed.), *The Encyclopedia of Religion* (New York: Macmillan Publishing Company, 1987).

5. Roux, *La Religion*, pp. 138–9, 151 and 158–9, and *Faune*, pp. 52, 60 and 207.

6. Roux, *Faune*, pp. 199, 211, 229, 246–9, 285, 298 and 315–16.

7. Denis Sinor, 'The legendary origin of the Turks', in Egle Victoria Zygas and Peter Voorheis (eds), *Folklorica: Festschrift for Felix J. Oinas* (Bloomington (Indiana): Research Institute for Inner Asian Studies, 1982), pp. 223–53.

8. Roux, *Faune*, pp. 403–6.

9. Roux, *La Mort*, pp. 46–8 and 103–9.

10. Ibid., pp. 120, 123, 140–1, 170, 172, 176 and 182–3; Roux, *La Religion*, pp. 267–8 and 277; Chavannes, *Documents*, p. 241.

11. Sinor, 'The establishment', p. 315.

12. Tang Chi, 'The religious and lay symbolism of the T'u-chüeh as recorded in Chinese history', in Klaus Sagaster (ed.), *Religious and Lay Symbolism in the Altaic World and Other Papers* (Wiesbaden: Harrassowitz, 1989), pp. 395–6.

13. Colin Mackerras, *The Uighur Empire* (Canberra: Australian National University, 1968), pp. 47–51 and 'The Uighurs', in Sinor (ed.), *The Cambridge History*, p. 335.

14. Roux, *La Religion*, pp. 139–40 and 235, *Faune*, pp. 61 and 202 and *La Mort*, pp. 24–5.

15. Roux, *La Mort*, pp. 111 and 176–7; Mackerras, *The Uighur Empire*, pp. 23–6, 33–6 and 117–19.

16. Wilhelm Schmidt, *Der Ursprung der Gottesidee* (Münster: Aschendorff, 1926–55), vol. 9, p. 45; Sinor, 'The establishment', p. 297.

17. Roux, *La Religion*, pp. 65–6, 110–15 and 127–8.

18. Ibid., p. 181; Roux, *Faune*, pp. 98 and 337–8.

19. Roux, *La Religion*, p. 255 and *La Mort*, pp. 108, 143 and 151.

20. Roux, *La Religion*, pp. 184 and 211–12.

21. Ibn Faḍlān, *Voyage*, pp. 18–25.

22. Ibid., pp. 28–30.

23. Roux, *La Religion*, pp. 31–2, 88–9 and 123; Vilhelm Thomse 'Dr. M. A. Stein's manuscripts in Turkish "runic" script from Mirz and Tun-huang', *Journal of the Royal Asiatic Society* (1912) 199, 2(and 205; Talât Tekin (ed. and tr.), *Irk bitig* (Wiesbaden: Harrassowit 1993), pp. 8–13.

24. Roux, *La Religion*, p. 217, *Faune*, p. 177 and *La Mort*, p. 9(Thomsen, 'Dr. M. A. Stein's manuscripts', pp. 190–214; Tekin (ed.) *Irk bitig*, pp. 7–27.

25. E. C. Sachau (tr.), *Alberuni's India* (London: Kegan Paul, 1910) vol. 2, p. 10.

26. Ibn Sīnā (Avicenna), *Livre de directives et remarques*, tr. Anne-Mari(Goichon (Paris: J. Vrin, 1951), p. 517.

27. 'Abd al-Ḥayy Gardīzī, *Tārīkh-i Gardīzī*, ed. 'Abd al-Ḥayy Ḥabīb' (Tehrān: Chāpkhāna-yi Armaghān, 1363–1984), pp. 256 and 260–3.

28. Roux, *La Religion*, pp. 68 and 95; Maḥmūd Kāshgharī, *Compen- dium of the Turkic Dialects*, tr. Robert Dankoff, Duxbury (Mass.): Harvard University Printing Office, 1982–85, part 1, pp. 213 and 236 and part 2, pp. 229 and 377; Robert Dankoff, 'Kašǧarī on the beliefs and superstitions of the Turks', *Journal of the American Oriental Society* 95 (1975)77.

29. Roux, *La Religion*, pp. 117, 121–2, 136–7 and 148; Kāshgharī, *Compendium*, part 1, p. 148 and part 2, pp. 343 and 350; Dankoff, 'Kašǧarī', pp. 72–3.

30. Roux, *Faune*, pp. 121–4 and 266; Kāshgharī, *Compendium*, part 1, pp. 107 and 269; Dankoff, 'Kašǧarī', p. 79.

31. Roux, *La Mort*, pp. 44 and 98 and *La Religion*, p. 271; Kāshgharī, *Compendium*, part 2, p. 172; Dankoff, 'Kašǧarī', pp. 71–2.

32. Abū Ḥamīd Muḥammad al-Ghazālī, *Mishkāt al-anwār*, tr. W. H. T. Gairdner (London: Royal Asiatic Society, 1924), p. 92; Julian Baldick, *Mystical Islam* (London: I. B. Tauris & Co Ltd, 1989), p. 21.

33. Michael the Syrian, *Chronique*, in *Recueil des historiens des croisades: Historiens orientaux* (Paris: Imprimerie Nationale, 1872–6), pp. 314–15; Roux, *La Religion*, pp. 85–6; *Itinerario di la gran militia, a la pavese*, in *Recueil des historiens des croisades: Historiens occidentaux*, vol. 5, ed. and tr. Paul Riant (Paris: Imprimerie Nationale, 1895, p. 659).

34. Denis Sinor, 'John of Plano Carpini's return from the Mon- gols', *Journal of the Royal Asiatic Society* (1957) 203–4; Jehan, seigneur de Joinville, *Vie de Saint Louis*, ed. Noel L. Corbett (Sherbrooke (Que- bec): Éditions Naaman, 1977), pp. 186–7.

35. Peter Jackson and David Morgan (trs), *The Mission of Friar William of Rubruck* (London: Hakluyt Society, 1990), pp. 95–6; Roux, *La Religion*, pp. 278–9.

36. Roux, *La Religion*, pp. 83, 102, 161 and 257–8 and *Faune*, pp. 26 and 57; Kaare Grønbech, *Komanisches Wörterbuch: Türkischer Wortindex zu Codex Cumanicus* (Copenhagen: Einar Munksgaard, 1942), pp. 141, 186, 191–2, 233, 257–8 and 262–3.

37. 'Alā' al-Dīn 'Aṭā Malik ibn Muḥammad Juwaynī, *The History of the World-conqueror*, tr. John A. Boyle (Manchester: Manchester University Press, 1958), vol. 1, pp. 55–7.

38. Roux, *La Religion*, pp. 196–7; Ronald E. Latham (tr.), *The Travels of Marco Polo* (Harmondsworth: Penguin Books, 1958), p. 89.

39. Juwaynī, *The History*, vol. 1, pp. 57–61.

40. Roux, *La Religion*, pp. 232–3.

41. Ibid., pp. 70–1.

42. Ibid., pp. 144–5.

43. W. Bang and G. R. Rachmati (eds and trs), 'Die Legende von Oghuz Qaghan', *Sitzungsberichte der Preussischen Akademie der Wissenschaften*, Phil.-Hist. Klasse 25 (1932) 683–724, lines 1–8; Paul Pelliot, 'Sur la légende d'Ughuz-khan en écriture ouigoure', *T'oung Pao* 27 (1930) 254–5.

44. Bang and Rachmati (eds and trs), 'Die Legende', lines 19–88.

45. Ibid., lines 89–309.

46. Ibid., lines 310–76.

47. Geoffrey Lewis (tr.), *The Book of Dede Korkut* (Harmondsworth: Penguin Books, 1974), p. 12; Baldick, *Homer*, pp. 15, 27, 30 and 32.

48. Lewis (tr.), *The Book of Dede Korkut*, pp. 60–87 and 202, n. 58; Faruk Sümer, Ahmet E. Uysal and Warren S. Walker (trs), *The Book of Dede Korkut* (Austin: University of Texas Press, 1972), pp. 40–69 and 193–4, n. 49.

49. Lewis (tr.), *The Book of Dede Korkut*, pp. 108–16 and 203–4, n. 73; Sümer, Uysal and Walker (trs.), *The Book of Dede Korkut*, pp. 89–97 and 196, n. 5.

50. Lewis (tr.), *The Book of Dede Korkut*, pp. 117–32.

51. Ibid., pp. 133–9.

52. Ibid., pp. 140–50; Baldick, *Homer*, p. 117.

53. Lewis (tr.), *The Book of Dede Korkut*, pp. 171–9, 208, n. 125 and 210, n. 135 and n. 137.

54. Hamilton A. R. Gibb et al. (eds), *The Encyclopaedia of Islam*, second edition (Leiden: E. J. Brill, 1960–), article 'Abū Muslim'; Irène Mélikoff, *Abū Muslim* (Paris: Adrien Maisonneuve, 1962), pp. 25–7

and 45–83.

55. Mélikoff, *Abū Muslim*, p. 97.

56. Julian Baldick, 'The Iranian origin of the *futuwwa*', *Institut Universitario Orientale, Napoli, Annali* 50 (1990) 345–61 and *Mystical Islam*, pp. 91–2; Henry Corbin, *En Islam iranien*, vol. 2 (Paris: Gallimard, 1971), pp. 81–96.

57. Mélikoff, *Abū Muslim*, pp. 116–43; Roux, *La Religion*, p. 254.

58. Abū Bakr Ibn al-Dawādārī, *Kanz al-durar*, ed. Hans R. Roemer (Wiesbaden: Franz Steiner, 1960–), vol. 7, pp. 219–27; Gunhild Graf, *Die Epitome der Universalchronik Ibn ad-Dawādāris im Verhaltnis zur Langfassung* (Berlin: K. Schwarz, 1990), pp. 59–63 of the Arabic text and 186–97 of the German section.

59. Julian Baldick, *Imaginary Muslims: The Uwaysi Sufis of Central Asia* (London: I. B. Tauris & Co., 1993), pp. 67–8.

60. Ibid., pp. 59–62 and 67–8; Deuteronomy 34: 6.

61. Baldick, *Imaginary Muslims*, pp. 77–80, 107–10, 137–9 and 163–6.

62. Ibid., pp. 50–4; Julian Baldick, 'The legend of Rābi'a of Basra: Christian antecedents, Muslim counterparts', *Religion* 20 (1990) 233–47.

63. Baldick, *Imaginary Muslims*, pp. 178–9 and 183–5 and 'The legend', pp. 239–40; cf below, p. 121.

64. Baldick, *Imaginary Muslims*, pp. 124 and 160; cf below, p. 154.

65. Strahlenberg, *An Historico-geographical Description*, pp. 355–6 and 380–3.

66. Johann Georg Gmelin, *Reise durch Sibirien* (Göttingen: Abram Vandenhoeck, 1751–2), vol. 2, pp. 491–7.

67. Ibid., vol. 2, pp. 498–9.

68. Ibid., vol. 2, p. 502.

69. Jean-Paul Roux, 'Le chaman altaïque d'après les voyageurs européens des XVIIe et XVIIIe siècles', *Anthropos* 56 (1961) 441, 443, 450–1 and 456.

70. Johann Gottlieb Georgi, *Russia* (London: J. Nichols, 1780–3), vol. 2, p. 169.

71. Ibid., vol. 3, pp. 279–80.

72. Alexei I. Levshin, *Description des hordes et des steppes des Kirghiz-Kazaks* (Paris: E. Charrière, 1840), pp. 330–7.

73. Ibid., pp. 337–8.

74. Ibid., pp. 370.

75. Vasilii V. Radlov, *Aus Sibirien* (Leipzig: T. O. Weigel, 1884), vol.

pp. 19–21.
76. Ibid., pp. 21–8.
77. Ibid., pp. 28–51.
78. Karl Reichl, *Turkic Oral Epic Poetry* (New York: Garland Publishing, 1992), p. 319.
79. Ibid., pp. 152–4; Alexander Chodźko (tr.), *Specimens of the Popular Poetry of Persia* (London: W. H. Allen & Co., 1842), pp. 30–5, 11–151 and 189–93.
80. Chodźko (tr.), *Specimens*, pp. 306–33 and 340–2.
81. Baldick, *Homer*, pp. 156–7.
82. Arthur Hatto (ed. and tr.), *The Memorial Feast for Kökötöy-khan* (Oxford: Oxford University Press, 1977), pp. 42–5.
83. Konstantin K. Yudakhin, *Kirgizsko-russkii slovar'* (Moscow: Sovetskaya entsiklopediya, 1965), s.v. töö.
84. Hatto (ed. and tr.), *The Memorial Feast*, pp. 58–61 and 145–6.
85. Ibid., pp. 62–83.
86. Arthur Hatto (ed. and tr.), *The Manas of Wilhelm Radloff* (Wiesbaden: Harrassowitz, 1990), pp. 73–143.
87. Nora K. Chadwick and Victor Zhirmunsky, *Oral Epics of Central Asia* (Cambridge: Cambridge University Press, 1969), pp. 100–4.
88. Ibid., pp. 114–15.
89. Vasilii V. Radlov (ed. and tr.), *Proben der Volksliteratur der Türkischen Stämme Süd-Sibiriens* (St Petersburg: Eggers et Co, 1866–1904), vol. 2 of the German translations, pp. 607–32.
90. Chadwick and Zhirmunsky, *Oral Epics*, pp. 131–4.
91. Radlov (ed. and tr.), *Proben*, vol. 4 of the German translations, pp. 443–76.
92. Baldick, *Homer*, pp. 8, 38–9 and 106–12.
93. Marie Antoinette Czaplicka, *Aboriginal Siberia* (Oxford: Oxford University Press, 1914), pp. 172–84.
94. Ibid., pp. 194–200 and 210–18.
95. Ibid., pp. 233–8.
96. Leonid Potapov, 'Shamans' drums of Altaic ethnic groups', in Vilmos Diószegi (ed.), *Popular Beliefs and Folklore Tradition in Siberia* (Bloomington: Indiana University, 1968), pp. 210–17 and 227–9.
97. Vilmos Diószegi, 'The problem of the ethnic homogeneity of Tofa (Karagas)', in Diószegi (ed.), *Popular Beliefs*, pp. 244–6, 293 and 301–5.
98. Ibid., pp. 306–9 and 324–5.
99. Jean-Paul Roux and Kemal Özbayri, *Les Traditions des nomades*

de la Turquie méridionale (Paris: Adrien-Maisonneuve, 1970), pp. 102
4 and 121–35.

100. Ibid., pp. 165–8, 179–80, 189–92 and 200–1.

101. Ibid., pp. 213–16 and 237–53.

102. Vladimir Basilov, 'Vestiges of transvestism in Central-Asian sha
manism', in Vilmos Diószegi and Mihály Hoppál (eds), *Shamanism ir*
Siberia (Budapest: Akadémiai Kiadó, 1978), pp. 281–7.

103. Ibid., pp. 288–9; cf Richard N. Frye (tr.), *The History of Bukhara*
(Cambridge, Mass.: The Mediaeval Academy of America, 1954), pp.
75–6.

104. Mariya Zhornitskaya, 'Dances of Yakut shamans', in Diószegi
and Hoppál (eds), *Shamanism*, pp. 362–5.

105. Ugo Marazzi (tr.), *Māday Qara* (Naples: Istituto Universitario
Orientale, 1986), pp. 29–82; Pindar, *Pythian Odes* IV. 93–119;
Apollonius of Rhodes I. 942–6, 982–4, 990–1011 and II. 178–489
and 528–647; Apollodorus, *Bibliotheca* I. 9. 16–22.

106. Marazzi (tr.), *Māday Qara*, pp. 82–105; Pindar, *Pythian Odes* IV.
71–92 and 220–41; Apollonius of Rhodes III. 401–1339; Apollodorus,
Bibliotheca I. 9. 23–7.

107. Marazzi (tr.), *Māday Qara*, pp. 106–138; Ovid, *Metamorphoses*
VII. 294–424; Apollodorus, *Bibliotheca* I. 9. 27–8.

108. Reichl, *Turkic Oral Epic Poetry*, pp. 59–60, 98 and 112.

109. Ibid., pp. 160–3; Lev Penkovskii (tr.), *Alpamysh* (Leningrad: Sov.
pisatel', 1982), pp. 220–39.

110. Reichl, *Turkic Oral Epic Poetry*, pp. 160–4; Penkovskii (tr.),
Alpamysh, pp. 239–364.

111. Reichl, *Turkic Oral Epic Poetry*, p. 214.

112. Ibid., pp. 295–8.

113. Ibid., pp. 333–42.

114. Cf Julian Baldick, *Black God: The Afroasiatic Roots of the Jewish,
Christian and Muslim Religions* (London: I. B. Tauris & Co Ltd, 1997),
p. 157.

115. Roux, *La Religion*, p. 102.

116. Deleuze and Guattari, *Mille Plateaux*, pp. 240–1 and 295–7.

Chapter 3: The Mongols

1. Urgunge Onon (tr.), *The History and the Life of Chinggis Khan*
(Leiden: E. J. Brill, 1990); Paul Ratchnevsky, *Genghis Khan* (Oxford:
Blackwell, 1991).

2. Onon (tr.), *The History*, pp. 1–14.

3. Ibid., pp. 21–2 and 31–3; Ratchnevsky, *Genghis Khan*, pp. 23–8.

4. Onon (tr.), *The History*, pp. 42–5; Ratchnevsky, *Genghis Khan*, pp. 40–1.

5. Onon (tr.), *The History*, pp. 46–60; Ratchnevsky, *Genghis Khan*, pp. 46–7, 54–5 and 63.

6. Onon (tr.), *The History*, pp. 77–92; Ratchnevsky, *Genghis Khan*, pp. 67–80.

7. Onon (tr.), *The History*, p. 105.

8. Ibid., pp. 107–10; Ratchnevsky, *Genghis Khan*, pp. 87–8.

9. Onon (tr.), *The History*, pp. 110–12 and 120, n. 1; Ratchnevsky, *Genghis Khan*, p. 89.

10. Onon (tr.), *The History*, pp. 135–40; Ratchnevsky, *Genghis Khan*, pp. 98–101.

11. Onon (tr.), *The History*, pp. 159–60; Ratchnevsky, *Genghis Khan*, pp. 141–2.

12. Onon (tr.), *The History*, pp. 162–4.

13. Ibid., pp. 9, 43, 94, 106, 153, 160, 164–5 and 173.

14. John of Plano Carpini, *Histoire des Mongols*, tr. Jean Becquet and Louis Hambis (Paris: Maisoneuve, 1965), pp. 32–8.

15. Ibid., p. 39.

16. Ibid., pp. 40–1.

17. Ibid., pp. 41–3.

18. Ibid., pp. 45–51 and 63.

19. Jackson and Morgan (trs), *The Mission*, pp. 75–6.

20. Ibid., pp. 90–2.

21. Ibid., pp. 133–3, 142, 193, 199 and 225.

22. Ibid., pp. 236–7.

23. Ibid., pp. 240–5.

24. Ibid., pp. 248–50.

25. Juwaynī, *The History*, vol. 1, pp. 39 and 59.

26. Ibid., vol. 1, pp. 204–6.

27. Ibid., vol. 1, pp. 186–9 and vol. 2, p. 569.

28. Ibid., vol. 1, pp. 231–2.

29. Ibid., vol. 1, pp. 22–30.

30. John A Boyle (tr.), *The Successors of Genghis Khan* (New York: Columbia University Press, 1971), p. 228.

31. Latham (tr.), *The Travels*, pp. 16 and 66–8; Roux, *La Religion*, pp. 135–6.

32. Latham (tr.), *The Travels*, p. 71.

33. Ibid., pp. 71–2.

34. Ibid., pp. 78–9.

35. Ibid., p. 80.

36. Ibid., pp. 87–90.

37. Ibid., pp. 109–111 and 127–9.

38. Roux, *La Religion*, pp. 37, 75, 238 and 268 and *La Mort*, pp. 121–2.

39. Walther Heissig, *The Religions of Mongolia* (London: Routledge & Kegan Paul, 1980), pp. 25–6 and 49–50.

40. Jean-Louis Bacque-Grammont (tr.), *Le Livre de Babur* (Paris: Publications Orientalistes de France, 1980), pp. 53 and 137; Wheeler M. Thackston (tr.), *The Babur nama* (Washington: Oxford University Press, 1996), pp. 45 and 136.

41. Šagdarin Bira, 'A sixteenth-century Mongol code', *Zentralasiatische Studien* 11 (1977) 20–1, 25, n. 9, 32, n. 84 and 33, n. 10.

42. Henri Serruys (tr.), 'Pei-lou fong-sou, les coutumes des esclaves septentrionaux de Siao Ta-heng suivi des Tables généalogiques', *Monumenta Serica* 10 (1945) 128–32.

43. Ibid. pp. 135–7.

44. Ibid., pp. 142–6.

45. Ibid., pp. 142–6.

46. Ibid., pp. 147–9.

47. Walther Heissig, 'A Mongolian source to the Lamaist suppression of shamanism in the 17th century', *Anthropos* 48 (1953) 494–6.

48. Ibid., pp. 496–500.

49. Ibid., pp. 522–3.

50. Heissig, *The Religions*, p. 18.

51. Georgi, *Russia*, vol. 3, pp. 251–2 and vol. 4, pp. 148–54.

52. Ibid., vol. 3, pp. 259–69 and 271–8.

53. Ibid., pp. 282–3.

54. Jorma Partanen (tr.), 'A description of Buriat shamanism', *Journal de la Société Finno-Ougrienne* 51 (1941) 3–8; Heissig, *The Religions*, pp. 54–5.

55. Partanen (tr.), 'A description', pp. 8–9.

56. Ibid., pp. 10–13.

57. Ibid., pp. 13–18.

58. Ibid., pp. 18–24.

59. Ibid., pp. 24–5.

60. Ibid., pp. 25–34.

61. Jeremiah Curtin, *A Journey in Southern Siberia* (Boston: Little, Brown & Co., 1909), p. 118.

62. Czaplicka, *Aboriginal Siberia*, pp. 283–5.

63. Demetrius Klementz, article 'Buriats', in James Hastings (ed.), *Encyclopaedia of Religion and Ethics* (Edinburgh: T. & T. Clark, 1908–26).

64. Garma Sanzheyev, 'Weltanschauung und Schamanismus der Alaren-Burjaten', *Anthropos* 22 (1927) 939–51.

65. Heissig, *The Religions*, pp. 10–11.

66. Ibid., pp. 10 and 46–58; Baldick, *Homer*, pp. 28, 33, 43 and 95.

67. Heissig, *The Religions*, pp. 69–76; Ellison B. Findly, article 'Agni', in Eliade (ed.), *The Encyclopedia of Religion*.

68. Heissig, *The Religions*, pp. 84–91.

69. Krystyna Chabros, *Beckoning Fortune: A study of the Mongol dalalgha ritual* (Wiesbaden: Harrassowitz, 1992), pp. 8–11, 21–5, 42 and 210–15.

70. Ibid., pp. 45–56, 81, n. 98 and 293–4.

71. Ibid., pp. 84–94, 220–9, 259 and 261.

72. Caroline Humphrey, with Urgunge Onon, *Shamans and Elders* (Oxford: Oxford University Press, 1996), pp. 12–13 and 64–5.

73. Ibid., pp. 13–16, 19–29 and 67.

74. Ibid., pp. 29–35 and 49–59.

75. Ibid., pp. 95–7.

76. Ibid., pp. 176–7.

77. Ibid., pp. 202–6.

78. Ibid., pp. 217, 254, 286 and 290–7.

79. Ibid., pp. 330–2 and 363–4.

80. Deleuze and Guattari, *Mille Plateaux*, pp. 435–6 and 492.

81. Friedrich Nietzsche, *Beyond Good and Evil*, tr. R. J. Hollingdale (Harmondsworth: Penguin Books, 1974), p. 32.

82. Baldick, *Homer*, p. 38; Nicholas J. Allen, 'Some gods of pre-Islamic Nuristan', *Revue de l'histoire des religions* 208 (1991) 141–68.

83. Baldick, *Homer*, pp. 30–2.

Chapter 4: The Tunguz and the Manchus

1. Édouard Chavannes, 'Voyageurs chinois chez les Khitan et les Joutchen', *Journal asiatique*, 9th series, 10 (1898) 395, 414, 431, 434–5 and 438.

2. Herbert Franke, 'Chinese texts on the Jurchen. I. A translation

of the Jurchen monograph in the San-ch'ao pei-meng hui-pen'
Zentralasiatische Studien 9 (1975) 129 and 135–7.

3. Ibid., pp. 137–8.

4. Ibid., p. 138.

5. Ibid., pp. 155–6; Paul Pelliot, 'Sur quelques mots d'Asie
Centrale', *Journal asiatique*, 11th series, 1(1913) 466–9.

6. Herbert Franke, 'Chinese texts on the Jurchen. II. A translation of Chapter One of the Chin-shi', *Zentralasiatische Studien* 12
(1978) 413–17.

7. Herbert Franke, 'Some folkloristic data in the dynastic history
of the Chin (1115–1234)', in Sarah Allan and Alvin P. Cohen (eds),
*Legend, Lore and Religion in China: Essays in Honor of Wolfram Eberhard
on his Seventieth Birthday* (San Francisco: Chinese Materials Center,
1979), pp. 138–9.

8. Ibid., pp. 139–53.

9. Lucien Gibert, *Dictionnaire historique et géographique de la
Mandchourie* (Hongkong: Imprimerie de la Société des Missions
Étrangères, 1934), pp. 646 and 860–1.

10. Stein, 'Leao-Tche', p. 135.

11. Jing-shen Tao, *The Jurchen in Twelfth-Century China* (Seattle: University of Washington Press, 1976), p. 12.

12. Roux, *Faune*, pp. 69, 110, 114, 198 and 218.

13. Gibert, *Dictionnaire*, p. 861; Jean-Paul Roux, *Le Roi* (Paris: Fayard,
1995), p. 88.

14. Gmelin, *Reise*, vol. 2, pp. 44–5, 82–9, 358–60 and 493.

15. Ibid., vol. 1, pp. 79–80 and vol. 2, pp. 206–16.

16. Georgi, *Russia*, vol. 3, pp. 85–6.

17. Ibid., vol. 3, pp. 100–115, 249, 256, 270 and 294; Herodotus
5: 3.

18. Czaplicka, *Aboriginal Siberia*, pp. 55–6 and article 'Tungus' in
Hastings (ed.), *Encyclopaedia of Religion and Ethics*.

19. Sergei M. Shirokogoroff, *Psychomental Complex of the Tungus*
(London: Kegan Paul, Trench, Trubner, 1935), pp. 43 and 52.

20. Ibid., pp. 70–7 and 113.

21. Ibid., pp. 122, 126–8, 141–2 and 164–5.

22. Ibid., pp. 179–80.

23. Ibid., pp. 190–206.

24. Ibid., pp. 218–19 and 226.

25. Ibid., pp. 224–76.

26. Ibid., pp. 288, 295, 299, 301–3, 310–11 and 326.

27. Ibid., pp. 319–32, 335–6 and 351.
28. Ibid., pp. 353–64.
29. Ibid., pp. 371–5.
30. Ibid., pp. 378–81.
31. Arkadii Anisimov, 'Cosmological concepts of the peoples of the North', in Henry N. Michael (ed.), *Studies in Siberian Shamanism* (Toronto: Arctic Institute of North America, 1963), pp. 85–92.
32. Ibid., pp. 100–3.
33. Ibid., pp. 103–5.
34. Ibid., p. 105.
35. Ibid., pp. 107–18.
36. Glafira Vasilevich, 'Early concepts about the universe among the Evenks (Materials)', in Michael (ed.), *Studies*, pp. 46–7.
37. Ibid., pp. 50–3 and 77, n. 10.
38. Ibid., pp. 60–9.
39. Ivan A. Lopatin, *The Cult of the Dead among the Natives of the Amur Basin* (The Hague: Mouton, 1960), pp. 26–44.
40. Ibid., pp. 56–7, 70–2 and 92–4.
41. Ibid., pp. 125, 129, 138–47, 150–4, 160–1 and 169–73.
42. Ibid., pp. 201–2.
43. Vilmos Diószegi, 'The three-grade amulets among the Nanai (Golds)', in Diószegi (ed.), *Popular Beliefs*, pp. 387–405.
44. Hans-Joachim Paproth, *Studien über das Bärenzeremoniell*, vol. 1 (Uppsala: K. Renner, 1976), pp. 11–21.
45. Ibid., pp. 77–91.
46. Ibid., pp. 95–123.
47. Ibid., pp. 273–4, 304–7 and 321–30.
48. Margaret Nowak and Stephen Durrant (trs), *The Tale of the Nishan Shamaness* (Seattle: University of Washington Press, 1977), pp. 1–25.
49. Ibid., pp. 25–87.
50. Cf Baldick, *Black God*, pp. 42–3, 49 and 65.
51. Cf Claude Lévi-Strauss, *La Potière jalouse* (Paris: Plon, 1985), pp. 23–8 and 120.
52. Cf Baldick, *Mystical Islam*, p. 8.
53. Deleuze and Guattari, *Mille Plateaux*, pp. 335–7.

Conclusions

1. J. Balázs, 'The Hungarian shaman's technique of trance induction', in Diószegi (ed.), *Popular Beliefs*, p. 64.

2. Georgi, *Russia*, vol. 3, pp. 20, 23–4 and 26–8.

3. Kai Donner, 'A Samoyede epic', *Journal de la Société finno-ougrienne* 30: 26 (1913) 3–8.

4. Marie Antoinette Czaplicka, article 'Samoyed', in Hastings (ed.), *Encyclopaedia of Religion and Ethics*; Toivo Lehtisalo, *Entwurf einer Mythologie der Jurak-Samoyeden* (Helsinki: Société finno-ougrienne, 1924), pp. 162 and 165.

5. Andrei Popov, 'How Sereptin Djaruoskin of the Nganasans (Tavgi Samoyeds) became a shaman', in Diószegi (ed.), *Popular Beliefs*, pp. 137–45.

6. Robert Austerlitz, article 'Samoyed Religion' in Eliade (ed.), *Encyclopedia of Religion*.

7. Uno Harva (né Holmberg), *The Mythology of All Races*, vol. 4 (Boston: Archaeological Institute of America, 1927), pp. 5, 41–3, 80–1, 95–7, 114, 140–1, 260–1 and 294–5.

8. Géza Róheim, *Hungarian and Vogul Mythology* (Locust Valley, N.Y.: J. J. Augustin, 1954), pp. 4, 13–17, 20–2 and 39.

9. Valerii Chernetsov, 'Concepts of the soul among the Ob Ugrians', in Michael (ed.), *Studies*, pp. 5–23.

10. Béla Gunda, 'The Hungarian shaman's technique of trance induction', in Diószegi (ed.), *Popular Beliefs*, pp. 41–51.

11. Tekla Dömötör, *Hungarian Folk Customs* (Budapest: Corvina Press, 1977), pp. 15 and 67–73.

12. Otto von Sadovsky, 'Linguistic evidence for the Siberian origin of the Central Californian Indian shamanism', in Mihály Hoppál and Otto von Sadovsky (eds), *Shamanism: Past and Present* (Budapest: Ethnographic Institute, 1989), pp. 165–84.

13. Harva, *The Mythology of All Races*, vol. 4, pp. 293–5.

14. Kaarle Krohn, article 'Finns (Ancient)', in Hastings (ed.), *Encyclopaedia of Religion and Ethics*.

15. Johannes Scheffer, *The History of Lapland* (London: T. Newborough, 1704), pp. 119, 152–3 and 308.

16. Ivar Paulson, *The Old Estonian Folk Religion* (Bloomington: Indiana University, 1971), pp. 160–2.

17. Leena Siikala, 'Finnish rock art, animal ceremonialism and shamanic worldview', in Mihály Hoppál (ed.), *Shamanism in Eurasia* (Göttingen: Edition Herodot, 1984), pp. 71–6.

18. Elias Lönnrot, *The Kalevala*, tr. Keith Bosley (Oxford: Oxford University Press, 1989), pp. 1–119.

19. Cf Matti Kuusi, 'Lemminkäinen', in Eliade (ed.), *The Encyclopedia of Religion*; Matti Kuusi, Keith Bosley and Michael Branch (eds and trs), *Finnish Folk Poetry: Epic* (Helsinki: Finnish Literature Society, 1977), pp. 214–20 and 538–9; Baldick, *Black God*, pp. 46–7.

20. Lönnrot, *The Kalevala*, pp. 187–357.

21. Ibid., pp. 358–431.

22. Ibid., pp. 432–96.

23. Ibid., pp. 497–514.

24. Ibid., pp. 515–648.

25. Ibid., pp. 649–66.

26. Cf Baldick, *Homer*, pp. 25–6 and 156–7, and Jean-Marc Pastré, *Structures littéraires et tripartition fonctionelle dans le Parzival de Wolfram von Eschenbach: La quête du Grâl* (Paris: Éditions Klincksieck, 1993).

27. Kuusi, Bosley and Branch (eds and trs), *Finnish Folk Poetry: Epic*, pp. 527–8; Jarig G. Oosten, *The War of the Gods* (London: Routledge & Kegan Paul, 1985); 1 Samuel 4–7.

28. Cf Baldick, *Homer*, pp. 29 and 33.

29. William F. Kirby (tr.), *The Hero of Esthonia* (London: John C. Nimmo, 1895), vol. 1, pp. 1–31.

30. Ibid., vol. 1, pp. 32–48.

31. Ibid., vol. 1, pp. 49–134.

32. Cf Carpenter, *Folk Tale, Fiction and Saga*, pp. 112–35 and 157–63.

33. Cf Roux, *La Religion*, p. 102.

34. Cf Baldick, *Homer*, pp. 139 and 151.

35. Cf Carpenter, *Folk Tale, Fiction and Saga*, pp. 117–19, 129–33, 162 and 187.

36. Vendidad 19.

37. Luke 4: 1–113; cf Matthew 4: 1–11.

38. J. Michael Stitt, *Beowulf and the Bear's Son* (New York: Garland Publishing, 1992); Stephen O. Glosecki, *Shamanism and Old English Poetry* (New York: Garland Publishing, 1989).

39. John R. Clark Hall (tr.), *Beowulf* (London: Allen & Unwin, 1967), pp. 35–63, 84–103 and 132–72.

40. Cf Baldick, *Homer*, p. 59.

41. Popov, 'How Sereptin Djaruoskin of the Nganasans became a shaman', p. 137; Grigorii Bongard-Levin, *The Origin of Aryans* (New Delhi: Arnold-Heinemann, 1980), pp. 111–17; Miguel Asin Palacios,

Islam and the Divine Comedy (London: John Murray, 1926).

42. Chabros, *Beckoning Fortune*, pp. 42 and 102, n. 39.

43. Deleuze and Guattari, *Mille Plateaux*, pp. 342–4 and 352–3.

44. Baldick, *Black God*, p. 155.

45. Ibid., pp. 85–6 and 106–109.

46. Cf Burnett James, *The Music of Jean Sibelius* (East Brunswick, NJ: Associated University Presses, 1983; Šandor Kovács, 'The Ethnomusicologist', in Malcolm Gillies (ed.), *The Bartók Companion* (London: Faber and Faber, 1993), pp. 51–63 and György Kroó, 'Cantata profana', ibid., pp. 424–37.

47. Cf Deleuze and Guattari, *Mille Plateaux*, p. 309; Christina Hole, *British Folk Customs* (London: Hutchinson & Co, 1976), pp. 46–7; Qur'an 5: 60; Baldick, *Imaginary Muslims*, pp. 78, 107, 163–6 and 229–30.

Bibliography

Baldick, Julian, *Mystical Islam: An Introduction to Sufism* (London: I. B. Tauris & Co Ltd, 1989).

—— *Imaginary Muslims: The Uwaysi Sufis of Central Asia* (London: I. B. Tauris & Co Ltd, 1993).

—— *Homer and the Indo-Europeans: Comparing Mythologies*, (London: I. B. Tauris & Co Ltd, 1994).

—— *Black God: The Afroasiatic Roots of the Jewish, Christian and Muslim Religions* (London: I. B. Tauris & Co Ltd, 1997).

Bang, W. and Rachmati, G. R. (eds and trs), 'Die Legende von Oghuz Qaghan', *Sitzungsberichte der Preussischen Akademie der Wissenschaften*, Phil.–Hist. Klasse 25 (1932) 683–724.

Carpenter, Rhys, *Folk Tale, Fiction and Saga in the Homeric Epics* (Berkeley: University of California Press, 1946).

Chabros, Dominique, *Beckoning Fortune: A study of the Mongol dalalga ritual* (Wiesbaden: Harrassowitz, 1992).

Chadwick, Nora K. and Zhirmunsky, Victor, *Oral Epics of Central Asia* (Cambridge: Cambridge University Press, 1969).

Czaplicka, Marie Antoinette, *Aboriginal Siberia* (Oxford: Oxford University Press, 1914).

Deleuze, Gilles and Guattari, Félix, *Mille Plateaux* (Paris: Les Éditions de Minuit, 1980).

Diószegi, Vilmos (ed.), *Popular Beliefs and Folklore Tradition in Siberia* (Bloomington: Indiana University, 1968).

—— and Mihály Hoppál (eds), *Shamanism in Siberia* (Budapest:

Akadémiai Kiadó, 1978).

Eliade, Mircea (ed.), *The Encyclopedia of Religion* (New York: Macmillan Publishing Company, 1987).

Franke, Herbert, 'Chinese texts on the Jurchen. I. A translation of the Jurchen monograph in the San-ch'ao pei-meng hui-pen', *Zentralasiatische Studien* 9 (1975) 119–86.

Georgi, Johann Gottlieb, *Russia* (London: J. Nichols, 1780–3).

Gibert, Lucien, *Dictionnaire historique et géographique de la Mandchourie* (Hongkong: Imprimerie de la Société des missions étrangères, 1934).

Gmelin, Johann Georg, *Reise durch Sibirien* (Göttingen: Abram Vandenhoeck, 1751–2).

Harva, Uno (né Holmberg), *The Mythology of All Races*, vol. 4 (Boston: Archaeological Institute of America, 1927).

Hastings, James (ed.), *Encyclopedia of Religion and Ethics* (Edinburgh: T. and T. Clark, 1908–26).

Hatto, Arthur (ed. and tr.), *The Memorial Feast for Kökötöy-khan* (Oxford: Oxford University Press, 1977).

Heissig, Walther, *The Religions of Mongolia* (London: Routledge & Kegan Paul, 1980).

Herodotus, *Le Storie*, Volume IV: *Libro IV, La Scizia e la Libia*, ed. Silvio M. Medaglia, tr. Augusto Fraschetti, with introduction and commentary by Aldo Corcella (Vicenza: Arnoldo Mondadori, 1993).

Hoppál, Mihály (ed.), *Shamanism in Eurasia* (Göttingen: Edition Herodot, 1984),

Hoppál, Mihály and Sadovszky, Otto von (eds), *Shamanism: Past and Present* (Budapest: Ethnographic Institute, 1989).

Humphrey, Caroline with Onon, Urgunge, *Shamans and Elders* (Oxford: Oxford University Press, 1996).

Ibn Faḍlān, *Voyage chez les Bulgares de la Volga*, tr. Marius Canard (Beirut: Éditions de la Méditerranée, 1981).

Ibn Rusta, *Les Atours precieux*, tr. Gaston Wiet (Cairo: Société de Géographie d'Égypte, 1955).

Jackson, Peter and Morgan, David (trs), *The Mission of Friar William of Rubruck* (London: Hakluyt Society, 1990).

Juwaynī, 'Alā' al-Dīn 'Aṭā Malik ibn Muḥammad, *The History of the World-conqueror*, tr. John A. Boyle (Manchester: Manchester University Press, 1958).

Kāshgharī, Maḥmūd, *Compendium of the Turkic Dialects*, tr. Robert Dankoff, Duxbury (Mass.): Harvard University Printing Office,

1982–5.

Latham, Ronald E, (tr.), *The Travels of Marco Polo* (Harmondsworth: Penguin Books, 1958).

Levshin, Alexei I., *Description des hordes et des steppes des Kirghiz-Kazaks* (Paris: E. Charrière, 1840).

Lewis, Geoffrey (tr.), *The Book of Dede Korkut* (Harmondsworth: Penguin Books, 1974).

Lönnrot, Elias, *The Kalevala*, tr. Keith Bosley (Oxford: Oxford University Press, 1989).

Lopatin, Ivan, *The Cult of the Dead among the Natives of the Amur Basin* (The Hague: Mouton, 1960).

Maenchen-Helfen, Otto J., *The World of the Huns* (Berkeley: University of California Press, 1973).

Marazzi, Ugo (tr.), *Māday Qara* (Naples: Istituto Universitario Orientale, 1986).

Michael, Henry H. (ed.), *Studies in Siberian Shamanism* (Toronto: Arctic Institute of North America, 1963).

Nowak, Margaret and Durrant, Stephen (trs), *The Tale of the Nishan Shamaness* (Seattle: University of Washington Press, 1977).

Onon, Urgunge (tr.), *The History and the Life of Chinggis Khan* (Leiden: E. J. Brill, 1990).

Paproth, Hans-Joachim, *Studien über das Bärenzeremoniell*, vol. 1 (Uppsala: K. Renner, 1976).

Partanen, Jorma (tr.), 'A description of Buriat shamanism', *Journal de la Société Finno-Ougrienne* 51 (1941).

Penkovskii, Lev (tr.), *Alpamysh* (Leningrad: Sov. pisatel', 1982).

Plano Carpini, John of, *Histoire des Mongols*, tr. Jean Becquet and Louis Hambis (Paris: Maisonneuve, 1965).

Radlov, Vasilii V., *Aus Sibirien* (Leipzig: T. O. Weigel, 1884), (ed. and tr.), *Proben der Volkslitteratur der Türkischen Stämme Süd-Sibiriens* (St Petersburg: Eggers et Co, 1866–1904).

Ratchnevsky, Paul, *Genghis Khan* (Oxford: Blackwell, 1991).

Reichl, Karl, *Turkic Oral Epic Poetry* (New York: Garland Publishing, 1992).

Roux, Jean-Paul, *La Mort chez les peuples altaïques anciens et médiévaux d'après les documents écrits* (Paris: Adrien-Maisonneuve, 1963).

—— *Faune et flore sacrées dans les sociétés altaïques* (Paris: Adrien-Maisonneuve, 1966).

—— *La Religion des Turcs et des Mongols* (Paris: Payot, 1984).

Sagaster, Klaus (ed.), *Religious and Lay Symbolism in the Altaic World and Other Papers* (Wiesbaden: Harrassowitz, 1989).

Serruys, Henri (tr.), 'Pei-lou fong-sou, les coutumes des esclaves septentrionaux de Siao Ta-heng suivi des Tables généalogiques', *Monumenta Serica* 10 (1945), pp. 117–208.

Shirokogoroff, Sergei M., *Psychomental Complex of the Tungus* (London: Kegan Paul, Trench, Trubner, 1935).

Sinor, Denis (ed.), *The Cambridge History of Early Inner Asia* (Cambridge: Cambridge University Press, 1990).

Stein, Rolf, 'Leao-Tche', *T'oung-Pao* 35 (1940) 1–154.

Strahlenberg, Philipp Johann von, *An Historico-Geographical Description of the North and Eastern Parts of Europe* (London: J. Brotherton et al., 1738).

Tekin, Talât, *A Grammar of Orkhon Turkic* (Bloomington: Indiana University, 1968).

Wittfogel, Karl and Feng Chia-Sheng, *History of Chinese Society. Liao (907–1125)* (Philadelphia: American Philosophical Society, 1949).

Index One
Names of Persons, Deities etc.

'Abbas 65
Abu Muslim 61–2, 66
Achilles 74
Admetus 59
Agni 117
Agricola, Michael 156
Ahmad of Uzgen 63–4
Ahura Mazda 106, 112
Alan-qo'a 93
Alpamysh, 86–7, 164
Altan Khan 107
Aphrodite 17–19
Apollo 17–18, 116
Ares 17–19
'Arrow-Breath' 65
Atagha Tengri 117
Athena 76
Attila 6, 20, 27
Avicenna 49–50, 88

Babur 106
Badshindai 115
Bajan Ami 134
Baraq Baba 56
Barhatakin 49

Bartók, Béla 170
'bear-spirit, the' 151, 165
Bektash 81
Beowulf 165–6
Biruni 49
'Black Image' 110
Bodonchar 93–4
Borough, Stephen 150–1
Buchu 143
Buddha, the 106
Bugha 134
Bukha Noyon 116
'Bull Prince' 116
Buqu Khan 54–5
Burqan Qaldun, Mount 93–5,
    103

Carpini, John of Plano 53, 98–
    100
Chagchi 113
Chaghan Tengri 73
Chodźko, Alexander 71
'Creator White God' 15, 124
Cyclops, the 60

Darius 15, 20–2
Dayichin Tengri 117
Death 59
Death, the Angel of 114
Debetsoy 115
'deer, the spirit of the' 32
Demon, the 158
Devil, the 67, 131, 141, 152,
  165
Digenes Akrites 72
'Divine Twins, the' 124
Djariuskin, Sereptie 152, 168
'dogs, the nine black' 79

Earth 17–18, 31–3, 36, 40, 43,
  94, 97–8, 108–9, 117, 128,
  147
'earth, the master of the' 80
'earth, the spirit-mistress of the'
  80
Elias 18
'Enemy God' 117
Erklik 45
Esege Malan 115–16

Fatima 81
'fire, the god of' 115
'Fire-Queen mother' 117

Gardizi 49–50
Genghis Khan 8–9, 20, 92–8,
  101–4, 117, 120, 123–4, 167
Gmelin, Johann Georg 67, 131
George, Saint 18
Georgi, Johann Gottlieb 68,
  110–11, 131–2, 151
Ghalakhan Eke 117
Ghazali, Muhammad 51
Gholumta Eke 117
Gish 19

God 18–19, 23, 39, 43, 46–7,
  50–1, 54, 57, 59, 64, 66, 74,
  98, 100–3, 105, 141, 159,
  161, 170
'Grandmother, the Very Old'
  110

'hearth, the deity of the' 119
'Hearth-Mother' 117
Heaven 3, 10, 22–4, 28, 31–2,
  36–7, 39, 43, 45, 76, 93–4,
  97–8, 106, 108–9, 116–17,
  120, 123, 127–30, 132, 134,
  147, 164, 167–8
Hephaestus 74
Heracles 17–18, 59, 161
Herodotus 5, 15–22, 35, 64, 82,
  103, 133
Hestia 17
Hippocrates 83
'horse, the spirit of the white'
  32
Hsiao Ta-heng 108–9
Hsü Meng-hsin 127–8
Hung Hao 127

Ibn al-Dawadari 62–3, 88
Ibn Fadlan 46–7
Ibn Rusta 29
Idrisi 52
Ilibemberti 152–3
Ilmarinen 157–62
Ilmun Khan 146
Indra 125
Ingdaqai 109–10
Isis 158
'Itoga' see Itugen
Itte 151–2, 165
Itugen ('Itoga', 'Natigai') 99,
  104

Jacob 64
Jamuqa 94–6, 98
Jason 83–5
Jayaghaghchi Tengri 112
Jelme 95
Jesus 152, 161–2, 165
Joinville, Jean de 53
Juwayni 54–5, 101–3

Kaidarakov, Roman 79
Kalervo 160
Kalev 162–3
Kaleva 157
Kara Tygan 75
Kashghari 50–1
Kerendo 141
Khan Shargay Hoyon 116
Khubilai 104–5
Kögüdäy Märgän 84–5, 89
Kökčö 74
Kökötöy 72
Koori 143
Korkut 58, 87
Köroğlu 71–2
Kreutzwald, Friedrich 162
Kubera 125
Kullervo, 160, 162

'Lady, the Divine' 32
Lemminkäinen 158–62
Levshin, Alexei 68–9
Linda 163
Lönnrot, Elias 157–8, 162
Luke 165

Mada'ini 46
Maday Qara 83–4
Makita Mangri 115
Manas 73–4
Mary 18, 65, 162

Medea 85
Michael the Syrian 52
Mitra 124
Möngke 100–3, 105
Möngke Tengri see Tengri
Moon (son of Oghuz) 57–8
'Moon, the White' 111
Moses 64
Mountain (son of Oghuz) 57–8
Mountain, the Black 32
'Mountain, Long White' 129–31
Movsês Kağankatouaçi 30
Muhammad 62–3, 65, 80–1

'Natigai' see Itugen
Nausicaa 59
Nestor 58
Neyichi Toyin 109–10
Nietzsche, Friedrich 124
'Nishan shamaness, the' 145–8
Northland, the Master of 159–60, 162
Northland, the Mistress of 157–61
Num 152

Odun Jayaghan Tengri 112
Odysseus 8, 59, 76–7, 86, 164–5
Oghuz 56–8, 65, 89, 91
Ögödei 97–8, 102–103
Olanger 75
Omosi-mama see Umay
Orion 79, 156
Oronggu 73
Osiris 158
Ötükän 39–40, 43, 104

Penelope 77
Polo, Marco 9, 29, 55, 103–5

Pozdneyev, Alexander 111
Prajña Sagara 109
'Providence, God of' 112

Qara Qula 84–5
Qormusta Khan Tengri
   (Qormusda) 106, 112

Radlov, Vasilii 74–6
Rashid al-Din Tabib 55–6, 58,
   96, 103
'Red Official God' 112
'Rich Father' 134
'road, the god of the' 48
Rubruck, Friar William of 53–4,
   100–1
'Ruler Light-Bay Prince' 116,
   124

Sari Kiz 81
Satuq Bughra Khan 64
Scheffer, Johannes 156
Scylla 86
Sea (son of Oghuz) 57–8
Seth 158
'shaman-master, the great' 80
Shara Tekhe 116
Shentäi 76
Shidurqu 97
Shih-tsu 128
Sibelius, Jean 170
Sirens, the 86
Sky (son of Oghuz) 57–8
Smallpox 18
Sohni 163–4
'Spirit, the Black Tutelary' 109–
   10
Star (son of Oghuz) 57–8
'Star-Fate God' 112
Strahlenberg, Philipp Johann

von 22, 66
Sube'etei 94–6
Südäi Märgän 75–6
Suksagal 75
Sülde Tengri 117
Sun, the 86
Sun (son of Oghuz) 57
Surkhayil 86
Synshy Sary Kus 76

Tamim ibn Bahr 43
Tašmat 82
Teb-tengri 97, 102
Teiresias 165
Tengri (Möngke Tengri) 23, 30,
   39–40, 43, 45–6, 48, 50,
   54,93, 97, 106 (Möngke
   Tengri), 116–17 (Möngke
   Tengri)
Theseus 85
Thor 66
'Time' 113
'Time, the white lion of' 113
'Time Man, the white old' 113
Toktai 21
Tolui 97, 103
Töshtük 74–6
Tyhost 18

Ulaghan Khan Tengri 112
Ülgen, Bai 70
Umay (Ome, Ome Barkan,
   Omi, Omosi-mama) 39, 50,
   122, 133–4, 146
Underworld, the Lord of the
   146, 163
Untamo 160
Unyany 141
Uways 63

Väinämöinen 157–62
Valikhanov, Chokan 72
Varuna 124–5
Verbitskii, Vasilii 70, 89

Wangdan Yumching 112
Wang-khan 95–6
War 31
'White God' 112
'wind, the earl of the' 32
'wolves, the seven blue' 79

'Womb Spirit' 122
'World White God' 115
Yama 125
'Yellow He-goat, the' 116
Yoldaš-oġli, Fazil 86

Zalmoxis 21
Zarathushtra 165
Zayan Sagan Tengri 115
Zeus 16–17, 117
Zurvan 113

Index Two
Names of Peoples

Ainu 21
Altaians 70, 79, 83, 88
Arabs 43, 46, 52
Arins 22
Armenians 30
Avars 6, 15, 28–9, 36
Azerbaijanians 71

Bashkirs 41, 47, 87–8, 90
Bulghars 6, 15, 30–1, 36, 51
Buryats 92–3, 110–12, 115–17,
    119

Chinese 22–5, 28, 34, 38–45,
    54, 92, 105, 107–8, 119, 122,
    124, 127–30, 148, 169
Chuvash 66–7
Cumans 52–4, 90

Daurs 120–2, 124, 169

Egyptians 16, 158
English 165
Eskimos 142
Estonians 150, 154–5, 157, 160,
    162, 164
Evenks 138, 140–1, 144–5, 158

Finno-Ugrians 11, 166
Finns 1, 4, 11, 73, 77, 141, 143,
    149–50, 153–7, 161
Franks 27, 101
French 53

Georgians 17, 58
Germans 53
Getae 20–1
Gilyaks 145
Golds 141–3, 147–8
Greeks 3, 5, 8, 16–18, 21, 27,
    59, 72, 82–5, 117, 132, 157,
    164, 166

Hsiung-nu 5–6, 15, 22–5, 27,
    35–7, 40, 42, 129
Hungarians 1, 4, 6, 11, 27, 29,
    31, 52–3, 66, 141, 150, 153–
    5, 170
Huns 1, 5–6, 15, 25–8, 30, 37

Indians 13–14, 27, 57, 77, 117, 124–5, 164
Indo-Iranians 12, 19, 125, 164, 166
Iranians 19, 21, 27, 29, 49, 51, 54–5, 61–2, 86, 92, 96, 101, 106, 112–13, 125, 165–6
Issedones 17, 36
Italians 52–3

Japanese 113, 125
Juan-juan 6, 15, 28, 38
Jurchens 10, 32, 97, 105, 126–30, 147–8, 169

Kachin Turks 75
Kalmucks 86–7
Karakalpak 82
Kazakhs 68–9, 72, 76, 82
Kerait 95
Khanty 141
Khazars 6, 15, 29–30, 33, 42, 51
Khitans 6, 15, 31–7, 51, 105, 120, 124, 126–7, 129–30
Kipchak 51, 55, 119
Kirghiz 7, 38, 44–5, 49, 72–4, 76, 86, 88–90
Kitinat Indians 141
Kysyl Turks 75

Lapps 155–6

Manchus 1, 10, 120, 126, 130–1, 133–7, 145, 147–8, 169
Mansi 153
Mo-ho 128–9
Mongols 1, 4–6, 8–9, 12, 17, 20–3, 25–8, 31, 37, 39, 52–3, 59, 65–6, 77, 92–125, 127, 149, 167–8

Nganasan 152
Norsemen 142, 162
Norwegians 155
Nuristani 19

Ob-Ugrians 153–5
Oghuz 46, 51, 56, 58, 61, 87, 90
Ossetians 5, 16–20, 36, 124

Pueblo Indians 83

Romans 13, 26–7
Russians 52, 98, 142, 155

Samoyeds 11, 77, 150–2, 165–6, 168
Scythians 1, 5–6, 15–23, 27, 35–6, 82–3, 89–90, 103, 167
Slavs 27, 30
Svans 17

Tahtaci 80–2
Tangut 97
Tatars 67, 76
Teleuts 68
Thracians 20–21, 132, 164–5
Tofa 80
T'o-pa 15, 25–6, 33, 37
Trojans 32
Tunguz 1, 6, 10, 31, 73, 77, 126, 129, 131–8, 140–5, 147–50, 152, 167–8
Turkmens 82
Turkomans 49
Turks 1, 5–8, 12, 17, 20, 23, 25–30, 37–92, 104, 110, 124–5, 143, 145, 148, 154, 164, 167–8
Türks 7, 23–4, 38–44, 47, 88–9

Ugrians 11
Uighurs 7, 38, 43–4, 48, 54–5,
    101
Uzbeks 82, 86, 88

Wu-sun 23

Yakut 66–7, 77–8, 83, 88–9,
    144–5
Yörük 80–2

Index Three
Subjects

ancestors 6, 17, 32–3, 36, 40–2,
  45, 47, 49, 53–6, 63, 73, 77,
  88, 91, 93, 98, 116, 119,
  128, 130, 133–5, 139, 143,
  151, 155, 157, 167
animals 2–4, 6–10, 14, 17, 19,
  23–4, 26–8, 32–3, 35–7, 40,
  45–6, 48, 51–2, 55–7, 60, 64,
  67, 74, 76, 81–3, 85, 88–92,
  94–9, 102–4, 107–11, 113–
  14, 117–24, 126, 128–32,
  134–5, 137, 139–44, 146–9,
  151, 153–4, 160–1, 167–70
antelopes 73, 107
apples 17, 62, 66
archery 8, 13, 58–9, 64, 69, 87,
  99, 109, 127, 129, 132, 146,
  148–9
armour 29, 108, 122, 140, 151
arrows 3–4, 6, 20–2, 23, 28–9,
  31–2, 34–5, 43, 52, 57–60,
  65, 87, 90, 94, 99, 108, 113,
  118, 127, 131–2, 136–7,
  145–6, 148

axes 4, 20
badgers 107
banners *see* emblems, heraldic
bears 2, 4, 10, 21, 33, 48, 51,
  57, 67, 75–6, 78, 88, 124,
  126, 131, 133–4, 137, 143–5,
  147, 149, 151–3, 155–6,
  159–61, 164–6
bees 158, 166
birds 4, 8, 21, 23, 34, 48, 54–5,
  67, 70, 75, 78–80, 83–4, 89,
  95, 99, 107, 109, 111, 121,
  126, 132, 134, 137, 139–41,
  143, 146–9, 151, 154, 156–7,
  161, 167
blood 19–20, 23, 30, 32, 35,
  95–6, 104, 110–11, 121–3,
  126–7, 131–2, 135, 145, 152,
  167, 169
boar, wild 32–3, 37, 48, 107
bones 23, 25, 27, 33, 45, 56, 75,
  94, 96, 98–9, 106–7, 111,
  114, 155, 161
bows 4, 34, 46, 57–9, 61, 79, 87,

98, 108–109, 115, 131–2,
137, 164
'brothers' (blood-brothers) 20,
34–5, 44, 87, 90, 92, 94–6,
98, 123
buffaloes 62

camels 2, 4–5, 48, 51, 59–60,
62, 73, 82, 85, 117–20, 123–
4, 133
cats 10, 51, 67, 88, 131, 147
cattle 2, 6, 13, 25–6, 28, 31–2,
34, 36–7, 39, 45–6, 48–9, 51,
56–7, 59, 67, 75, 77, 82, 85,
91, 94, 98, 106–7, 109, 111–
12, 116–19, 124, 127–8, 130,
132, 147,154, 160–1
caves 21, 24, 26, 40–1, 45, 49,
56, 60, 63, 73, 84, 159, 164,
166
chickens 34, 46, 58, 82, 146
colours 6, 9–10, 22–3, 25, 31–4,
36, 39–41, 43–4, 48, 52, 54–
5, 57–9, 63, 65, 69, 73,
75–81, 84–5, 89, 92–4, 96,
99–102, 104–6, 109–17, 119,
122–31, 142, 146–8, 152,
155, 157, 168
cranes 47, 80, 82, 91, 146
cups 16, 19–20, 23, 31, 34, 36,
47, 53, 85, 100, 104–5, 124,
128, 149, 167

daggers 4
deer 4, 6, 28, 32–3, 35, 37, 48,
57, 64, 73, 93, 113, 123,
130, 139, 170
demons 31, 67, 69, 76, 85, 99,
101–102, 122, 131
divination 9, 13, 19–20, 22, 27,

30–1, 35, 39, 42–3, 49–50,
52, 54, 67–9, 78–80, 82–3,
88, 90, 92, 99–102, 105, 114,
121, 124, 128, 132, 140,
143, 146, 148, 154–5, 161,
169
dogs 6, 10, 30, 32–4, 36, 49,
51–3, 56, 67, 74, 77–9, 88–9,
93, 102–3, 109, 120, 123,
127, 129, 131–2, 134–5,
142–3, 146–7, 151
doves 76
dragons 56, 72, 74–7
drums 25, 30, 43, 56, 66, 68,
70, 78–80, 101, 104, 107,
110–11, 114, 136, 139, 146,
149, 151, 153–5
ducks 4, 136

eagles 4, 23, 35, 48, 74–6, 87,
89–90, 132–4, 157, 159–61,
163, 167
earth, the 3, 13–14, 21–2, 24,
31–2, 35, 39–41, 43, 45, 47,
56, 59, 63, 67, 69, 73–6, 77,
79–80, 84, 88–90, 96, 98,
102, 104, 115, 124, 128,
141, 148, 152, 156, 158–9,
164–8
eelpouts 139
'elders' 9, 120–1
elephants 4
elk 2, 4, 77, 126, 137, 139, 141,
153, 156–8
emblems, heraldic (banners,
flags, standards) 3, 9, 41, 69,
88, 92, 96, 98, 106, 111,
113, 117, 122, 167
enthronements 26, 29, 33–4,
40, 42, 102, 106

falcons 48, 74, 96, 124, 153
fertility 2, 9, 12–13, 16, 18, 29,
    33, 63, 71, 78, 86, 89–90, 95,
    98, 112, 115–17, 119, 124,
    132, 156–7, 159, 161–3, 166,
    168–9
fire 27, 30–1, 35, 39, 49, 67,
    69–70, 76, 80–1, 86, 88–9,
    92, 98–100, 104–6, 111, 114,
    117, 121, 123, 137–8, 140,
    143, 152, 161, 167
fish 4, 23, 32, 37, 47, 52, 96,
    121, 124, 126, 130, 135,
    138–40, 151, 156, 161, 167
fishing 4, 14, 32, 84, 96, 130–2,
    138–9, 143, 148, 150–1, 156,
    168
flags see emblems, heraldic
force (strength) 12–13, 16, 18,
    23, 33, 35–6, 39, 48, 57, 71,
    76, 86, 89–90, 95, 109, 112,
    115–16, 151, 154, 156, 159–
    61, 163, 165–6, 168
fortune 23, 30, 32, 40, 44, 47–
    8, 50–1, 62, 97, 109, 112,
    117–18, 123
foxes 2, 22–3, 46, 48, 122, 132–
    3, 147
frogs 21, 79
funerals 6, 20, 23–4, 26–31, 33,
    35–6, 40, 42, 44–6, 49, 51,
    53, 61–7, 69, 90, 99, 103,
    108–10, 120, 126–9, 131–3,
    142–3, 147–8, 151, 155, 167

gazelles 62
geese 6, 32, 70, 80–1, 88, 141
goats 2, 4, 81–2, 98, 107, 111,
    114, 116, 133
grouse 154–5

hair 23, 27, 57, 76,78, 111, 120,
    122, 157
hares 22–3, 32–3, 48, 64, 68, 70
hawks 76, 83, 89, 130
hearth, the 17, 119, 124, 135
horses 2–6, 8–9, 13, 20, 23–7,
    30–7, 39–40, 42, 47–8, 51,
    53, 58–9, 61, 66–70, 72–8,
    80, 82–5, 87–90, 92, 94–5,
    98–9, 101–4, 107–12, 114–
    15, 117–19, 121, 124,
    127–33, 135, 145, 147–8,
    154–5, 157–8, 167
hunting 3–4, 6, 14, 21, 32–3,
    35–7, 45, 48, 57–8, 64–5, 73,
    80, 91–2, 94, 97, 102–3,
    107–9, 118–21, 123, 126,
    130–2, 134, 137–8, 141,
    143–5, 148–50, 153, 156,
    158, 167–8

images 9, 17, 25, 27, 55–6, 66,
    70, 98, 100, 104, 109–11,
    114, 120–1, 131–3, 135,
    138–40, 146, 153

javelins see spears

lakes 21, 28, 57, 80, 93, 130,
    151, 156, 161
lances 29, 86, 88, 99
larks 161
left side, the 5, 24–5, 34, 127
lemmings 2
lice 73, 94, 99
light 23, 57, 81, 89, 93, 99, 106,
    122, 169
lightning 30, 50, 99, 102, 108
lions 46, 59–60, 67, 88, 113,
    146

lizards 79, 156

magic 4, 12–13, 17, 25, 29–30,
    34, 44, 50, 68, 75, 95, 99–
    101, 109–10, 124, 142–3,
    155, 157, 159
magpies 50, 130
mammoths 4
marmots 96, 124
marriages 24, 29, 34, 41–2, 44,
    58–61, 65, 69, 75–8, 82–3,
    85, 87, 93, 98, 100, 104,
    108, 117, 127–8, 130, 132,
    147–8, 151, 155, 157–9,
    161–3
mice 21, 51
moon, the 25, 30, 33–4, 37, 45,
    58, 70, 79, 98–9, 113, 141,
    149, 161
mountains 2–3, 6, 9–10, 14, 23,
    25–6, 29, 31, 33–4, 39–41,
    43, 47, 50, 52, 55, 57, 63,
    65–6, 75, 80–1, 83–4, 87–90,
    92–5, 102–4, 111, 113, 117,
    120–1, 123–5, 127, 129–32,
    140, 147, 152–4, 158, 165–6,
    170

numbers 4, 7, 20, 22–4, 28–34,
    37, 40–5, 47, 52–5, 60, 62,
    64–6, 69–71, 73–4, 77, 79,
    86, 92, 94, 100–2, 104–10,
    112–16, 121–2, 127–8, 134–
    6, 141–2, 146, 148, 151–2,
    154, 160, 162–4, 166–7, 170

oaths 6, 20, 27–8, 44, 53, 81,
    94–6, 98, 126, 131–2, 144,
    147
owls 80, 111, 156

panthers 143–4, 148
parrots 65
peacocks 100
pigs 10, 33–4, 127
pike 126, 139, 153, 159, 161
placenta, the 39, 50, 152–3
poles 10, 53–4, 68, 98, 109,
    111, 129–32, 140, 146–9
porcupines 50

rain 7, 31, 41, 43, 47, 50, 63,
    79, 88, 90, 102, 127, 130
rats 23, 94, 99, 124, 167
ravens 48, 144–5
reindeer 2, 80, 83, 89, 126,
    132, 135–6, 138–40, 147,
    150–3
rivers 2–3, 14, 27–9, 32, 40–1,
    43, 47, 62–3, 65–7, 87–90,
    93, 121, 125, 138–40, 146,
    152, 158–9, 163–4, 168
roads 25, 30, 44, 47

sable 57
sacrifices 6, 9–10, 16–20, 22–6,
    30–7, 39–40, 42–4, 47, 51,
    66–8, 70, 79, 90, 94, 96–8,
    102, 111–12, 114–15, 117–
    19, 123, 127, 129–32, 135,
    139–40, 143, 145, 147, 149,
    151–2, 155, 165, 167, 169
salmon 157
salmon-trout 126, 138–9
scalping 19, 35–6, 154, 167
scorpions 165
seas 2–3, 14, 83–4, 89, 96, 100,
    124, 151, 157–61, 163, 167
shamanesses 10, 25, 28, 31, 54,
    67, 88, 93, 109–10, 114, 122,
    124, 126, 128, 132, 137,

145–9

shamans 4, 8–10, 20, 27, 31, 34–5, 39, 43–5, 49–51, 54–6, 66–70, 74–5, 77–80, 82–3, 85–6, 88–93, 97, 99, 101–2, 104–5, 109–16, 119–24, 126–8,131–9, 142–5, 147–59, 166–70

sheep 2, 6, 25, 27, 31–4, 39, 46, 58, 60, 69, 81–2, 98, 100, 103, 107, 111, 114, 117–18, 121, 131

singing 5, 8, 27, 31, 51, 54, 69–71, 78, 82, 85, 88, 104, 117, 128, 136, 145, 155, 157–61

skulls 17, 19, 23, 29, 31–3, 36–7, 41, 167

sky, the 3, 8, 13–14, 16, 21–2, 25–6, 28–9, 31–2, 35, 37, 39, 41, 45–7, 54, 56–9, 65–6, 68, 70, 74, 76, 78–9, 84, 87–90, 95, 98, 103–104, 106, 113, 115, 120–2, 124, 128–30, 132, 134, 136, 138, 140–1, 147–9, 152–3, 156, 158–9, 161, 164–8

smallpox 18, 108, 113

smiths 13, 74, 78, 115, 157

snakes 47, 65, 77, 79, 111, 113–14, 132–3, 156, 159, 165

sovereignty 12–13, 16–18, 23, 33, 35–6, 57, 63, 71, 76, 89–90, 112, 116, 125, 148, 156, 161, 163, 165, 168

spears 20–1, 113, 138–9

spirits 8–10, 17–18, 22–3, 26, 28, 31–2, 34–5, 37, 44, 57, 63–5, 67, 69–70, 74, 77–80, 82–3, 88–9, 92, 95–7, 104, 109–10, 114–16, 119–22,

124, 129, 131, 133–40, 142–4, 146–9, 151–2, 154–6, 165, 167–70

staffs 4, 52, 55, 64, 69, 113

stoats 139, 147, 161

stones 4, 7, 30, 40–3, 47, 50, 53, 55, 64, 67, 69, 95, 100, 114, 120, 135, 154, 157, 160, 163, 165

summer 2, 33, 35, 40–3, 47, 63, 88, 90, 102, 108, 117, 167, 169

sun, the 25, 30, 34, 37, 44–5, 58, 63, 70, 79, 81, 89, 94, 98–9, 102, 105, 113, 127, 131, 141, 149, 158, 161

swallows 75

swans 41, 47–8, 75, 83, 158, 160

swords 3, 16, 19–20, 25, 27–8, 30, 53, 60, 74, 100, 104, 108, 151, 155, 159–60, 163–4

taboos 9, 18–19, 32, 78, 81, 92, 99–100, 102, 107–108, 126, 145, 147, 149, 166

tents 5, 20, 27–8, 32–4, 37, 40, 44, 46, 54–5, 57, 61, 69–70, 80, 93, 98–100, 102, 104, 108, 110, 118–20, 123, 126, 138–40, 149, 151–2, 158, 168

thresholds 81, 99

thunder 21, 28, 66, 100, 102, 108, 110–12, 117

tigers 2, 75, 126, 134, 137, 143–4

time 39, 113

tombs (graves) 3–6, 9, 14, 20–

21, 23–4, 27–31, 33–5, 42,
44, 46–7, 51, 53–4, 60–1, 64,
68, 74, 103, 108, 110, 133,
142, 155, 159, 164, 167
trees 2–4, 6, 8, 14, 19, 24, 29–
31, 33–4, 40–1, 43–4, 47,
50–1, 54–8, 65–7, 70, 74–5,
79, 81, 89, 93, 98, 105, 113–
14, 117, 120–2, 125, 127,
129, 131–2, 135–6, 138–9,
141, 143, 149, 151–2, 154,
156–61, 170

underworld, the 13, 21, 45, 54,
74, 76, 78–9, 84, 89–90, 122,
126, 134, 136, 138–40, 142–
3, 146, 148. 152–3, 158–9,
161, 163–6
unicorns 57

vultures 51, 89

war 3, 18–19, 22, 27, 31, 37, 41,
43–4, 55, 57, 60, 66, 69, 86,
95–7, 101–4, 107, 117, 122–
3, 127, 133, 137, 153, 163,
167–8
warriors 3, 5, 7, 12–13, 16, 19,
29, 33, 37, 41, 51, 60, 62,
71–2, 74, 86, 89, 109, 117,
123, 151, 153, 155, 162–3,
167–8

water 3–4, 21, 26–8, 30, 35, 39–
40, 47, 49, 62, 64, 81, 89, 95,
97–8, 100, 102, 110, 114,
140–1, 146, 156, 169
wealth 13, 57, 72–3, 75–6, 109,
119, 125, 137–8, 152, 160
weapons 3, 20, 26, 44, 61, 71,
74–5, 82, 114, 117, 122, 137,
140, 165
weasels 23
whales 155
wind 32, 41, 43, 47, 49, 54, 63,
88, 90, 118, 158
winter 2, 32–3, 35, 41–2, 44,
47, 63, 88, 90, 102, 167, 169
wolves 7, 9, 23–4, 37, 40–1, 43,
45, 49, 51, 57, 78–9, 88, 93,
102, 117, 122–3, 132, 139,
147, 159–60, 166
womb, the 39, 50, 120
women 6, 17–18, 29, 31, 40,
58–60, 65–6, 69, 71–4, 78–9,
82–3, 86, 88, 94, 97, 99, 102,
108, 120–2, 124–5, 127–8,
132, 134, 142–3, 145, 147,
151–2, 154, 159–60, 167–8
worms 51, 79
wrestling 30, 58–9, 69, 76, 97,
146, 149

yaks 106